SHADY RETREATS

20 plans for colorful, private spaces in your backyard

BARBARA W. ELLIS

ILLUSTRATIONS BY GARY PALMER

ARCHITECTURAL PLANS BY JULIE BURNS

STOREY
BOOKS

The mission of Storey Publishing is to serve our customers by publishing practical information that encourages personal independence in harmony with the environment.

Edited by Gwen Steege and Karen Levy
Designed by Wendy Palitz
Art direction by Cynthia McFarland
Production assistance by Susan Bernier

Painted garden illustrations © Gary Palmer
Architectural plans by Julie Burns
Additional illustration page 12 by Carolyn Bucha

Indexed by Peggy Holloway

Printed in Singapore by CS Graphics
10 9 8 7 6 5 4 3 2 1

Library of Congress Cataloging-in-Publication Data

Ellis, Barbara W.
    20 plans for colorful shady retreats : how to plan, plant, and grow with shade as the theme / Barbara W. Ellis.
        p. cm.
    ISBN 1-58017-472-8 (alk. paper)
    1. Gardening in the shade. 2. Gardens—Design. I. Title: Twenty plans for colorful shady retreats. II. Title.
SB434.7 .E45 2003
635.9'543—dc21
                                            2002151301

Photograph Credits
Cover photographs
© Joseph De Sciose: spine
© Alan Detrick: front cover top left
© Global Book Publishing Pty. Ltd.: front cover top right
© Saxon Holt: front cover bottom
© Maggie Oster: back cover

Interior photographs
© Joseph De Sciose: i, 71 (top and bottom), 95 (center)
© Alan Detrick: 2
© Liz Ball/POSITIVE IMAGES: 83
© Gay Bumgarner/POSITIVE IMAGES: 7 (bottom)
© Crandall and Crandall: 14, 76
© Barbara Ellis: v, 41 (second from top), 100, 106 (center), 113 (top), 137 (bottom), 143 (center)
© Catriona Tudor Erler: vi, viii, 3 (bottom), 4 (right), 7 (top), 142
© Roger Foley: 16, 17, 46, 124
© Global Book Publishing Pty. Ltd.: vii, 29, 35 (center and bottom), 41 (all except second from top), 47 (center and top right), 58, 65, 71 (second from top), 77, 82, 88, 95 (top and bottom), 101, 106 (left), 113 (bottom), 119, 125 (top and bottom), 130 (top, second from top, and bottom), 137 (top and center), 143 (bottom), 146, 163, 165, 166
© Saxon Holt: ii, 1, 6, 11, 18, 40
© Rosemary Kautzky: 20, 21, 53, 59,118, 136, 144
© Janet Loughrey: 15, 34, 89, 94
© MACORE, Inc.: 35 (top), 52 (left and lower right), 71 (third from top), 106 (right), 113 (second and third from top), 125 (center), 130 (third from top), 143 (top)
© Maggie Oster: 112, 131
© Jerry Pavia: 70
© Neil Soderstrom: 10, 64
© Mark Turner: 3 (top), 4 (left), 13, 23, 28, 107

dedication

For my aunt Hattie, Harriet Nace, whose garden harbored the earliest shady retreats I remember and who identified me as a gardener when I was far too young to know what that meant.

For my mother, Jane Ann Ellis, who forgave me for building a fort on top of her fern garden and who helped me make my first garden.

For my husband, Peter Evans, who embraces it all with humor and understanding — gardens, dogs, parrots, cats, and me.

contents

introduction viii

PART 1: creating a shady garden refuge 1

PART 2: designs for 20 shady retreats 23

clearing on a woodland edge 25

two shady spaces for a small lot 31

cozy nook on a terrace 36

berm for instant privacy 42

tempting, shaded terrace 49

mulched terrace under trees 55

gazebo at a forest's edge 60

a deck in the woods 66

relaxing pool house 72

ceiling of leaves and sky 78

arbor and lattice sitting area 85

an inviting place to putter 90

pergola for strolling 96

pavilion in a terraced garden 102

private space in a busy yard 109

shady seating in a formal garden 114

clearing in the woods 120

old-fashioned front porch 127

a perch in the trees 132

private gathering place 138

PART 3: favorite shade plants 145

perennials 146

annuals, biennials, and tender perennials 162

shrubs, small trees, and vines 166

index 176

why shade?

Children instinctively understand the importance of private, shady spaces. Secret playhouses, whether tucked under an evergreen with branches sweeping the ground or patched together in an unused part of the backyard, are a childhood rite of passage. One of the earliest shady retreats that I treasured was on the front porch of my aunt Hattie's house, a grand old place surrounded by flowers. The porch was furnished with a glider and hidden from view behind a veil of maypops (*Passiflora incarnata*) and other vines. It was a wonderful spot for drinking lemonade, playing house, or visiting with my aunt.

All too often, adults have forgotten the magic of these shady childhood retreats. When it comes to landscaping, we're more likely to think about what will look neat and tidy — or will blend in with the neighborhood — than to recollect the treasured spaces of childhood. Planning a garden that recaptures those secret spaces isn't just a whimsical idea, however. Children have the right idea about

yards: They aren't supposed to be just pretty pictures to look at or places to toil away with a lawn mower and hedge shears. They're spaces to use and enjoy, whether that means growing things, playing in the shade under a tree, eating an impromptu picnic outdoors, or building a secret clubhouse.

I am not talking about re-creating forts or other childhood spaces down to the plywood walls or cement-block chairs, though. Instead, my goal — and the theme of this book — is to capture the essence of a special space and use that as inspiration for landscape design. Putting things on an adult scale is a first step. Try to identify what makes a space special, then translate cement blocks into comfy chairs, a childhood clubhouse into a charming toolshed or summerhouse, and a rough circle of logs into a dining area surrounded by shrubs.

My own yard features several shady retreats that are each unique and distinct. On the north side of the house, I have a shady bluestone terrace tucked up next to an arborvitae. There's also a hammock slung beneath a willow tree whose overhanging branches nearly conceal it from the house. The branches form a ceiling and walls that look like a green fountain spilling overhead as you lie in the hammock. I've also created a shady "room" that is screened on two sides by mixed shrub and perennial borders. It's outfitted with Adirondack chairs atop a carpet of lawn.

All of these are quiet, peaceful spaces, but shady retreats don't have to be quiet and peaceful. I have another favorite shady spot that's completely different. Set out in the shade of a giant old walnut tree in the big fenced area where our dogs play, the space consists of a bench and several inexpensive lawn chairs. While there, I spend most of my time throwing a Frisbee and kicking balls for our dogs rather than sitting, though I do manage occasional sips of coffee. Still, it is a relaxing shady retreat, because it takes me far away from my desk and computer.

While the spaces in my garden are all quite different, they share many essential characteristics that make them appealing, enjoyable, and restorative. Obviously, shade is a must, as sitting in full sun is neither enjoyable nor healthy. If you don't have mature shade trees to work with, however, don't despair. Throughout this book you'll find hundreds of ideas and suggestions for figuring out what will work best in your yard, including how to create a shady retreat even if your yard doesn't currently offer any shade at all!

Privacy is also very important. A shady space hidden behind shrubs or walls is pleasant to use,

whereas a table set out in the middle of the yard where the neighbors can watch your every move isn't at all compelling. The type and style of screen will vary according to where you live and how much protection from neighbors and noise you need. Because we live in the country and don't have many neighbors, I don't worry about screening spaces on all sides. Instead, I aim for spaces that have a comfortable, enclosed feel but still have a good view of the garden and surrounding area.

In fact, giving a space a sense of enclosure goes hand in hand with creating privacy. This is another principle that children understand instinctively. After all, one of the first things they do when creating a space is mark its outline, thus separating and defining it (my nephew's fort is outlined with bricks from a pile in the backyard). The photographs and designs in this book offer a wealth of possibilities for enclosing space. You'll probably want to use something more than a row of bricks but less than four solid hedges with a door on one side. Spaces can be enclosed with a mix of trees and shrubs, trellised vines, fencing, real walls, or a combination of several elements. In the pages that follow, you'll find ideas for creating all manner of shady retreats, from small to large, from rustic to formal.

A ceiling for shade and green walls for privacy are just one part of the puzzle. You should also think about how you want to use your shady retreat. You can create an outdoor space for eating, reading, visiting, gardening, birdwatching, meditating, playing — anything that appeals to you and your family. How you plan to use the space will determine how it is furnished and decorated. This book has examples of spaces used for all sorts of activities.

Time is another factor to consider. Depending on the clarity of your vision for the space, as well as the time and money you have available, you may choose to create your shady retreat in a single weekend. Or it may become a long-term project that takes several years to complete. Don't let having a finished, perfect space become your main objective. Kids certainly aren't hampered by such practicalities, and to a large extent, you shouldn't be either. The important thing is to get started, so that you will have even a simple shady retreat to enjoy. You can always fine-tune the design, add plants, upgrade the furniture, and decorate the space as inspiration, time, and money allow. Remember how much fun it was to build a playhouse or discover a secret place to play in the backyard? It's still fun, so get out there and enjoy the process!

PART 1

creating a shady garden refuge

A garden provides its creator with a beautiful vista to behold, plus a fun and fascinating place to dig, grow things, experiment with design, and simply enjoy the outdoors. But gardens also can offer sanctuary — retreats where peace, quiet, and privacy are the main attractions. A spot protected from the sun by an overhanging tree or sheltered by an arbor makes a delightful outdoor living space. Screen that space from the outside world with shrubs, a fence, or a wall, and you have a peaceful inner sanctum. Add a few pieces of furniture, and you have a treasured place to visit daily to steal a few minutes — or hours — of sanctuary.

If looking out your windows reveals little more than a sea of grass punctuated by a tree or two, creating a shady retreat may seem like an impossibility. Fortunately, you don't need professionals or even a giant budget to make one. That's because a shady retreat doesn't have to be grand or expensive to be successful. As long as it offers shade, privacy, and some basic furnishings, even the smallest space can provide a welcome respite from this all-too-busy world. In its simplest form, a shady retreat need be nothing more than a rustic bench nestled beneath the branches of a tree, with a few shrubs or even a trellis to add a bit of privacy.

Even if you've never designed a garden, you have an inner reservoir of images that will prove invaluable. They're based on places that appealed to you as a child. Tap into those images (see Why Shade? on page viii for ideas) for a lifetime of memories to inspire you.

making
shady spaces

Shady retreats are as different as gardeners and their gardens — their very uniqueness is part of the charm and appeal. These are not spaces meant to impress the neighbors, nor are they designed to be just pretty pictures to look at from a distance. They're private outdoor living spaces to be used and enjoyed, whether that means relishing them alone or sharing them with close friends.

Because shady retreats are personal spaces, it pays to think carefully about what kind of space will make you happy. Not only will a successful shady retreat reflect your taste and be designed for your use and comfort, but it also will be inspired by the characteristics of your yard and garden. If you'd prefer to work with a professional landscape designer rather than develop a shady retreat by yourself, find someone who'll listen to you and who asks questions about what you'd like to have. Then look carefully at the plans he or she develops to make sure they reflect your personality. After it's installed, you'll still want to add decorations or other touches that make it really your own.

Whether you have a yard that's basically a blank slate or have already picked out the perfect spot for a shady retreat, spend some time thinking about how you would like to use the space. (See Useful Spaces, Peaceful Places on page 5 for some suggestions to get you started.) Consider the amount of space you'll need — room for one or two people or for a larger gathering.

Think about what you have the time and money to do now, but don't overlook what you want the space to look like in a few years. The most intriguing shady retreats often aren't planned per se; they evolve as plants and other features are added over time.

That's not to say you can't create a retreat in a single weekend, and it's certainly possible to get the basics in place in short order. But consider developing and changing the space as your time, budget, and inclination allow. If you need more trees or shrubs for shade or screening, put them at the top of your "to-do" list. The sooner you plant, the better. Phase in other improvements, such as upgrading furniture, exchanging mulch for paving, and replacing an umbrella with a vine-covered arbor, as you use the space and learn more about your needs.

Simple comforts. Depending on the size and style of your garden, your shady retreat may be a bench set against a hedge of oakleaf hydrangeas (*Hydrangea quercifolia,* left), a spot on a patio shaded by an umbrella (top right), or a bench in a woodland garden (right).

picking the perfect spot

Once you have some ideas about how you'd like to use your shady retreat, take a good look at your yard to scout out potential sites. Look first for areas that are already shady and see how they could be modified to create a retreat. If you don't have any usable shade, see Shade: Natural or Constructed? on page 10 for ideas. Areas under trees are obvious choices. Don't overlook potential spaces that are covered up by low tree branches or ones that are hidden or completely filled in by overgrown shrubs. Sometimes limbing up a tree or removing a shrub or two is a great way to carve out space for a shady retreat.

Forgotten or unused spots also make great shady retreats. Look for a nook next to the garage or an overlooked spot in a side yard, for example. If you're thinking about a space where traffic might be a problem — a spot directly in the path that runs from house to compost pile, perhaps — think again. Unless you can redirect traffic easily, avoid such sites since a place that kids cut through routinely won't ever be very serene!

I've found that shady retreats are best planned from the inside out — inside the space, that is. So stand in potential spaces, if you can, and try to estimate how big they could be when cleared out. Visualize how they might look when screened, shaded, and outfitted with some furniture. For ideas

on creating different types of spaces and dealing with myriad landscapes, look through the garden designs in part 2.

As you look at potential spaces, don't forget how you want to use your shady retreat. A secluded sitting area for one or two people can be tucked away in a corner of the yard; a shady dining area with a table for six needs a much larger space. Plus, if you plan on entertaining in your shady space, consider how close it is to the kitchen to make it easy to carry out trays of food and other necessities.

Your search may uncover several potential shady retreats. If so, consider making more than one — a tiny spot for one person to sit and a larger space for friends and family to enjoy, for example.

Off the beaten path. Chairs and a table set on a tiny, shaded patio (left), or a large terrace sheltered by an arbor (above), both make very compelling shady retreats.

useful spaces, peaceful places

A shady retreat can be used in many ways. The list below is designed to help you think about how you want to use yours. The furnishings and other features you'd like to have can help you determine how big it should be.

I would like to use a shady retreat to:

☐ Read and write

☐ Sit quietly

☐ Sleep

☐ Garden

☐ Enjoy the view

☐ Stretch or do other types of exercises

☐ Meditate

☐ Get away from the phone, TV, and other distractions

☐ Watch birds and other wildlife

☐ Study, work, or use the computer

☐ Keep an eye on children playing elsewhere in the yard

☐ Visit with friends and family

☐ Play board games or cards

☐ Play with dogs or other pets

The types of dining and entertaining that I plan to do are:

☐ Eat informally (snacks and drinks)

☐ Eat more formally (dining table and chairs)

☐ Entertain small groups of two to four people

☐ Visit with friends. How many people should the space accommodate? _____

☐ Entertain larger groups. How many people should the space accommodate? _____

The amount of privacy I need can be accomplished by:

☐ Shrubs, small trees, large perennials

☐ Hedge

☐ Fence or wall

☐ House or other building

☐ Something overhead, such as an arbor

☐ Distance (no nearby neighbors on that side)

The available shade sources are:

☐ Overhead trees in yard

☐ Overhead trees in neighbors' yard

☐ Shade cast by house or building

☐ Shade cast by fence

☐ Vines on arbor

☐ Umbrella

☐ Awning

The types of furniture I will need are:

☐ Small garden bench

☐ Chairs or loveseat

☐ Table and chairs

☐ Picnic table

☐ Hammock or hanging chair

☐ Side tables

☐ Coffee table

☐ Footstools

☐ Counter or serving space

☐ Storage bench

☐ Barbecue grill

The other types of features I will need are:

☐ Lights or candles

☐ Screens or other bug protection

☐ Water spigot

☐ Electric outlet/lighting

☐ Fire circle or chimnea

☐ Water garden

☐ Fountain

☐ Sculpture or other focal point

☐ Shady flower bed

☐ Low-maintenance ground covers

Use these general measurements to estimate the amount of space you need:

Bench: 2' x 4–6'

Single chair: 2' x 2' to 2½' x 2½'

Sitting area with two chairs: 5' x 5'

Sitting area with four chairs: 7½' x 7½' to 8' x 8'

Table (square) with two chairs: 6' x 8'

Table (square) with four chairs: 6' x 6' minimum; ideal size, 8' x 8' to 9' x 9'

Table (round) with six chairs: 10' x 10'

Table (rectangular) with eight chairs: 8' x 12'

Hammock: Hanging distance varies from 13' to 18', depending on the model, and each model will have minimum and maximum hanging distances; necessary width to accommodate a hammock is 6' to 8', depending on the hammock, to allow for swing

Hammock stand: 12' to 13' long; 5' to 7' wide

Hanging chair: 3½' x 3½'; allow at least 2' extra on all sides to accommodate swing movement

Chimnea or Mexican fireplace: 5' square minimum

Grill (2' x 2') and counter area (2' x 4'): 4½' x 4½' minimum; more is better. Be sure to locate a grill where prevailing winds will not blow smoke toward sitting areas.

Picnic table, small, for six: 5' x 6' minimum; ideal size, 7' x 8'

Picnic table, large, for eight: 5' x 7½' minimum; ideal size, 7' x 9½'

what makes a welcoming outdoor room?

Whatever their size or style, the most successful shady retreats are outdoor rooms that have a comfortable, clearly defined feeling. When planning your retreat, think in terms of creating a room that is enclosed by walls for privacy, has a level floor to make it easy and safe to use, and is shaded by a ceiling that gives the space a sheltered character. Decorate with plants but also use other materials in an interesting way. Mix shrubs and sections of fence for walls, or combine flagstones with mulch. Augment the shade cast by trees with a vine-covered arbor.

A. floors Mulch, pea gravel, crushed stone, pavers, brick, flagstone, and bluestone are all possibilities for creating a level surface. The material you choose depends on the style of space and on your budget. Consider a deck if level ground is at a premium. Decks are most often attached to a house, but freestanding ones are ideal for making a level space anywhere in the yard on sites that range from slightly uneven to steeply sloping. Decks can be installed with minimal damage to trees and are also perfect for making a shady (and dry) retreat on sites where the soil is boggy or wet. On a sloping site, building a series of terraces is another way to create level floors.

B. walls Shrubs; fences; vine-covered trellises; and stone, brick, or cement walls all can be used to enclose a shady space. Don't overlook existing buildings, either: A shady retreat can be tucked against the wall of a house or garage, for example. If blocking street noise or the sounds of a neighbor's swimming pool is an issue, a shrub border or a solid wall is best because it blocks more noise than does a fence or trellis. Shrubs planted along a wall are extremely effective in reducing sound. A space that's almost entirely enclosed will have a very intimate, private feel, whereas a space that's enclosed on only one or two sides will still seem quite private but have a more open, expansive quality.

C. ceilings Overhead tree branches, a timber-framed arbor, even a conventional roof are all options for creating a canopy. A low ceiling makes a space feel more cozy and intimate, while a high one — with tree branches spanning overhead, for example — creates a lofty sense of space. Whether you are building an arbor or using branches as your ceiling, plan on a minimum of 7½ to 8 feet for the ceiling height; even higher — 10 or 12 feet or more — is usually better. A solid roof is a good choice if you want to be able to use your retreat in all types of weather, especially if you live in an area with rainy summers.

Outdoor living spaces. Each space on these pages is unique, but all have walls, floors, and other features that make them appealing. Walls are made of plants or lattice screens. Floors are constructed of pavers or crushed gravel. Trees, an arbor, or a pleached canopy provide shade, while comfortable furnishings complete the design.

D. furnishings and decoration These elements transform a shady outdoor space into a room as cozy and pleasant as a den or family room. Simple benches, tree stumps, or even a circle of logs may suffice for a rustic spot. For a space designed for reading, visiting with friends, or eating, choose comfortable chairs made of wood, all-weather wicker, tubular aluminum, cast aluminum, cast iron, or wrought iron. For a finishing touch, add decorations such as potted plants, a special sculpture, wind chimes, and any other items that appeal to you.

shady retreats through history

Shady retreats have been popular for centuries. In the past, some were completely fanciful features of large pleasure gardens; others were used daily. Although some of these terms and concepts are no longer commonly used, all of the following types of spaces can inspire ideas and offer a great way to bring a sense of history to your garden plan. Many, such as gazebos, pergolas, and summerhouses, are once again becoming popular features of landscape design.

allées. These narrow walks bordered by evenly spaced trees or shrubs provide areas for strolling and talking. In the past, allées unified the garden and joined structures within it. The largest one led to the house, but narrower ones provided lanes shaded by trees or shrubs that arched overhead or were pleached (interlaced) to form a leafy roof. Narrow allées often ended at an alcove or summerhouse. Windows were cut through the greenery along the sides to provide views of the garden.

arbors. The term *arbor* refers to a variety of structures that enclose space to create a shady retreat, such as galleries and pergolas. Usually square or rectangular in shape and constructed of wood ranging from rustic branches to sturdy timbers, arbors have open roofs and commonly support vines. Typically, they shelter a single bench set against a fence or wall or two benches that face each other. Arbors also can be erected over decks and terraces to shade tables and larger seating areas.

decks. These seemingly modern structures actually started as extensions of porches and verandas. They also bear a relationship to Japanese viewing platforms, which are constructed to highlight a particular vista or to watch the moon. Modern decks are still commonly attached to the house, and they serve as an extended outdoor room that often replaces more expensive stone or brick terraces. Decks are ideal for creating level space on hilly sites because they are relatively easy to build on slopes. They also can be constructed around existing trees to take advantage of a natural shade canopy (hire an expert and allow plenty of room around the tree trunks for expansion and sway).

follies. A type of garden house, follies were popular in the grand landscaped parks of mid-eighteenth-century England. Follies were odd- or exotic-looking buildings that took the form of towers, pyramids, huts, or artificial ruins. They were designed as points of interest to be enjoyed while touring the garden.

A *hermitage,* an especially popular type of folly, was a very roughly built hut, often constructed of plastered-over roots, with a thatched roof and an earthen floor.

galleries. These were lightweight arched tunnels covered with vines or other plants trained over lath or metal frameworks. They provided a shady area for walking.

garden houses. Characteristic garden features for centuries, garden houses have always come in many different styles and sizes. In general, they are designed to protect visitors from the weather. For example, Chinese garden houses, called *chai,* were originally used by poet-scholars as places to write. Originally, *chai* were rustic huts in the mountains, but they could also be quite elegant, complete with lattice-covered windows. In England, owners of large landscaped parks built garden houses that resembled cottages, huts, or mills. These were often used to escape the hustle and bustle of the main house for a few days. In the United

States, garden houses took the form of small cottages or playhouses. Architecturally, they often echoed elements of the main house. *See also* Summerhouses.

gazebos. Modern-day gazebos were inspired by Victorian garden structures, which, in turn, were based on Dutch garden houses. The original Dutch gazebos were solid-sided structures built at the corner of a property overlooking both garden and adjoining canals. Victorian gazebos were open-air buildings with a solid roof and usually five to eight sides that offered a comfortable, shady place to sit. Chinese gardens featured a similar open-air structure, called a *t'ing,* which had a tile roof and sides that were either open or surrounded by a low wall. *Pavilions* are gazebo-like structures most often found in public parks and gardens.

grottoes. Designed to resemble caves, grottoes have origins in both China and Europe. These usually artificial structures were either above or below ground and quite fanciful. Grottoes were decorated, often elaborately, with rocks, shells, statues, plants, and fountains.

pergolas. Once again popular, these are tunnel-like, flat-topped arbors built of vertical pillars and horizontal beams. Like arbors and galleries, pergolas are covered with vines and provide a shady walkway to enjoy.

sheltered seats and alcoves. Popular in the late eighteenth and early nineteenth centuries, sheltered seats were constructed in a wide range of styles, from Chinese to Victorian, from rustic to cottage-like. They featured a solid roof sheltering a shaded seat that overlooked a view or other notable spot in the garden.

summerhouses. Less elaborate but more open and airy than a garden house, a summerhouse is a perfect shady retreat for sitting and reading or chatting with friends. Historically, summerhouses were more enclosed and private than gazebos. Summerhouses with lattice sides became popular in the American South in the mid-eighteenth century, as they provided a shady sitting area that could still take advantage of the breeze. The Victorians especially enjoyed creating rustic- or cottage-style summerhouses. More modern summerhouses echo the architectural style of the main house.

tool- and potting sheds. For putterers, these may be the perfect shady retreat. Utility buildings were originally kept out of the garden, but in the eighteenth century they quickly became quirky, fanciful structures. Modern utility buildings generally reflect the architecture of the house, but a tool- or potting shed can be as plain or fancy as its owner sees fit. Such buildings are often heavily decorated with window boxes and other ornaments.

tree houses. Often overlooked as structures for modern gardens, tree houses were especially popular during the sixteenth and seventeenth centuries and usually had a solid roof, walls, windows, and a door. These uniquely appealing shady retreats are built above ground either in or around a tree, and they offer seclusion, shade, and a bird's-eye view of the garden. Each one is different because it is designed to fit a specific tree or trees. A *crow's nest* is a similar structure, but it does not have a roof.

shade: natural or constructed?

When you're planning a shady retreat, studying shade can become an obsession. Naturally shaded spaces — those under existing or newly planted trees — can be created by making a clearing in a woodland, installing a small garden room under a stand of trees, planting several trees to shade a particular area, framing a space with a mix of shrubs and trees, or carving out a sheltered pocket under a limbed-up tree. Adding shade trees to enlarge a shady space or to cast shade at a particular time of day is another option. Don't overlook shade trees on adjoining properties as a source of much needed shelter.

You don't necessarily have to start with an area that's under trees, though, because you can create shade where you most want it. Constructed shady spaces offer an interesting range of options and frequently are the fastest way to create shade on an otherwise sunny lot. Erect an arbor over a terrace or deck and cover it with vines, and you've got a shady space to enjoy in relatively short order. You can always suspend a piece of shade cloth or awning material

Canopy options. Large, mature trees aren't a requirement for creating a shady retreat. Small ornamental trees cast substantial shade, too (above). Or consider adding a gazebo, a summerhouse, an arbor, or even an umbrella to make a shady retreat (left).

under the arbor until the vines fill in if the area is too sunny to use at first. Arbors also are more space efficient than are trees or shrubs, an important consideration if your yard is small. Other types of constructed spaces include pergolas, gazebos, porches, summerhouses, potting sheds, and even tree houses.

Some of the best shady retreats take advantage of both natural and constructed shade. Add an umbrella in a spot with dappled shade, perhaps, or a vine-covered arbor to augment the shade cast by a grove of young trees. Or create a sheltered refuge on the shady side of a garage or other structure that also receives some shade from

nearby trees. Many of the gardens pictured in this book combine elements of both natural and constructed shade, so you'll find plenty of ideas to consider in the photographs and paintings.

mapping shade

To plan a successful shady retreat, you'll need to understand the sun and shade patterns in your yard. Most gardeners have a good idea where the hot, full-sun sites are located, as well as where deep shade makes it hard to grow anything. The in-between areas, in shade for part of the day, are often another matter. Having a general idea of where the sun is in the sky at any given time of day will help you pick a site for your retreat. It will also be invaluable as you position trees, arbors, or other structures to cast shade when and where you want it.

To figure out sun and shade patterns, make a simple drawing like the one shown below. Draw the outline of your property or just the area where you'd like to create your shady retreat. Locate north on the map. Then sketch in the shade pattern several times during the course of a day — at 10 A.M., noon, 3 P.M., and 6 P.M. To plan shade patterns for new trees or other features, sketch them in (use a piece of tracing paper as an overlay if you don't want to write directly on your drawing). Then draw their projected shade patterns.

Keep in mind that the sun's angle in the sky changes throughout the year. The sun is lower in the sky in winter, so shadows are wider and longer than they are in summer, when the sun travels high overhead. If you're planning your retreat in any season other than summer, you'll need to adjust the shade patterns accordingly. Remember that areas of shade are narrower and shorter in midsummer than they are at any other time of year — and that's when you'll most want to use your shady retreat.

assessing privacy

A shady retreat wouldn't be a retreat without privacy. As you look at potential spaces, consider your options for screening them from the outside world. You don't need a solid hedge with a door on one side — like the garden Mary discovered in *The Secret Garden* — but screening that blocks off the outside world makes a shady retreat seem secluded and peaceful. The best style of screening will vary depending on your yard; you'll see lots of options in the garden plans in part 2.

As you stand in potential sites and examine them from the inside, think about what kinds of privacy screens you will need. A shrub or two or a vine-covered trellis may add all the privacy you want. Or perhaps you'll decide on a shrub border, a hedge, or a wall. Be sure to examine spaces from the outside, too. City gardeners may need trees, arbors, or other overhead structures for privacy if surrounding buildings overlook their gardens.

One advantage of fences and solid brick, stone, or cement walls is that they provide privacy as soon as they are erected. They are also very space efficient, making them a good choice for small yards. On the other hand, they are expensive and can block the breeze. On windy sites, solid barriers don't filter wind as shrubs do; instead, wind hits the barrier, then travels up and over it, thus creating turbulence on the other side.

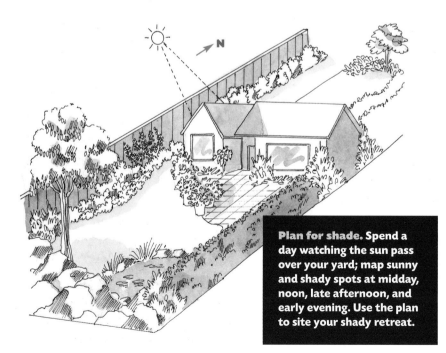

Plan for shade. Spend a day watching the sun pass over your yard; map sunny and shady spots at midday, noon, late afternoon, and early evening. Use the plan to site your shady retreat.

On a windswept site, consider using openwork fences (such as shadow box–style) or openwork brick or stone, and try to combine such solid barriers with shrubs. Stone, brick, and cement walls also trap and hold heat. This is a good characteristic if you're planting early-blooming bulbs, but on a sultry summer day all the stored heat will be released during the evening hours. On a south- or west-facing site, the heat can scorch plants on hot days, too.

A shrub border or a hedge is a good, relatively inexpensive option for adding privacy to any yard, provided space isn't at a premium. Shrub borders need to be fairly wide to be effective — usually at least 15 feet — and hedges should be at least 5 feet wide. Both shrub borders and hedges can take a few years to become established, so they will require more patience on your part than would a fence or conventional wall. Cost varies according to the species and size of the plants you select. Shrub borders and hedges can block the breeze, but not to the extent that a solid structure, such as a fence, will. On a windswept site, the wind will pass through them and be softened and reduced in the process. See Green Walls and Ceilings on page 15 for more information on planning for privacy.

considering the view

You may want to highlight nearby scenery or a view of the garden from your shady retreat — after

Pretty privacy. The vine-covered lattice wall behind this bench creates an appealing, private place to sit and enjoy a view of the garden.

all, a room with a view can be a delightful place to spend time. A flower bed, water garden, or piece of sculpture set in a drift of ground covers all will make wonderful views when framed through an opening in a shrub or a window cut in a trellis. Also, look beyond the boundaries of your property for views you can "borrow." It's worth doing some selective pruning or reorienting the design of

your shady retreat to capture the right vista. Spectacular views are wonderful — think of a secluded shady seat looking out at a distant mountain or lake — but don't overlook more subtle ones. Highlighting a trellis, specimen tree, or perennial bed in your yard or your neighbor's yard can be effective, too. While you're at it, make notes about views you'd like to hide, and think about tentative solutions.

designing your shady retreat

Although you can use graph paper, a tape measure, and colored pencils to design your retreat, planning on paper is an option, not a necessity. Using a more hands-on approach is fun and a very creative way to plan — more like constructing the forts and clubhouses that many of us built as children.

Start by clearing out and cleaning up the space you've selected. You may want to mark off the space with stones, stakes, or bricks to see where you're clearing. Don't be afraid to remove trees or shrubs

to make the space large enough to use, or adjust the space slightly to accommodate them. By the same token, take your time and make sure you don't rip out a plant that might be useful later — it's easier, and less expensive, to remove more plants in a few months or a year than it is to replace ones removed in haste. In addition to double-checking the shade pattern before you cut (so you don't remove something crucial), try to identify the plants you are thinking of keeping, then keep the best

ones. Choose spindly oaks over weedy ailanthus or Norway maples, for example. Giving a lanky, overcrowded plant a bit more space, along with some judicious pruning or training, can make all the difference in its appearance, so be patient. You can always remove a plant later, as your retreat develops, but there's no sense in replacing plants you don't need to.

The gardens in part 2 feature a variety of techniques that will help you create your shady retreat, from options for leveling out a site to making flower beds. For a technique that will help you visualize your space and experiment with where furniture and plants should go, see Clearing on a Woodland Edge on page 25.

Planning on paper is a good idea if your design calls for an arbor, a summerhouse, or an extensive paved area along with brick, stone, or concrete walls. If you have a large yard or want extensive new plantings for screening a retreat, a simple drawing may be in order. A scale drawing will help you design and locate structures, explain your plans to contractors, and estimate the amount of material you'll need (such as bricks or bluestone).

A rough map also makes it easy to draw in various options to determine where large-scale plantings might work best. Another idea is to take pictures of the space with a conventional or digital camera. Make copies or scan the shots into your computer and use them for sketching ideas.

green walls and ceilings

The plants you can use to screen a shady retreat run the gamut. Shrubs such as forsythias and privets (*Ligustrum* spp.), which can be sheared as hedges, are fine, as are viburnums, mock oranges (*Philadelphus* spp.), and weigela (*Weigela florida*). For year-round screening, think about needle- or broad-leaved evergreens. For a dense hedge that doesn't need regular shearing, consider a compact evergreen with a narrow, pyramidal shape. Several forms of arborvitae (*Thuja occidentalis*) fit the bill, including 'Pyramidalis', 'Rosenthalii', and 'Wintergreen'. For a less formal look, plant a shrub border of compact and weeping evergreens and flowering shrubs. Keep in mind that most compact evergreens grow slowly, so you'll probably want to invest in good-size plants from the start. To learn more about shade-loving

Planning options. While retreats under trees are fairly easy to create with careful clearing and planting, a scale drawing — or calling in a professional — is best if you are planning a structure such as a gazebo and pond (left) or a vine-covered arbor (right).

shrubs to plant in your retreat or to use as screens in partial to full shade, see Shrubs, Small Trees and Vines in part 3 on page 166.

Arbors are often covered with sun-loving vines. Climbing roses, clematis, wisteria, grapes, and Dutchman's pipe *(Aristolochia macrophylla)* all thrive in sun and, with a little patience on your part, will cast good, dense shade. See page 82 for more information on vines vigorous enough to clothe arbors and tips on how to start them climbing. Less vigorous vines, such as hybrid clematis, and even tender perennials, including morning glories *(Ipomoea* spp.) and scarlet runner bean *(Phaseolus coccineus),* can be used on trellises that form the walls of your shady retreat.

gardening in the shade

A shady retreat should be planted the way you want — fancy perennial beds are an option, not a necessity. Planting no-nonsense, low-maintenance ground covers is a good choice if you'd rather spend your time reading or meditating than gardening. No matter which kinds of plants you want, before you buy anything, take time to examine your site and think about where planting beds could go. If you are blessed with oaks and other deep-rooted trees, you can carpet the ground around your shady retreat with a lush shade garden. On the other hand, if shallow-rooted trees, such as maples and beeches, are the pre-

dominant species, planting near them may be nearly impossible.

Take a spade out to the site and dig a few test holes, but dig carefully to avoid damaging tree roots. If you find masses of roots that leave little space for perennials, your best bet is to pull any weeds and spread a layer of mulch on the soil to discourage their return. Don't pile soil on top of tree roots to create new planting beds: Not only will the tree roots reinvade the new soil, but changing the grade around a tree can damage or kill it as well.

Container gardens are a good way to add spots of color on sites where tree roots prevent planting in the ground. Set large tubs (half whiskey barrels work well) on top of the mulch and plant them with annuals or shade-loving perennials, such as hostas. If your budget allows, consider installing a ground-level deck over root-clogged soil and terracing it with planters to level an uneven site. See the garden designs in part 2 for other ideas on creating flower beds in shady sites.

On sites with tree roots that aren't so dense as to make planting impossible, you can prepare among roots pockets of soil that are perfect for accommodating a perennial or two. Take care to avoid damaging tree roots, though. Once the garden is planted, mulch it regularly with chipped hardwood or chopped leaves to discourage weeds, keep the soil moist and rich in organic matter, and give the planting a

Shady beds and borders. Plant drifts of shade-loving annuals, perennials, bulbs, and shrubs to decorate around your retreat — or to enjoy your walk along the path that leads to it.

woodsy look. See part 3 for information on plants to grow in shade. For plant combinations and other decorations that will brighten up shady spots, look for the Color in the Shade boxes that appear throughout this book.

planning the journey

The best garden designs offer places to go — paths to follow, secluded benches to perch on, shady nooks to discover — and a shady retreat is one of the most delightful of those destinations. With a little planning, the journey to a retreat can be half the fun of arriving there.

If you have enough space, indulge in the luxury of a path — long and winding or short and sweet. Mark the start with a specimen plant, a flower bed, a sculpture, a gate, an archway, or just an opening in a shrub border or hedge. Because often you can't see a retreat from the house (these are secluded places, after all!), a path can serve as a reminder that there's a quiet, peaceful place outside that's waiting to be occupied.

A path that has an obvious beginning but disappears from sight around a shrub or other planting is intriguing and tempting to follow. To create a path that's interesting and fun to trace, design a winding route with unexpected turns along its length. Decorate it with pockets of plants or interesting objects. Changing the path's covering, such as from flagstone to mulch, or its width (from

A shady stop. Walking to a shady retreat can be half the fun. Plan a path with twists and turns along the way, decorate it with beds of flowers, and include spots to sit and enjoy the view.

wide to narrow) also adds interest. Let the path become an essential part of how you experience your retreat. As you walk along it, try to clear your mind, begin to relax, and shed the cares of the day.

Even if your retreat is only a step or two from the back door, decorate the entrance to it with flowers, herbs, a container garden, rocks, an archway, or a gate. Con-

sider using this entry as a boundary between the outside world and a quiet place. Once there, you may choose to ban all electronics so cell phones and pagers won't ring. This ban would also force you to leave behind your computer, work, and E-mail. The result is a private sanctuary occupied by you and your guests, as well as birds and other creatures.

outfitting your shady retreat

Any room needs comfortable furnishings to make it appealing and useful, and an outdoor room is no different. You may already have an idea of what sorts of pieces you want for your shady retreat — a bench, several chairs, a hammock, or a table for two, perhaps. Settling on the exact materials and style can take time, though, as there are so many options from which to choose.

Above all, outdoor furniture needs to be able to withstand the weather, especially sun and rain, and that means it must be constructed of durable materials. Wood furniture made of teak, redwood, cedar, or pine is popular. Outdoor furniture is also constructed of several types of metal, including cast iron, tubular steel, tubular aluminum, wrought iron, wrought aluminum, and cast aluminum. All-weather wicker is a relatively new option. While conventional wicker furniture can't withstand wind and rain, all-weather wicker is made of polypropylene resin, vinyl, or fiberglass woven over a metal frame. Finally, if your heart is set on a hammock or hanging chair, you'll find both cotton and nylon models to choose from.

Regardless of the material, you'll want to consider both comfort and style when choosing furniture for any outdoor space. Sleek, modern-looking chairs may look great, but they won't compel you to linger in your shady retreat if they're not really comfortable. The same goes for charming twig chairs as well as antique cast-iron ones (or reproductions thereof). If they're lumpy and bumpy, they'll quickly become unused pieces of garden sculpture. Save such items for nooks where the furniture is meant to be looked at, not necessarily sat upon, and they'll be fine.

For most shady retreats, the goal is to have chairs that are comfortable enough to nestle into for an hour or two. It's important, therefore, to test furniture before you buy anything, if at all possible. If your taste exceeds your budget (some outdoor furniture can be quite expensive), don't put off outfitting your shady retreat until you can afford the perfect piece. Buy comfortable furniture that's in an acceptable style, then upgrade when you can.

finishing touches

Decorations and other features are as important outdoors as they are indoors, and all sorts of ornaments can add character to your shady retreat. Hard-core gardeners may just want a bed of choice dwarf shade-loving plants to decorate their space; bird lovers may decide to put up feeders. Displaying collections outdoors is fun too, whether you collect shells, rocks, watering cans, or birdhouses, which can be mounted on posts.

Or consider decorating a space with a striking sculpture or a collection of smaller related pieces. Wind chimes and other hanging items are appropriate, and don't forget to embellish nearby walls or fences with pots, wall hangings, trellises, or even painted trompe l'oeil scenes. Cement walls also can be adorned with mosaic tiles affixed directly to them. Temporary decorations are nice, too. Display a bucket of flowers, for example, or just a dish of water with one perfect bloom floating in it.

Water in any form, whether it's in a still, shallow bowl or moving in a fountain, makes a wonderful addition to an outdoor space. Consider leaving a birdbath or a dish of water on the ground to reflect the sky. (Keep in mind that you'll need to dump out the water every few days to eliminate mosquito larvae; birdbaths need scrubbing every few days, too.) You can enjoy moving water in a fountain even if you don't have a water garden (see page 111 for details). Moving water adds sparkle to a shady retreat, and it also introduces white noise, which can help mask the sounds of the outside world.

If you plan to use your shady retreat at night, candles or oil lamps are a nice touch. Consider ones where the flame is protected by a glass hurricane. Marine stores also carry lanterns, for both oil and candles, that don't blow out even in a fairly stiff breeze.

Above all, have fun decorating your shady retreat. Experiment with changing it around, adding and taking away items, and trying something completely different. The more your retreat expresses your personality, the more you'll want to use it.

Show your style. Express your style and interests — whether that means watering cans, rare plants, or objects collected at favorite vacation spots. Here, a birdbath adds a touch of color (left) and a large sculpture with Thurber-like figures dance in a shady corner (right).

designs for 20 shady retreats

PART 2

Sometimes, all you need to get started on a project is a great idea. In this section, you'll find hundreds of them! The following twenty plans for shady retreats are guaranteed to get you thinking about your own backyard and where you can carve out that perfect, private, shady space. You'll find a painting of each retreat followed by a detailed plot plan of the yard. There also is information about special features of each space and a list of suggested plants. Refer to the Color in the Shade boxes to help you inject color into any shady spot, and turn to the Ideas for Great Design sidebars for design principles to use when developing your own ideas for a shady retreat.

Instead of trying to copy these designs exactly, think about them as puzzle pieces that fit together to make many different pictures. Look for elements that would work in your yard — an arbor or a gazebo to add the shade you've always wanted or a deck that would level out a sitting area under trees, for example. Combine elements from different designs, too. Use the central sitting area from one design, the screening shrubs from another, and the hummingbird garden theme from a third. Don't overlook your own yard's features, either. Use the ideas presented here to renovate an unused terrace, or create a shady retreat next to the garage, then decorate the garage wall. If your dreams are bigger than your budget, make a small sitting area to use now, then start planning a larger shady retreat down the road. The main goal is to use these designs and ideas and get started.

clearing on a woodland edge

Despite the fact that this shady space is only a few steps from the house, part of its appeal is a secluded, "away from it all" feeling. The space itself is hidden from the house. In fact, the only sign of it from the back door is a mulched path that winds out of sight. Follow the path into the shade, and it reveals a quiet space outfitted with a hammock for snoozing plus comfortable chairs for sitting and reading or chatting with friends. The end result is a woodland clearing that seems far away from an otherwise ordinary backyard.

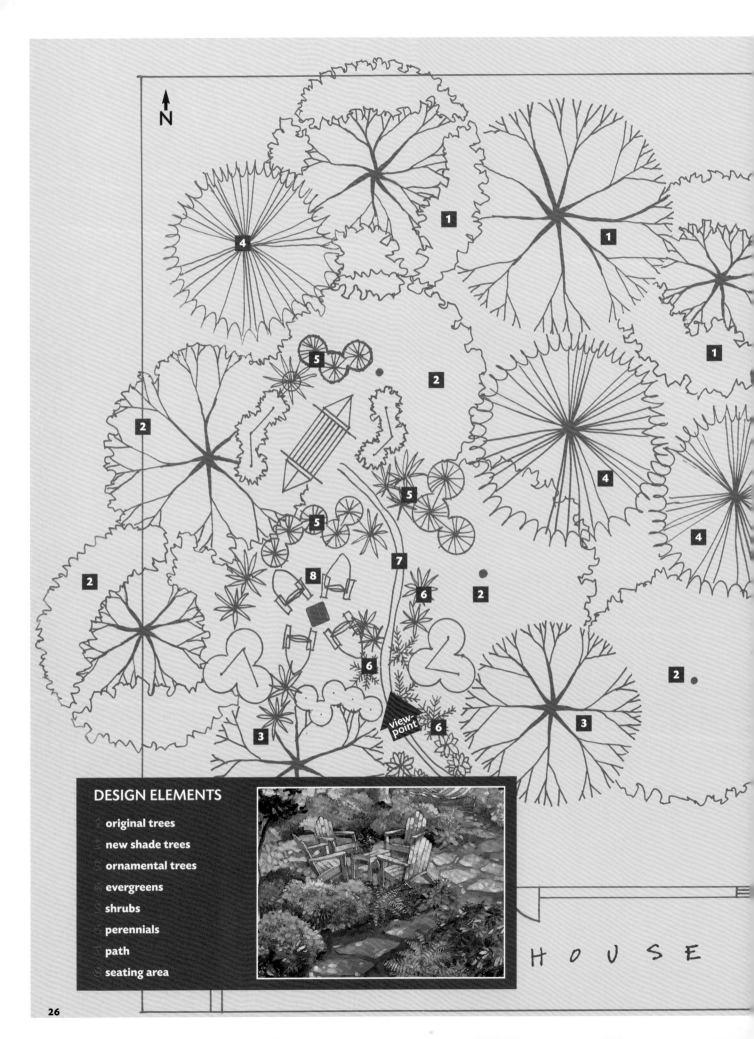

N ↑

1

1

4

1

2

5

2

2

5

4

5

5

7

8

6

2

4

2

6

6

2

3

view-point

6

3

DESIGN ELEMENTS

1 original trees

2 new shade trees

3 ornamental trees

4 evergreens

5 shrubs

6 perennials

7 path

8 seating area

H O U S E

WHILE TREES lining the back of this suburban property (1) gave it a wooded feel, the yard didn't always offer a shady, private haven. That's because the original stand of trees ran along the north side of the property, and the property faces south. As a result, even branches that hung out over the yard didn't cast much shade, leaving the yard baking in the sun from morning until night. Almost as important, the property was open on both sides and didn't offer any secluded areas that were screened from neighboring houses.

The yard did have a woodsy feel, which served as the inspiration for this secluded retreat, despite the lack of shade. Six new shade trees (2), two smaller ornamental flowering trees (3), four evergreens (4), and a mix of shrubs (5) were added to create this retreat. Careful placement of each new plant also helped screen the yard to make it more private. The plantings are much more than simple hedges, however. They surround and shelter a private clearing that has become a welcoming outdoor room. The new plantings also help bring the woods out into the yard, rather than leaving them marching along the back lot line. This gives the whole property more of a woodland feel. Drifts of vigorous, easy-care perennials carpet the ground (6), filling space once planted in grass.

planning for shade

Sun and shade patterns are fairly simple in any south-facing yard, and this yard was no exception. In order for trees to cast usable shade, they need to be planted out in the yard, closer to the house, because the most usable shade will be on the north side. Since spreading trees around a yard creates only a patch of shade here and another there, these trees are grouped to create a large area that's shaded for most of the day. While the key shade trees play the biggest role in blocking the sun, smaller ornamental trees help out, too. Shrubs in the plan add privacy, but they also contribute essential shade late in the day when the sun is low in the sky.

A planting like this one is actually easy to plan out right on the ground — although you can draw it out on paper if you want. To plan without resorting to paper, you'll need some stakes and string plus buckets, plastic bags full of leaves, or other miscellaneous items to stand in for shrubs. Start by locating the shade trees. Have helpers stand where you think trees should go. As you position your helpers, be sure to keep in mind where the sun will be traveling across the sky at high summer. You want the trees to block the sun, especially during the hottest part of the day.

First, examine the site from several sides, making sure you give each tree (currently a helper!) plenty of room to spread horizontally, although in a few years you'll want the branch tips to begin touching so they'll weave denser shade. Pound in stakes to mark their locations.

Next, use stakes and string to mark off the clearing, plus a winding path (7) that will lead from your house to the emerging shady retreat. Use more stakes to locate smaller ornamental trees — keep them on the edges so their ornamental features show to best effect. Arrange the buckets or what-have-you to stand in for shrubs that will screen the space and mark off the path. To help visualize how the space will work, set lawn chairs in the shady retreat you're creating.

Walk down the marked-off path to the seating area (8) and try to imagine how it will look. Are the shrubs in the right place to properly screen the space and create privacy? Will the trees cast enough shade? Keep moving the stand-in "shrubs" around — or the stakes that indicate where trees will go — until you're satisfied with the arrangement. You can then transfer the plan to paper or mark the spots where shrubs will go with short stakes until you plant.

Pick out the shade trees first; oaks (*Quercus* spp.) are deep rooted and easy to garden around. Ornamental trees like crab apples (*Malus* spp.) or cherries (*Prunus* spp.) bring spring flowers and other features to the outer edge of the woods you're creating. Select a mix of evergreen and deciduous shrubs suitable for your climate. Azaleas and rhododendrons are great shrubs for shady sites — see the listing on page 172 for more good ideas.

Depending on your budget and time available, you can plant the area yourself or hire a nursery to do the planting for you. Another option is to have the nursery install the trees, then plant the shrubs yourself. If you need to phase in the plantings, buy the biggest shade trees you can afford, and get them in the ground first.

an easy-care carpet

The floor of this space is covered with drifts of vigorous perennials to replace the high-maintenance grass that won't grow well in shade anyway. If you're planting the whole area at once, rent a sod cutter and remove the lawn. Otherwise, dig up sod and plant in sections once the trees are in place. All of the Plants to Choose From (page 29) spread to form large clumps or they self-sow. You'll need to weed regularly for a few seasons until the plants fill in; after that, they'll just need attention once or twice a year. Avoid invasive spreaders like bishop's weed (*Aegopodium podagraria* 'Variegatum'), which will take over the space, and English ivy *(Hedera helix),* which spreads everywhere and also climbs up trees.

color in the shade

Leaves and flowers aren't the only things that will brighten up a dark and shady spot. Consider adding colorful furniture, such as a bright red chair, to create a splash of color in your shady retreat.

plants to choose from

BLUE BUGLEWEED (*Ajuga genevensis*). Slower-spreading than vigorous *A. reptans*, this species produces blue flowers in spring and handsome, spinachlike leaves.

EPIMEDIUM (*Epimedium* spp.). *E.* × *perralchicum*, *E.* × *perralderianum*, and *E.* × *versicolor* are all good, tough, steady spreaders that grow in shade.

FERNS. Plant spreaders, such as Japanese painted fern (*Athyrium nipponicum* var. *pictum*), male fern (*Dryopteris filix-mas*), ostrich fern (*Matteuccia struthiopteris*), flowering ferns (*Osmunda* spp.), maiden ferns (*Thelypteris* spp.), broad beech fern (*T. hexagonoptera*), and New York fern (*T. noveboracensis*).

HELLEBORES, LENTEN ROSES (*Helleborus* × *hybridus*). Self-sown seedlings appear around the clumps in summer; dig them up in midsummer and spread them out to fill new spaces as needed.

HOSTAS (*Hosta* spp.). Choose vigorous, large-leaved cultivars, such as 'Francee' or 'Frances Williams', or smaller-leaved, vigorous selections, including 'Golden Tiara'.

VARIEGATED SOLOMON'S SEAL (*Polygonatum odoratum* 'Variegatum'). A handsome plant grown mostly for its clumps of erect, white-edged leaves, which are pretty from spring to fall.

VINCA (*Vinca minor*). This can be a very vigorous spreader; variegated forms, such as 'Alba Variegata' with white-edged leaves, are more restrained and quite ornamental.

Matteuccia struthiopteris

Helleborus x hybridus

Vinca minor

ideas for great design

cooling a hot site
Trees and shrubs that are arranged in groups create large, usable areas of shade. They also soften the edge of the woods and make the whole yard seem wooded.

on-the-ground planning
This space can be planned without resorting to complicated drawings. In fact, planning it out right on the ground makes it easy to visualize where the plants need to go.

hide-and-seek pathway
Although the path to this space isn't long, winding it out of sight behind shrubs and trees makes it interesting to follow and makes the shady retreat seem farther away from the real world.

cutting back on lawn
Mowing around trees and shrubs takes time and energy, and grass doesn't grow very well in shade anyway. Here, space under and around all the trees and shrubs is filled with a mix of vigorous perennials for a low-maintenance landscape.

two shady spaces
for a small lot

Efficient use of space is the reason this cheerful, cozy garden is so successful. The small, L-shaped lot features two shady outdoor rooms that are side by side, thus creating lots of useful and flexible space for outdoor living. The terrace, which adjoins the house, is outfitted with a table and chairs and is perfect for a meal alfresco, a game of cards, a craft-making session, or a visit with friends. An arbor over the sitting area gives it a comfortable, roomlike feel. Containers, and two-dimensional plantings in the form of vines trained on trellises, add color and appeal to both areas without taking up too much space.

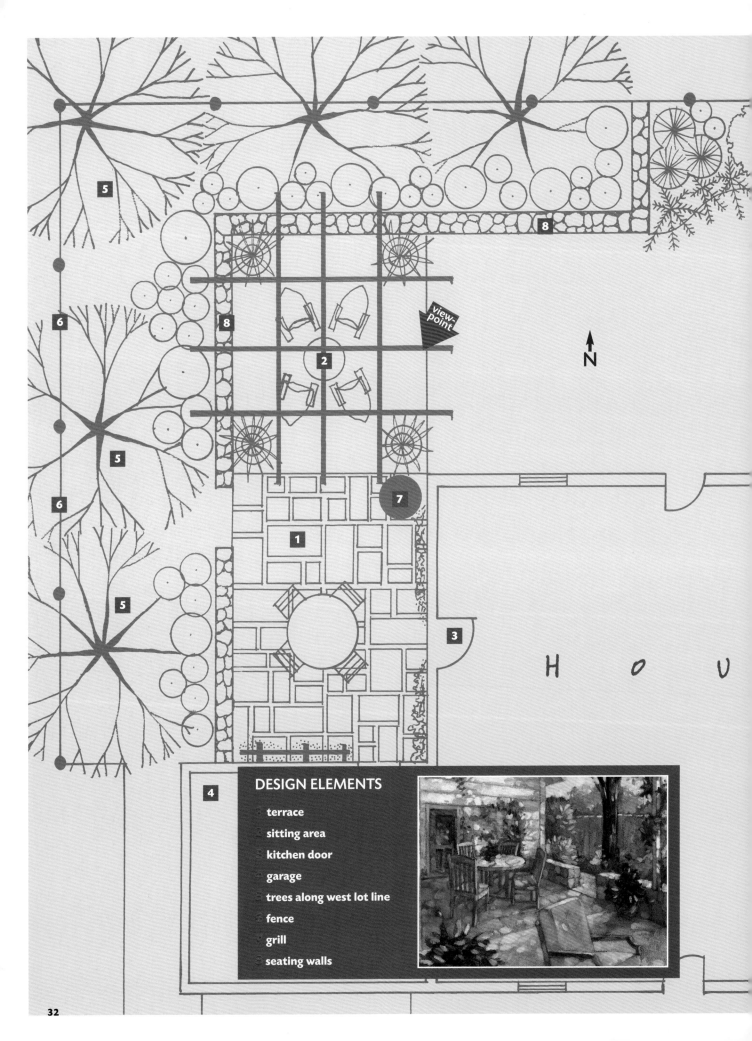

N

view-point

DESIGN ELEMENTS

1 terrace
2 sitting area
3 kitchen door
4 garage
5 trees along west lot line
6 fence
7 grill
8 seating walls

H O U

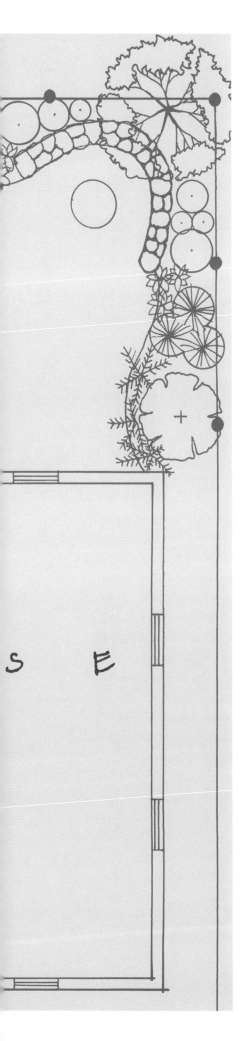

GOOD PLANNING is a key ingredient in this design — especially since it features two shady spaces. The terrace (1) and sitting area (2) are designed as distinct, but adjoining, outdoor rooms. They can be used either separately or together.

Convenient access is a primary feature of both spaces. Often, an area adjacent to the kitchen and garage is relegated to utility use (such as storage for garbage cans) or just lawn, and the main garden is located in back of the house. Here, since both spaces are easily accessible from the kitchen (3) and garage (4), location becomes an asset. It's easy to carry food and drinks out onto the terrace, and gardening equipment stored in the garage is handy, too.

Much of the shade that makes these spaces appealing is created by the location. In the morning, the house shades the terrace and much of the sitting area, while a row of trees along the west lot line (5) protects both spaces from the sun in the afternoon.

A vine-covered arbor over the sitting area augments the shade from the trees. (On a city lot, an arbor can also provide some much-needed privacy from above, where tall buildings overlook a garden.) Shrubs under the trees, along with a fence just inside the west lot line (6), contribute late-day shade and also make both spaces completely private. All these factors add up to a spot that's nice and shady even on a hot, sunny afternoon.

design for adjoining spaces

Making room for two shady retreats in this small yard not only makes the design more interesting, but it also gives each space a more intimate and appealing feel. Like adjoining rooms, the two spaces are decorated and furnished so each is distinct, yet together they form a harmonious whole.

Two types of "flooring" help set the spaces apart, just like flooring in a kitchen might be tile and the adjoining family room might be carpeted or have a wood floor. Here, the outdoor terrace and dining area is paved in bluestone — which gives the area a formal feeling — while the floor of the adjacent sitting area is pea gravel.

Although the furniture in each area is similar in style, the terrace is designed for eating, while the sitting area is arranged to make conversation a main focus. A grill (7) sits between the two spaces. The arbor overhead also sets the sitting area apart from the terrace. It is high enough (8 feet) to make walking under it comfortable, yet it gives the sitting area an enclosed feel. Together, the two outdoor rooms are flexible spaces for a wide variety of activities.

A 2½-foot-tall seating wall (8) connects the two spaces and the entire yard, for that matter; it frames the area and provides extra seating space for parties. The wall extends out beyond the arbor, then ends in the middle of the north lot line. To unify the design, another section of seating wall curves around a millstone table in the northeast corner of the yard. The table, wall, and adjacent plantings create a focal point to enjoy from the shady sitting area but also serve as an informal sitting area in the sun.

If you're on a budget or are a do-it-yourself gardener, think about installing a design like this and upgrading features in stages. That way, you can spread out the cost and the work. For example, pave the entire area in pea gravel — or pea gravel in one area and mulch in the other — until you can put in a proper bluestone terrace. Start with a basic pine table (or even plastic), then trade up as your budget allows. The important thing is to get the space started. Using it, even if you don't have it decorated as you'd like, will give

you even more ideas and help fine-tune the design.

plants for summerlong color

Space is at a premium in this garden, so plants on the terrace are restricted to narrow beds along walls to allow adequate room for chairs and walkways. Wax begonias, coleus, polka-dot plant (*Hypoestes phyllostachya*), and caladiums create a pink, white, and burgundy color scheme. All provide color for the entire season if they are kept watered in dry weather. The large containers under the arbor are filled with coleus, whose foliage contributes bright color and interesting texture throughout the summer.

Flowering vines trained up trellises add color higher up, while Dutchman's pipe (*Aristolochia macrophylla*) growing on the arbor shades the sitting area. (See Plants to Choose From, page 35, for more vines suitable for covering an arbor.) Vertical gardening — growing plants on trellises attached to the walls — is a great way to dress up a small area without taking up much space.

For lots of flowers that fit right in with this color scheme, consider combining woodbine honeysuckle (*Lonicera periclymenum*), with fragrant, white to yellow flowers, and a white-flowered form of black-eyed Susan vine (*Thunbergia alata*), which will bloom all summer long. Both bloom in shade, albeit less than they would in sun.

color in the shade

Add color to a shady spot by decorating fences or walls — especially in a small garden. Consider a folk art piece, like this sun-and-moon, hang wreaths or banners, or paint a design directly on the fence. All brighten up a dark spot without taking up space. Fancy trellises, with or without vines, are another great option.

plants to choose from

HARDY KIWI (*Actinidia* spp.). These have fragrant spring flowers and edible grape-size fruit in fall. Normally male and female plants are required for fruit set, but the cultivar *A. arguta* 'Issai' is self-fertile. Variegated kiwi *(A. kolomikta)* is grown for its leaves marked with white and/or pink; it is somewhat less vigorous than *A. arguta*.

FIVELEAF AKEBIA *(Akebia quinata)*. This vigorous, sometimes invasive, climber needs regular pruning. It has fragrant, brown-purple spring flowers and handsome leaves that stay on the plants until early winter. It is semievergreen in the South.

WISTERIA (*Wisteria* spp). These woody vines are the ultimate in vigorous climbers. Japanese wisteria *(W. floribunda)*, Chinese wisteria *(W. sinensis)*, and hybrid *W. x formosa* are popular. For a native species, consider American wisteria *(W. frutescens)* or Kentucky wisteria *(W. macrostachya)*. All sport clusters of fragrant, spring-borne flowers in lilac, violet, or white. Named cultivars bloom best. Make sure wisterias have an extremely sturdy arbor.

AMERICAN BITTERSWEET (*Celastris scandens)*. Plants have small, inconspicuous flowers in June followed by showy, orange-red berries and yellow foliage in fall.

For more vigorous vines for arbors, see Ceiling of Leaves and Sky on page 78.

Akebia quinata

Wisteria x formosa

Actinidia kolomikta

ideas for great design

efficient use of space
Careful planning yields two distinct shady spaces in a small area that can be used comfortably either separately or together.

location, location, location
Easy access to both the kitchen and the garage makes these spaces very practical, and the plan allows plenty of room for walkways, so it's easy to move around.

vertical gardening
Adding narrow beds filled with long-blooming annuals and trellised vines along the walls adds color and appeal to the terrace without taking up too much room or blocking walkways.

room with a view
The millstone table and the seating walls become attractive focal points to enjoy from the sitting area, and they also offer other pleasant places to sit when the sun isn't too hot.

cozy nook
on a terrace

While rectangular terraces are most common, this curvilinear one has its own appeal. The large area next to the house is suitable for parties and family gatherings, while a small shady retreat — perfect for quiet conversation or reading — is tucked into an alcove of the terrace toward the back of the yard. Lushly planted beds surrounding this space, plus a fence around the property, create a cozy, enclosed feel. Although this retreat is open at the front, the bed in the terrace near the house screens it from view, thus creating an inviting private space despite the relatively open entrance.

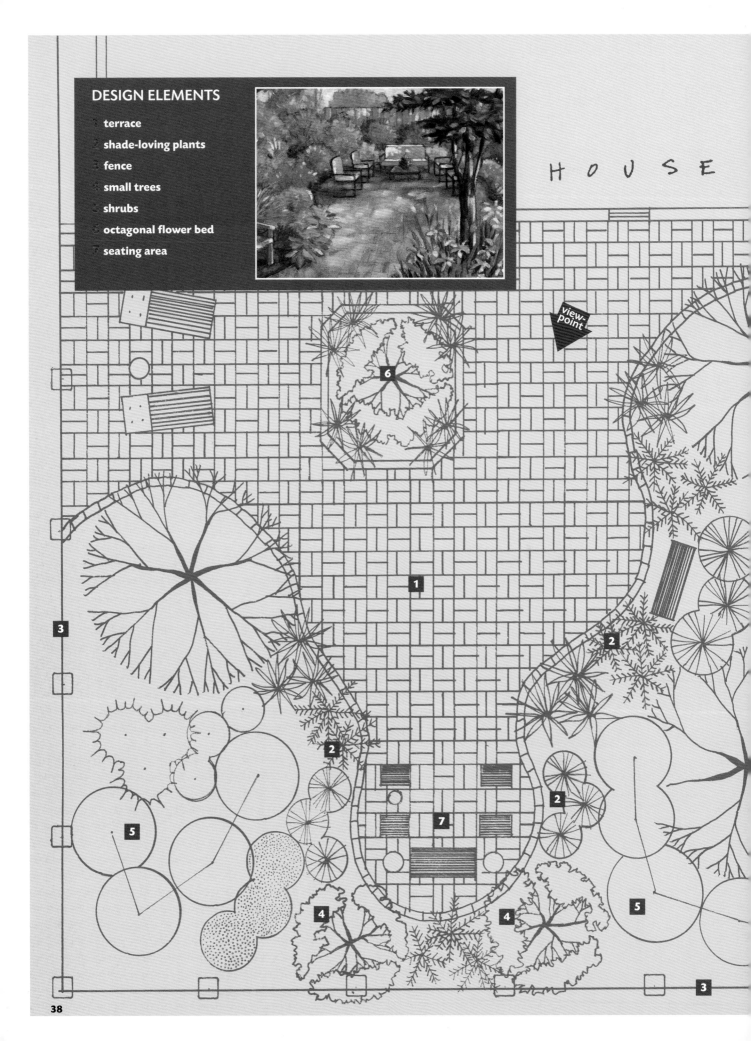

DESIGN ELEMENTS

1 terrace
2 shade-loving plants
3 fence
4 small trees
5 shrubs
6 octagonal flower bed
7 seating area

HOUSE

view-point

6

3

1

2

2

2

5

7

4

4

5

3

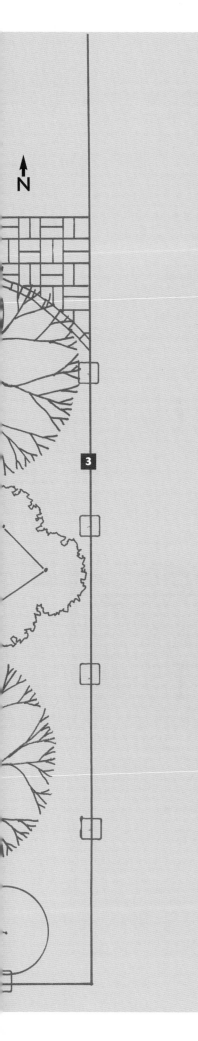

Once planted in scraggly grass with just a few trees, this yard began a transition from boring to beautiful when the lawn was replaced by a free-form terrace (1) flanked with beds bursting with shade-loving plants (2). Eliminating traditional grass, which doesn't grow well in shade anyway, has yielded a yard with plenty of room for gardening and an attractive, practical terrace — plus no lawn-care chores!

A north-facing site such as this one can be very shady, and shade was certainly an important factor in this design. A fence (3) and trees eliminate direct sun except near the house, leaving most of the planting beds in full shade all day long, with patches of dappled shade. A challenge in many gardens, shade is turned into an advantage in this design. Because there's no need for an arbor or umbrella for extra shelter from the sun, the shady sitting area has an airy and open feel. Brighter patches of dappled shade are filled with perennials that benefit from the extra light.

Along the back and sides of the yard, small trees (4) and a mix of shrubs (5) help screen the space from nearby neighbors. However, the fence that runs around the perimeter of the yard provides the most privacy. A solid board fence, such as this one, makes an ideal privacy screen, especially if space is at a premium. (A fence also can provide some shade late in the day.) Plantings of shrubs and small trees in front of the fence help soften its appearance and also muffle any noise from nearby neighbors.

A garage or other building makes an effective wall for a shady retreat, and a space like this one could be tucked up against a larger structure. The fence or wall surrounding a retreat becomes an opportunity for decorating: Paint it with a mural, adorn it with a trellis with or without vines, or use it as a place to hang a pretty plaque or another object.

a subtle screen

The wide opening at the front of this space could leave it too exposed — resembling a department store window. In fact, a completely wide-open front could easily reduce this cozy space to a pretty garden scene that's admired from afar but is rarely used.

The octagonal bed (6) in the center of the terrace solves that problem. Attractive in its own right, it also provides an important screening function and gives this shady retreat a much-needed sense of privacy and enclosure. The bed makes it possible to catch a glimpse of the sitting area (7) from the back windows of the house but keeps it out of full view, making the retreat a more tempting place to visit. From inside the retreat looking out, the bed screens the house and makes it seem farther away. The octagonal bed also serves as a centerpiece for the main patio, without blocking walkways or restricting guests' movements. Plus, it creates an attractive view to admire from the shady sitting area.

A small tree such as a paperbark maple *(Acer griseum)* or cornelian cherry dogwood *(Cornus mas),* at the center of the octagonal bed provides the bulk of the screen. (Careful pruning is necessary so it doesn't block walkways on the terrace.) Surrounding the tree are plants with edible flowers and herbs that tolerate part shade. Plants here include daylilies

(Hemerocallis spp.), cilantro *(Coriandrum sativum),* borage *(Borago officinalis),* sages/salvias *(Salvia* spp.), Johnny-jump-ups and pansies *(Viola tricolor* and *V.* x *wittrockiana),* Swiss chard *(Beta vulgaris* ssp. *cicla,* especially colorful 'Bright Lights'), and pot marigolds *(Calendula officinalis).*

plants for a terrace garden

Despite daylong shade, this north-facing site doesn't lack for color. A mix of plants with variegated foliage keeps the color coming all season long. (See Plants to Choose From, page 41, for ideas.) Drifts of shade-loving ornamental grasses and ferns mingle with hostas.

Color echoes help unify the plantings. For example, the gold stripes in the leaves of variegated hakone grass *(Hakonechloa macra* 'Aureola') pick up the bright tones in the foliage of hostas such as 'Great Expectations' and 'Inniswood'. In addition, combining a mixture of textures and forms also keeps the planting interesting, as mound-shaped hostas with rounded leaves contrast with lacy ferns, astilbes, and bleeding hearts. All the plants in this garden thrive in rich, evenly moist soil that's well-drained. Deeply dug soil amended with plenty of organic matter, such as compost, helps ensure healthy looking foliage that remains attractive throughout the growing season.

color in the shade

Plants grown in containers add a spot of color anywhere in the garden, and they are especially valuable in shady spots. Here, a collection of caladiums and begonias bring colorful flowers and foliage to a simple sitting area. Pot-grown plants also are ideal for brightening up a shady bed or border. Plant these shade-loving specimens in the ground, or pot them up in ordinary nursery containers and then sink the pots to the rim in the soil. Keeping tender perennials like begonias and caladiums in pots makes it easier to overwinter them indoors and grow them for another year.

plants to choose from

FRINGED BLEEDING HEART (*Dicentra eximia*). For summerlong production of the dainty flowers, remove spent blooms and keep the soil moist. A spot with morning sun and afternoon shade is best.

HAKONE GRASS (*Hakonechloa macra* 'Aureola'). This species forms large mounds of stunning green-and-yellow striped leaves. In addition, it makes an ideal container plant.

HOSTA (*Hosta* spp.). Use small-leaved cultivars such as 'Golden Tiara' or 'Grand Tiara' along the edges of a flower bed, with larger variegated plants such as 'Great Expectations', 'Gold Standard', and 'Inniswood' farther back. *H. tokudama* 'Flavo Circinalis' is stunning, too. 'So Sweet' has fragrant white flowers and white-edged leaves.

JAPANESE PAINTED FERN (*Athyrium nipponicum* var. *pictum*). This plant is frequently grown for its handsome leaves.

ORNAMENTAL TREES. Several small ornamental trees would make handsome additions, including Eastern redbud (*Cercis canadensis*), flowering dogwood (*Cornus florida*), cornelian cherry dogwood (*C. mas*), and Japanese maple (*Acer palmatum*). Shade-tolerant shrubs include summersweet (*Clethra alnifolia*), evergreen Japanese plum yew (*Cephalotaxus harringtoniana*), and leatherleaf viburnum (*Viburnum rhytidophyllum*).

Hakonechloa macra 'Aureola'

Hosta tokudama 'Flavo Circinalis'

Athyrium nipponicum var. *pictum*

Cornus florida

ideas for great design

divided space
Dividing a large area, such as a terrace, into smaller subspaces helps organize the site by directing traffic and setting aside spots for conversation or other pursuits. In any sitting area, chairs are best arranged in a semicircle and should be no more than 8 to 10 feet apart.

off the beaten path
While this sitting area is convenient to the house, it is off the main terrace and away from any walkways to eliminate cut-through traffic and give it a private feel.

foliage a feature
Since summer-blooming flowers that thrive in shade are at a premium, these beds feature perennials with variegated foliage. This ensures the garden will remain colorful throughout the growing season.

color echoes
Repeating colors in flowers and foliage throughout a garden is a strong unifying design element. Shades of yellow, white, or bronze are good colors for echoing in foliage.

berm for instant privacy

Surrounded by shrubs and blooming perennials, this charming gazebo offers a shady spot in the middle of an otherwise sunny garden. The gazebo is nestled up against a berm that is heavily planted in shrubs, tough ground covers, and a few trees. The berm partially encloses the gazebo and creates a wall of greenery that protects this spot from the sights and sounds of nearby neighbors. Beds curving around the base of the gazebo make it an integral part of the garden — a perfect shady vantage point for enjoying the sun-loving flowers, butterflies, and other garden delights.

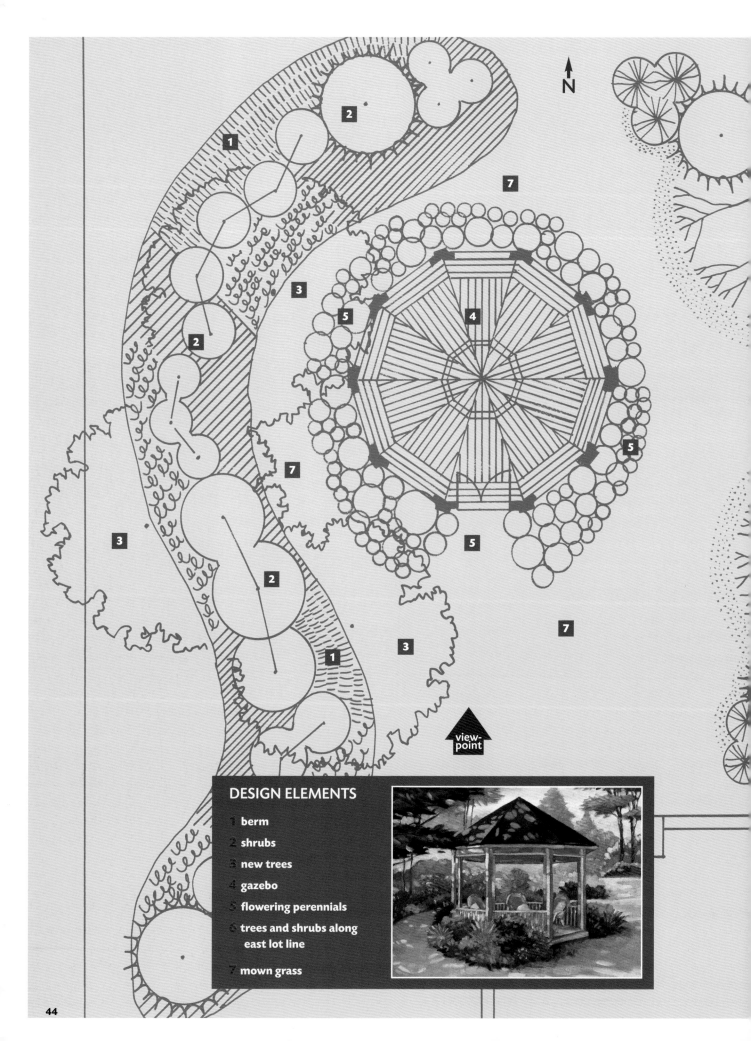

N

7

1

2

7

3

2

5

4

5

2

5

3

7

1

3

view-
point

DESIGN ELEMENTS

1 berm
2 shrubs
3 new trees
4 gazebo
5 flowering perennials
6 trees and shrubs along
   east lot line
7 mown grass

44

THIS LUSH YARD began life as a nearly featureless, flat-as-a-pancake square of lawn that looked more like a soccer field than a garden. Close neighbors on the west side, along with an unattractive view off the west corner, made the yard far too public and noisy. A private, shady space seemed like an impossibility.

Fortunately, one thing the property had going for it was plenty of space, and building a berm of soil (1) offered an immediate solution to the problems this yard presented. Even before it was planted, the berm effectively blocked the view and provided some much-needed privacy. A berm is a very effective noise barrier, too, especially when planted with shrubs (2). The berm also made the yard more interesting by adding a grade change and giving it a more rolling character.

instant shade

While trees (3) planted along the berm will one day add some shade, the gazebo (4) is the main reason this retreat is shady. Like the berm, it provided an immediate solution to this yard's shortcomings by adding a shady sitting area as soon as it was set in place. Unlike gazebos plopped down in the center of a lawn (which generally look too exposed), this one fits into the landscape beautifully.

Nestled in the curve of the berm and surrounded with plantings of shrubs and flowering perennials (5), it is an inviting outdoor room that offers a patch of cool shade right in the middle of the garden. Plantings around the gazebo, plus the berm, add to the private, secluded feeling so essential to any shady retreat.

The berm also solves another inherent problem: Large, flat, empty yards, such as this one, become an intimidating design challenge. It's hard to know where to start since there are few, if any, clues to guide you. Here, the berm provides an overall organizing principle that puts all the elements of the design in context. For example, the arc of trees and shrubs along the property's east side (6) echo the same curve of the gazebo's position in the curve of the berm. Together they outline and enclose the yard's central space. The result is a harmonious and balanced design.

Berms aren't suitable solutions for small yards, however, since they take up considerable space. The slope on a finished berm should range from 5:1 (five horizontal feet for each foot in elevation in the slope) to 4:1. That means a 6-foot-tall berm with a 5:1 slope will need to be 30 feet wide (5 horizontal feet x 6 vertical feet = 30 feet). Flowing, natural shapes are the easiest to build and plant. The base of the berm can be constructed of fill dirt or subsoil, but make sure the top foot or two is made of good screened topsoil so that it's easy to plant. Even newly planted shrubs on top of a berm add privacy, and once they begin to reach mature size they'll form a substantial barrier.

low-maintenance plants

This sunny garden is designed to keep maintenance to a minimum. The berm is planted with a mix of sun-loving shrubs — both decidu-ous and evergreen — and three ornamental shade trees along the edges. Vigorous ground covers fill the space underneath, and both shrubs and ground covers spill off the edges of the berm to soften it and make it look more natural.

Beds around the gazebo are planted with ornamental grasses, daylilies, (*Hemerocallis* spp.), core-opsis, purple coneflowers, *(Echinacea purpurea),* and catmints *(Nepeta)* — all tried-and-true perennials that perform well with a minimum of fuss. To develop a low-maintenance plant list for your own garden, look first to native plants that grow naturally in your area. They'll generally thrive with the amount of moisture and soil type your garden has to offer. Add improved cultivars of natives, along with other plants that grow well in the sun, soil, and exposure your garden offers.

The berm is planted with vigorous ground covers instead of grass, which reduces lawn care; they are mulched to keep weeds under control. This way, the homeowners can mow all the way around the outside of the berm instead of fussing with a lot of mowing and trimming of individual plants. Occasional weeding on the berm is a must the first few years until the ground covers fill in. Soaker hoses installed under the mulch make it easy to water the shrubs while they're getting established.

Vigorous ground covers, like the ones planted on the berm and in Plants to Choose From, page 47, need to be used with care, since they can quickly take over your garden. Combining different ground covers works here, since they're equally vigorous and one won't swamp the other. Mowing around the entire berm keeps them from spreading into the lawn and beyond.

Parts of the berm that are clos-est to the perennial plantings sur-rounding the gazebo are planted with less-aggressive ground covers including lilyturf (*Liriope* spp.), epimediums (*Epimedium* spp.), and hostas. Berm and perennial plantings are also separated by a strip of mown grass (7).

color in the shade

Don't be afraid to have some fun when selecting sculpture for your garden — serious, classical-looking pieces aren't for every-one! These funky dinosaurs, which are marching through a bed of perennials, add a whimsical touch that's sure to make visitors laugh out loud. They also bring in much-needed color. The blue-and-white pattern of the dinosaurs is echoed in the gazing ball behind them for even more light and color.

plants to choose from

BUGLEWEED *(Ajuga reptans).* This low-growing perennial forms wide-spreading mats of spinach-like leaves, and spikes of bright purple-blue flowers appear in early summer.

CREEPING BELLFLOWER *(Campanula rapunculoides).* Showy, but very invasive and difficult to eradicate, this bellflower sports violet-purple blooms in summer.

PACHYSANDRA, JAPANESE SPURGE *(Pachysandra terminalis).* This wide-spreading species is grown for its evergreen leaves. Plants spread but are fairly easy to pull up if they roam to where they are not wanted.

PLUMBAGO *(Ceratostigma plumbaginoides).* Another fast spreader, plumbago produces brilliant blue flowers from late summer onward, and the leaves turn bright red and orange in fall.

VARIEGATED BISHOP'S WEED *(Aegopodium podagraria* 'Variegatum'). This fast-spreading perennial forms a dense mat of pretty green-and-white leaves. Dig up any sections of the clumps that revert to green.

VINCA, CREEPING PERIWINKLE *(Vinca minor).* Rounded evergreen leaves and pretty flowers in shades of lavender or white make vinca an attractive, if fast-spreading, ground cover.

Ajuga reptans

Ceratostigma plumbaginoides

Pachysandra terminalis

ideas for great design

instant privacy and shade

A berm is a good privacy barrier suitable for a large, flat area. Here, coupled with a gazebo, it creates an appealing shady space in an exposed, featureless yard.

big berms are best

Little berms often look contrived and out of place, so build one that is substantial — even 5 or 6 feet tall. If there isn't room for a good-size berm, consider using a fence or retaining wall instead.

close spacing

Instead of setting plants at the recommended distances and waiting for them to fill in, plant densely, at perhaps half the recommended distance. Close spacing makes it harder for weeds to get a foothold. To prevent erosion, cover the soil with burlap, then cut holes through it for planting.

growing gracefully

As plantings in this garden mature, the yard will become shadier. As the amount of shade increases, more lawn can be replaced with ground covers and perennials.

tempting, shaded terrace

Cool, shady, and elegant, this arbor-covered terrace is a perfect spot for entertaining friends and family, whether that means a formal dinner party or an informal game night. In addition to the main dining table, comfortable chairs tucked into a corner make a space for quiet conversation or reading. Simple, classic design throughout makes this small terrace seem larger than it really is. Sleek, somewhat modern-looking furniture and neat plantings around the terrace are arranged formally. This area also becomes a pretty picture to look at from indoors, through windows in the house that overlook it.

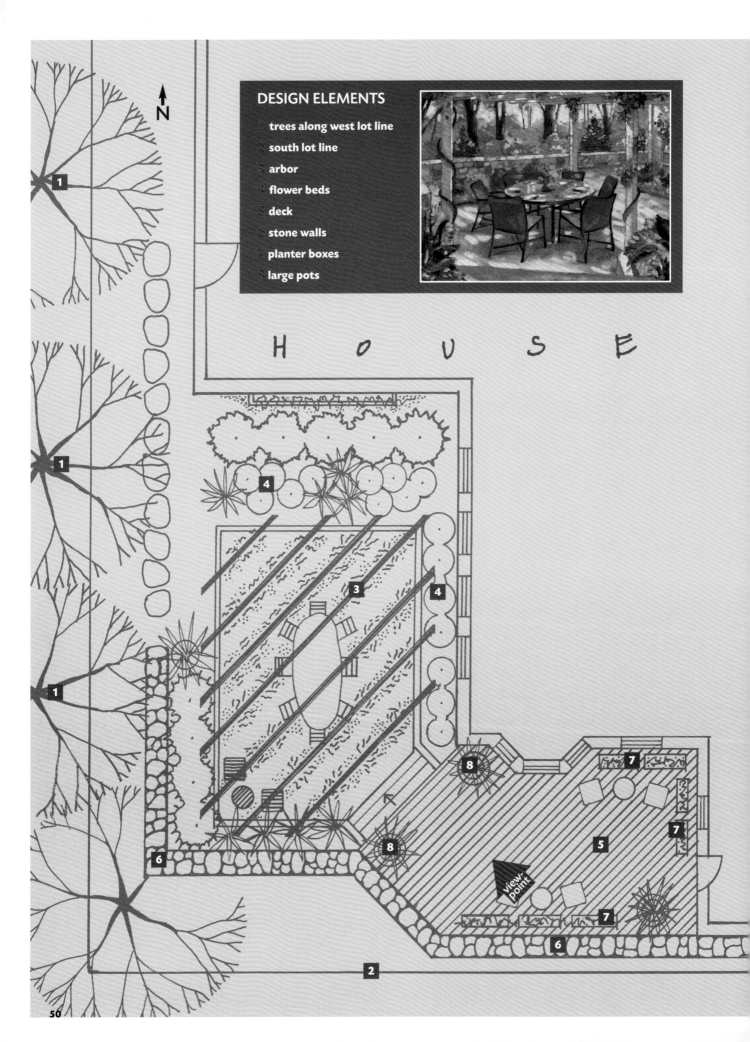

DESIGN ELEMENTS

1. trees along west lot line
2. south lot line
3. arbor
4. flower beds
5. deck
6. stone walls
7. planter boxes
8. large pots

H O U S E

view-point

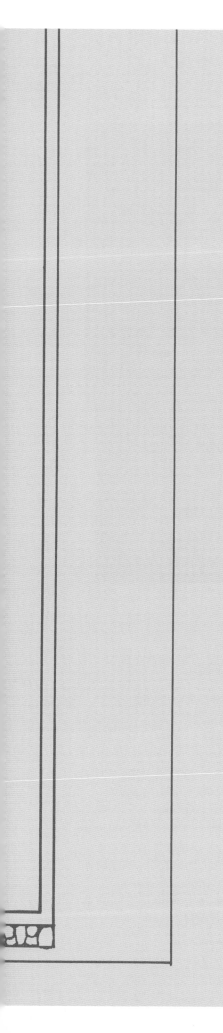

REDESIGNING an existing terrace or other outdoor living space is often an excellent and economical way to make it more useful. Although it was shaded in the morning by the house and in the late afternoon by the row of trees along the west lot line (1), this terrace was hot and sunny during the day. Heat that built up during the day was released in the evening, making it uncomfortably hot even after dark. Access was a problem, too, since the property drops off on the south side (2). The only way out to the terrace was via an uneven row of pavers across an awkward slope that was difficult to maintain.

The retrofit began with the construction of a sturdy arbor (3) over the terrace to provide shade during the hottest part of the day. The arbor also gives the terrace an intimate, enclosed feeling, and it ensures privacy even from close neighbors. It doesn't extend over the beds along the house (4), thus allowing some light to reach the plants. Since the terrace is several steps below the deck, the arbor is tall — a full 12 feet high. This ensures that visitors won't have to duck when stepping down onto the terrace. It also keeps the view from deck to terrace open and inviting. In addition, since the arbor is covered with wisteria, its tall height allows plenty of head-

room so the long clusters of flowers don't hit visitors on the head.

Soil in the beds around the terrace got an upgrade, too. Previously, scraggly plants in these beds struggled to survive in subsoil topped with a few inches of topsoil. The old plants were pulled out, and compost and topsoil were brought in to replace the tired soil. The new beds offer 2 feet of improved soil over loosened subsoil that was amended with compost.

making connections

To create a really usable connection between the terrace and the house, a deck (5) was added between the two to replace the uneven pathway. This enlarges the usable outdoor space in this small yard and also makes a welcoming entrance to the terrace. It's now easy to walk out to the terrace, even while carrying trays of food. A stone wall (6) squares off the southern and western edges of both deck and terrace, giving them a finished, formal look. Large planter boxes (7) on the sunny deck are perfect for a kitchen garden. They're used to grow herbs, choice vegetables, edible flowers, and salad crops.

Two large pots (8) of purple-leaved cannas, salvias, dwarf petunias, and other annuals mark the transition between deck and terrace.

Rhododendron 'Hino Crimson'

Taxus cuspidata 'Capitata'

Hydrangea quercifolia

Tsuga 'Cole's Prostrate'

DWARF AZALEAS (*Rhododendron* spp.). A wide variety of azaleas that need little, if any, pruning to stay compact is available. Flowers grow in shades of pink, red, fuchsia, yellow, orange, and white. The best choices are ones that thrive in your region of the country, so consult a local botanical garden, arboretum, or garden center. Azaleas bloom best in partial shade.

FIVE-LEAF ARALIA (*Eleutherococcus sieboldianus*). This tough, little-known shrub is primarily grown for its foliage and adaptable habit. Plants tolerate severe pruning, full shade, and dry soil, yet still maintain their good looks.

GLOSSY ABELIA (*Abelia* x *grandiflora*). A good screen or hedge plant, this species contributes glossy leaves and white or pale pink flowers to the garden from spring through summer. Plants bloom best in partial shade. 'Compacta' is a dwarf cultivar.

HEMLOCKS (*Tsuga* spp.). These needled evergreens are perfect for shade and are most often grown as trees. Look for dwarf cultivars such as 'Jeddeloh' or even ground-covering 'Cole's Prostrate', which reaches 12 inches. Plants grow well in shade and tolerate pruning.

JAPANESE PLUM YEW (*Cephalotaxus* spp.). For small gardens, choose a compact cultivar of this handsome evergreen. 'Duke Gardens' reaches about 3 feet tall and spreads from 3 to 4 feet. Plants tolerate full shade and pruning.

OAKLEAF HYDRANGEA (*Hydrangea quercifolia*). Showy white flower panicles in summer, bright red fall foliage, and interesting bark make this an excellent ornamental that brings four-season interest to shady spots. Plants bloom best in partial shade. 'Pee Wee' grows to 3 feet; 'Snowflake', reaches about 8 feet in height.

YEW (*Taxus* spp.). Tough and tolerant, these needled evergreens are excellent screening plants for spots in partial to full shade. They tolerate severe pruning, but for a small garden like this one, a compact or fastigiate cultivar is best. *T.* x *media* 'Densiformis', which grows to 4 feet and spreads from 4 to 6 feet, is one cultivar to consider for a tight spot.

This showy mix also calls attention to the steps leading down to the terrace. Giving visitors such clues that a level change is ahead helps eliminate tripping and missteps. In addition to pots marking a level change, a change in pattern from the deck to the steps also helps make the transition obvious.

plants for easy elegance

The simple plantings surrounding this terrace give it a lush feel, but with a minimum of maintenance. A privacy screen of evergreens was planted along the western side of the terrace. Shrubs along the house are grown for foliage or flowers.

By starting with dwarf cultivars and keeping plants trimmed in a natural shape — not sheared into cubes and gumballs — it's possible to maintain them at an appropriate size for this small space with a minimum of pruning. Shaping shrubs so they're slightly wider at the base

than at the top helps prevent them from losing lower branches and leaves. The wisteria on the arbor needs regular attention with pruning shears to keep it in bounds, but otherwise needs little care. See Two Shady Spaces for a Small Lot on page 31 and Ceiling of Leaves and Sky on page 78 for more vines suitable for an arbor.

Climbing the south-facing wall is Japanese hydrangea vine *(Schizophragma hydrangeoides)*, a shade-tolerant climber that produces white flowers in summer. To echo the white flowers all summer, impatiens or begonias could be planted along the front edge of the beds.

In a site like this one, it's important to carefully study the amount of sun and shade each part of the bed receives. Spots next to the house, which are shaded until mid-afternoon, will be much shadier than those near the lot line. Plants grown for their flowers bloom best when planted in the brightest spots.

ideas for great design

a terrace retrofit
Redesigning an existing space makes it possible to take advantage of its strengths but correct its shortcomings. Here, the arbor and deck add shade and vital access.

easy access a must
The deck leading from the house makes this terrace much more inviting. A space that's easy to get to — especially when carrying trays of food and other essentials — is far more compelling.

simple, sleek design
A formal style and sleek, modern-looking furniture make any small space seem larger. Plantings arranged in straight, formal rows plus a subtle, understated color scheme create a space that feels quiet and restful.

shrubs for a small space
In any small garden, shrubs can be a challenge because they either take up so much space or need to be pruned ruthlessly to keep them in bounds. Finding compact cultivars eliminates hours of pruning down the road.

color in the shade

Gazing balls glisten in the shade, bringing light to dark spots. They also reflect the plants around them. Glass models come in a variety of colors, with many types of stands — from simple to ornate — for displaying them. Display copper and stainless-steel gazing balls on stands, or set them right down among the plants.

mulched terrace under trees

Sitting in the shade under a clump of trees with branches arching high overhead is one of the most relaxing ways to spend time outdoors. Birdsong, rustling leaves, cool shade, and dappled patches of sun give this shady retreat all the appeal of a woodland clearing. Mulched with shredded bark and outfitted with comfortable furniture, this is a perfect spot for whiling away a summer afternoon. Feeders that are kept full year-round entice birds to visit, too, creating a fascinating, never-ending show. Shade-loving shrubs surrounding the terrace add privacy for the human visitors, cover for birds, and flowers in spring.

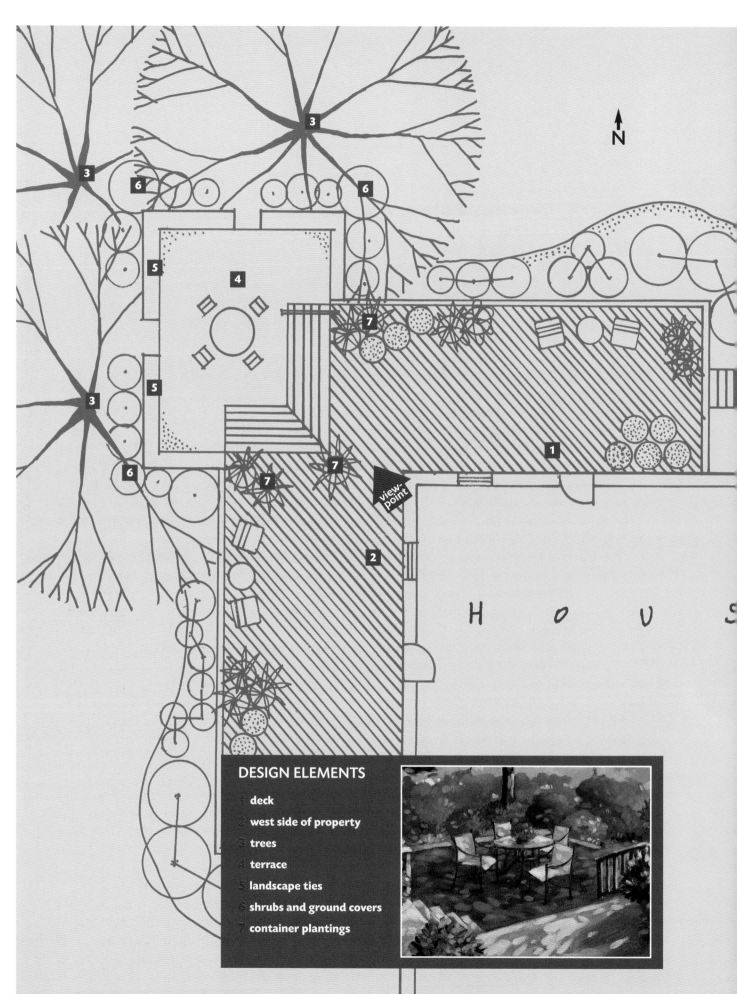

N

DESIGN ELEMENTS

1 deck
2 west side of property
3 trees
4 terrace
5 landscape ties
6 shrubs and ground covers
7 container plantings

view-point

H O U S

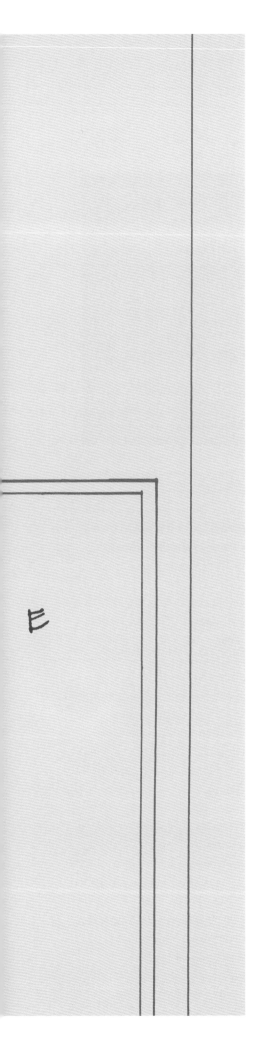

LEVEL SPACE was at a premium on this lot, until the deck (1) was added along the back of the house to create a large area for outdoor entertaining and other activities. While the deck certainly solved the problems of usable space on a sloping lot, it didn't offer much in the way of shade. Areas on the north side of the house are fairly well shaded, but the west-facing exposure (2) was sunny all day.

Erecting an arbor or installing an awning were certainly options for creating shady space here, but this design used another approach. To take advantage of the existing shade provided by the small clump of trees below the deck (3), the northwestern corner of the deck was removed and replaced with steps that led down under the trees. Tucking a terrace under the trees (4) makes use of a lovely shady spot, and it also expands the outdoor living space by creating a private retreat with a character all its own.

The terrace has a rustic, woodsy character due largely to the thick layer of shredded bark mulch that forms the floor. Landscape ties (5) frame the space and hold the mulch in place but minimize disturbance to tree roots. A deck could also have been installed around the trees with minimal damage. (For information on building decks around trees, see A Deck in the Woods on page 66.)

To create an arching entrance and ensure plenty of headroom for visitors, the trees were limbed up on the side nearest the deck. On the north and west sides, low branches were allowed to remain to augment the privacy screen. (On a site with a nice view, limbing up on both sides might be in order.) Maintenance is minimal. The area needs occasional weeding, and the mulch layer has to be replenished periodically.

To augment the woodsy feel and make the space even more private, grass was replaced with shade-loving shrubs and ground covers (6). A few perennials add colorful flowers and foliage to the mix. Replacing the grass with plants that thrive in shade also reduced maintenance, especially time spent mowing and trimming.

a wildlife haven

The underbrush also attracts birds and other wildlife to the area, and the space has become a perfect spot for watching birds. Birdfeeders hang from the trees; a tray or platform feeder offers fare for a wide variety of species; and suet feeders attract woodpeckers, chickadees, and nuthatches. Hanging birdhouses offer places for them to set up housekeeping; a birdbath set on the mulch encourages all manner of wildlife to stop in for a drink or a bath.

Viburnum rhytidophyllum

Kalmia latifolia

Hamamelis x intermedia 'Jelena'

CLIMBING HYDRANGEA

(Hydrangea petiolaris). This woody climber bears glossy green leaves and flat-topped clusters of white flowers in early to midsummer. Plants also have handsome, cinnamon-brown exfoliating bark. They can reach 60 to 80 feet with support and grow in full sun to partial shade in rich, evenly moist, well-drained soil. Do not train these plants onto walls that require periodic painting, as they attach themselves by clinging holdfasts. They are very slow to establish after transplanting, so be patient.

LEATHERLEAF VIBURNUM *(Viburnum rhytidophyllum).* This species bears clusters of creamy white flowers in spring. Plants reach 15 feet and feature evergreen leaves, making them excellent plants for screening. Plants will grow in heavy shade and in acidic or alkaline soil.

MOUNTAIN LAUREL *(Kalmia latifolia).* Many improved cultivars of this native shrub are now available, with flowers in shades from white to deep pink. These plants are still wild-collected, and buying a named cultivar is an easy way to make sure a plant is nursery grown. Blooms appear in early summer and the foliage is evergreen. Plants require moist, well-drained, acidic soil.

NANNYBERRY VIBURNUM *(Viburnum lentago).* White flowers in late spring followed by blue-black berries that attract birds make this a nice addition to shrub borders. They spread by suckers and are good screening plants for moist or dry soil.

SUMMERSWEET *(Clethra alnifolia).* Grown for its upright clusters of fragrant, white flowers, this species spreads by suckers and forms broad mounds. Plants do best in wet conditions or in average, well-drained soil.

SWEETSHRUB, CAROLINA ALLSPICE *(Calycanthus floridus).* Blooming from late spring to midsummer, this species produces small, red-brown flowers that have a rich fruity fragrance. It grows in acidic or alkaline soil.

VIRGINIA SWEETSPIRE *(Itea virginica).* This species bears bottle-brush-shaped clusters of white, lightly fragrant flowers in early summer. Plants grow in wet soil as well as in moist, well-drained conditions.

WITCH HAZELS *(Hamamelis* spp.*).* Depending on the cultivar, these bloom from late fall to early spring and have excellent fall foliage color. They are large shrubs, growing to 20 or 30 feet, and are excellent for screening. Plants grow in acidic or alkaline soil.

In addition, a conventional birdbath without the pedestal makes a fine ground-level model, or you can use something as simple as a large terra-cotta plant saucer. Be sure to clean it out thoroughly every other day or so and refill it with fresh water. In addition to encouraging visitors, all the feeders and birdhouses are decorations that give this retreat a character all its own.

Containers overflowing with annuals and tender perennials at the top of the steps (7) make the terrace below more private by hiding the entrance somewhat. They also help mark this transition, call attention to it, and make it safer. Structural clues also mark the transition. Here, the diagonal decking contrasts with the steps themselves. The steps also are illuminated with low-voltage lighting at night.

a layered screen

Layers of plants were added to recreate the underbrush that was torn out when the house was built. Drifts of daffodils, Spanish bluebells *(Hyacinthoides hispanica)*, and grape hyacinths *(Muscari* spp.) provide fresh, spring color. A mix of ground covers fills in around the shrubs, which form the backbone of the planting. These include ferns, hostas, bigroot geranium *(Geranium macrorrhizum)*, woodland phlox *(Phlox divaricata)*, and lungworts *(Pulmonaria* spp.).

Flowering shrubs that thrive in partial shade and bloom over a long season, like the ones in Plants to Choose From, page 58, form the nucleus of the plantings around this retreat. All are adaptable plants that prefer moist, loamy, acidic soil.

color in the shade

Birdhouses make wonderful garden ornaments for brightening any shady spot. Painted wooden houses are always charming, but try to find ones that open up for cleaning, so the old nest can be removed each year. Try painting your own designs, or decorate a house by attaching twigs, seedpods, and other found items with waterproof glue.

ideas for great design

tree-friendly design
Digging the foundation required for a stone or brick terrace can kill trees. Here, landscape ties help level out the site, and mulch creates soft, fairly level footing.

limbing up
In a shady retreat sheltered by trees, remove any branches that could pose a threat to visitors. Remove large branches to create plenty of headroom, but also look for twigs that could poke an eye or scratch someone's face.

bring in a free show
Well, almost free, since it does cost money to keep birdfeeders filled! Birds and other wild visitors make a shady retreat extra special.

consider the view
Evaluate what there is to look at from a retreat, then screen and reveal as needed. Larger shrubs, especially ones that spread by suckering, make great informal screens. Remove some lower tree branches to open up views you want to enjoy.

gazebo at a forest's edge

Sheltered by trees and surrounded by lush-leaved perennials, this gazebo has transformed a boggy, hard-to-maintain site into a lovely garden destination. The stepping-stone path leads through beds of moisture-loving perennials and makes it possible to get to the gazebo with dry feet, even in spring, when the spot is decidedly swampy. Many perennials that thrive in wet or boggy soil feature large, showy leaves, which give this garden an exotic appeal. A ground-level birdbath and birdhouses invite woodland creatures to visit, and the screened gazebo is enjoyable to use on buggy summer evenings.

WET SPOTS can be wonderful gardening opportunities in disguise, but they often start out as maintenance nightmares. They're a headache to mow because lawnmowers bog down in the lush growth and mucky soil. Since loads of wonderful perennials thrive in damp soil, wet spots can be transformed into spectacular gardens.

Once covered with weedy underbrush, this damp woodland is now filled with moisture-loving perennials and shrubs. The gazebo (1) at the center of the garden provides a dry spot that makes a perfect viewing platform right in the center of the action. It's a wonderful, quiet place to sit alone or with a few friends and enjoy the flowers, birds, butterflies, and chimnea (2) on cooler nights.

Careful siting is one thing that makes this gazebo so special. It is tucked under the trees (3) in a spot that's always a few degrees cooler than the sunny backyard. Trees provide most of the shade, but the gazebo's roof ensures the sitting area is completely shaded. Wrapping the gazebo with plants also makes it an integral part of the landscape. There's no doubt that this is a welcoming — and interesting — place to spend time and enjoy the garden.

The curving path (4) leading through the beds of perennials (5) is designed using the principle of hide and reveal, which makes any garden path more alluring. While a straight path allows visitors to see the destination clearly, the curvilinear design blocks the view of the gazebo from some points along the path and allows glimpses of it from other points. This makes the path more intriguing to follow and encourages visitors to enjoy the plants along the way. It also gives them time to let go of everyday concerns, relax, focus on the moment, and enjoy being outside in a beautiful garden.

Well-designed paths help make visitors feel cared for and safe, and this one allows them to journey out to the gazebo even in very wet weather without risk of soaking their shoes in a puddle or ruining them in mud. The path is set slightly above grade level, and the pavers are set in gravel, making it possible to stay high and dry even in soggy weather.

a lush, wet garden

A wonderful mix of perennials thrives in wet soil and shade. When starting a garden on a site like this one, it's best to develop it in sections. Wet soil is heavy, so you may want to hire extra help for this task. Dig weeds or remove grass and loosen the soil. Work in plenty of organic matter, such as coarse compost, to improve drainage — especially if you find you have heavy clay. You may want

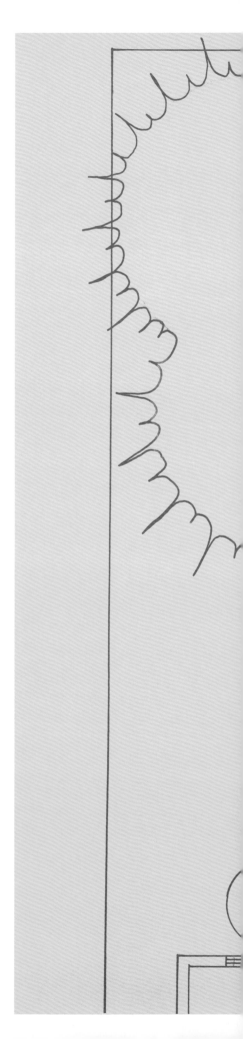

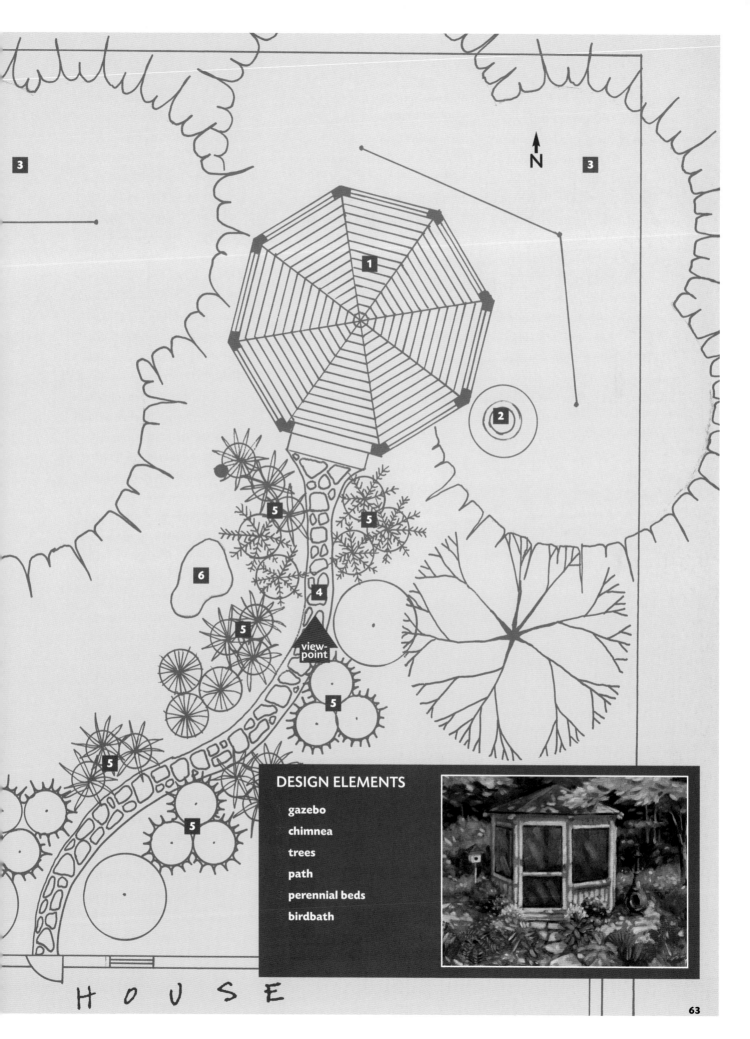

3

N

3

1

2

5

5

6

5

4

view-
point

5

5

5

5

DESIGN ELEMENTS

gazebo

chimnea

trees

path

perennial beds

birdbath

H O U S E

to add some pavers or flat rocks throughout the garden beds so you can get in to weed and care for plants without getting your feet wet and muddy.

It's also a good idea to study the lay of the land during a rainstorm, since that's the best time to see where water stands, where it runs off, and where it needs to flow. Dig trenches to direct runoff. If a site has excessive runoff, consider building a natural pond (without a liner) to hold it while it percolates into the soil. Surprisingly, installing an artificial water garden on a wet spot like this one isn't a good idea. Although it might seem like a perfect place, groundwater fills the hole under the installed liner and will either push a fiberglass liner right out of the ground or else cause large, water-filled bubbles to form under flexible liners. This garden plan features a ground-level birdbath (6) in a well-drained spot.

For screening a shady retreat, select shrubs that thrive in wet, shady spots, including swamp or sweet azalea *(Rhododendron viscosum)*, which produces white flowers flushed with pink in summer. There are hollies for damp shade, too, including inkberry *(Ilex glabra)*, an evergreen, and winterberry *(I. verticillata)*, a deciduous species. Need trees for a wet location? Consider planting pin oak *(Quercus palustris)*, tupelo *(Nyssa sylvatica)*, swamp chestnut oak *(Quercus michauxii)*, common baldcypress *(Taxodium distichum)*, river birch *(Betula nigra)*, sweetgum *(Liquidambar styraciflua)*, or American planetree *(Platanus occidentalis)*.

Think foliage to keep any shade garden interesting all season. Look for plants with contrasting leaf shapes, sizes, colors, and textures, and combine them to highlight their differences. Bold-leaved hostas like 'Sum and Substance', with chartreuse leaves, are stunning with grassy-leaved variegated hakone grass *(Hakonechloa macra 'Aureola')*, for example.

Bold-leaved perennials give this garden a very lush tropical look. Plus-size hostas like 'Big Daddy', 'Krossa Regal', and 'Regal Splendor' are truly spectacular when grown in damp soil, as are moisture-loving ferns such as cinnamon ferns *(Osmunda cinnamomea)* and royal ferns *(O. regalis)*. Truly boggy conditions make it possible to keep stunners like ligularia *(Ligularia stenocephala, L. dentata, or L. przewalskii)*, Chinese rhubarb *(Rheum palmatum)*, and umbrella plant *(Darmera peltata)* thriving. Plants to Choose From, page 65, suggests other perennials for wet soil and shade.

color in the shade

A birdbath brightens a shady spot because light is reflected off the water. Although cast-concrete birdbaths are most common, this ceramic model also contributes bright blue color to the garden. Copper ones are available, too. All birdbaths should be cleaned thoroughly and refilled every few days. Store them indoors over the winter, or turn the bowl upside down to keep it dry. Otherwise, freezing water will cause it to crack. The wind chimes hanging over this birdbath add an interesting vertical element to this spot.

plants to choose from

ASTILBE (*Astilbe* spp.). Plumy, early-summer flowers and glossy, fernlike leaves make these plants handsome additions to any shade garden. Give them damp soil, where selections such as *A. chinensis* var. *taquetti* 'Superba' can grow 4 feet tall.

GOAT'S BEARD (*Aruncus* spp.). Compact 10-inch-tall *A. aethusifolius* and the 6-foot-tall *A. dioicus* are both handsome. They have ferny leaves and loose clusters of white flowers that resemble astilbes.

LOBELIA (*Lobelia* spp.). Scarlet-flowered cardinal flower *(Lobelia cardinalis)* and great blue lobelia *(L. siphilitica)* produce spikes of flowers that attract hummingbirds. Both self-sow in good conditions.

MASTERWORT (*Astrantia major).* This species bears clusters of buttonlike pink, maroon, or green flowers over mounds of handsome, lobed leaves.

MEADOW RUE (*Thalictrum* spp.). These handsome perennials produce tiny, petalless flowers in huge showy clusters above mounds of delicate-looking, blue-green leaves. *T. delavayi* and *T. rochebrunianum* are popular species.

SIBERIAN IRIS (*Iris sibirica).* In early summer, these popular perennials produce showy flowers in shades of white, violet, purple, blue, and yellow. The clumps of grassy leaves remain attractive all season. Plants grow with up to about 2 inches of standing water over the crowns.

Astrantia major

Thalictrum delavayi

Iris sibirica

TURTLEHEAD (*Chelone* spp.). These wildflowers bear clusters of showy, two-lipped flowers in pink, purple, or white. They will grow in heavy clay and spread to form 2-foot-wide clumps.

ideas for great design

match plants to site
Instead of trying to drain a wet site, use the conditions to advantage by filling it with shrubs and perennials that will thrive there naturally.

hide-and-reveal pathway
Curving a pathway through plantings makes the trip out to a shady retreat more interesting and exciting. It also makes the ultimate destination more intriguing.

user-friendly paths
Paths should make visitors feel cared for: Do make them level, to eliminate danger of tripping, but consider varying the surface to keep them interesting. Also avoid or remove low overhead branches that might get in the way.

evening comforts
Screens keep bugs at bay in this gazebo, and a chimnea is available for fires that warm up the area in spring or fall. Candles (and a watertight tin for matches) would also make this site perfect for an outdoor evening.

a deck in the woods

Although commonly attached to the back of a house, a deck can be a wonderful addition anywhere in a yard. This one takes advantage of existing shade by carving out level space in the middle of a clump of trees toward the back of the property. The deck is designed to fit around existing trees, and one tree actually comes up through the floor of the deck itself. Partially hidden from the house, the deck is surrounded by shade-loving shrubs and wildflowers that create privacy yet reveal an attractive view. The sitting area that results is suitable for a variety of activities, from family gatherings to chatting with friends or simply snoozing.

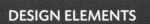

DESIGN ELEMENTS

1 deck built around tree
2 tree growing up through
  the deck
3 west lot line
4 shrubs and wildflowers
5 ground covers
6 lawn
7 archway

N

3

3

4

4

2

5

5

1

7

6

viewpoint

H O U S E

THIS SHADY outdoor living space started out as a sloping, uneven patch of ground under a nice clump of oak and maple trees. The site has a pretty view of the mountains in the distance, but they are not easy to see from the house, so creating a sitting area to enjoy the view made perfect sense.

Installing a terrace here was out of the question — digging the required foundation would have killed or damaged the trees — and the site was too uneven for a simple arrangement of mulch and landscape ties. A ground-level deck (1) proved to be the perfect solution, making it possible to create plenty of level space in the shade. With a canopy of tree branches forming the roof, shrubs around the area screening the sides as walls, and openings to enjoy the view, this deck is a very special and practical outdoor living space.

level space, anywhere

Whether attached to a house or freestanding in the yard, decks are excellent options for creating an outdoor space with a level floor under trees. That's because their design can be adapted to the specific site, so they can be constructed with minimal disturbance to tree roots. Spans between posts and the size of the joists are adjusted to accommodate tree roots and trunks and minimize damage to them. Decks also can be designed to allow existing trees to come up through the floor of the deck, as one does here (2).

Freestanding decks also are great options for creating sitting space in areas with boggy soil, another place where terraces aren't practical. There, they can be surrounded by lush, tropical-looking bog plants. For a deck in either kind of location, consult a skilled contractor or landscape architect who has experience dealing with such sites. During construction, be sure to protect trees that are near the site by erecting snow fencing or other barriers around them outside of the dripline (where the tips of the branches end). Before the deck is finished, limb up trees or erect barriers (such as railings around a trunk) so that guests will not hit their heads on low-hanging branches or a trunk that leans at an odd angle.

This deck is at ground level for the most part, although it's higher off the ground in some places than others because of the uneven terrain. It was installed first, before any of the surrounding gardens. After the deck was in place, patches of grass and English ivy (Hedera helix), which were threatening to take over the entire area, were replaced along the west lot line (3) and along the south side of the deck. These areas are now planted with a mixture of small trees and shrubs to make them seem more wooded and create a more effective privacy screen. North of the deck, the area is planted with lower-growing shrubs and wildflowers that add color and interest without blocking the view (4).

Low ground covers along the east edge of the deck (5), which receive a half day of sun, eliminate the need to trim grass, and the open front makes it easy to keep an eye on young children playing on the lawn (6). In time, this entrance to the deck will be planted more heavily so it is screened and much more private. A vine-covered archway (7) marks this east entrance to the deck. It serves as a symbolic marker separating the play yard and lawn from the quiet sitting area under the trees.

Whether you have children or not, boundaries like this one may make sense for a shady retreat. You may want to set personal rules about leaving work, computers, cell phones, or pagers behind when entering your retreat. Or you may want to make restrictions on activities — card games and art projects may be okay, but loud roughhousing or sports off-limits.

pockets of wildflowers

The design of the shade gardens around this deck depends to a great extent on the type of trees growing overhead. While deep-rooted oaks make it easy to find room to fit in flowers, there are also maples in this grove, which are notoriously shallow rooted and difficult to plant under.

Here, the areas under the maples have either just been weeded and mulched, or vines from nearby spots with deeper soil have been allowed to fill the area. English ivy can survive under maples, but unfortunately, it climbs the trees and is too rampant to leave. The vines that are allowed to scramble over the ground under these trees include climbing hydrangea (*Hydrangea petiolaris*) and sweet autumn clematis (*Clematis terniflora*).

Rich, moist soil under the oak on the north side of the deck is a perfect spot for growing an array of native wildflowers. There are also several plumleaf azalea (*Rhododendron prunifolium*), a native species with red to red-orange flowers in midsummer. The garden is planted around the roots of the oak tree, and the area is mulched with chopped leaves for a natural look. While loads of wildflowers fill this garden in spring and early summer, a few are still stunning late in the season. All of the perennials in Plants to Choose From, page 71, are attractive from midsummer to fall.

color in the shade

Water gardens are usually located in full sun, because most water-garden plants don't tolerate shade. But light reflecting on water brightens the shade, and fish are always fun to watch. A fountain would add even more sparkle to this garden.

plants to choose from

ALLEGHENY SPURGE (*Pachysandra procumbens*). This species forms broad mounds of handsome, semi-evergreen leaves that are mottled with maroon and green. Creamy white flowers appear in spring.

AMSONIA (*Amsonia hubrectii*). A shrubby perennial with pale blue spring flowers, Amsonia is spectacular in fall, when the billowing clumps of very narrow leaves turn golden-yellow.

HARDY AGERATUM (*Eupatorium coelestinum*). With its fluffy, flat-topped clusters of lilac-blue flowers, this species looks just like a tall ageratum. Plants reach 2 to 3 feet and spread to form broad clumps.

NORTHERN SEA OATS (*Chasmanthium latifolium*). An ornamental grass that thrives in shade, this species bears bamboolike leaves and drooping clusters of green seeds that turn brown in fall. Plants self-sow with enthusiasm.

PINK COREOPSIS (*Coreopsis rosea*). Although normally a plant for full sun, coreopsis will grow in partial shade. This species produces tiny pink, yellow-centered daisies from summer to fall.

SNAKEROOT, BUGBANE (*Cimicifuga* spp.). Two species of cimicifuga are native wildflowers: American bugbane (*C. americana*), which blooms from late summer to fall, and black snakeroot (*C. racemosa*), which blooms in midsummer. Both sport spikes of fluffy white flowers.

Amsonia hubrectii

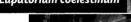
Chasmanthium latifolium

Eupatorium coelestinum

Cimicifuga racemosa

ideas for great design

forge a flat space
Decks are often overlooked as options for creating a flat space out in the yard, yet they're practical and relatively economical. Today, they can be constructed of recycled plastic wood.

flexible furniture
If you plan on moving outdoor furniture from place to place, consider purchasing lightweight, sturdy tubular-aluminum pieces.

don't fight the site
Trying to dig planting holes under a shallow-rooted tree like a maple is an exercise in frustration. It's much better to cover these areas with mulch and/or vines scrambling on the ground, and look for better sites to garden elsewhere.

planting pockets
To find spots for perennials under shade trees, poke around in the soil with a small trowel looking for spaces between larger roots. Loosen the soil in pockets and amend it with compost. Try not to cut tree roots.

relaxing pool house

This deeply shaded pool house makes a lovely retreat from spring to fall. Open on the southern and western sides to give a clear view of the pool, it has arbors extending from the eaves to ensure that the entire space remains cool and shady. A ceiling fan swishes overhead on hot days, and cushioned chairs provide comfortable seating. The solid roof makes it a nice place to spend time outdoors even on a rainy day. To give the area the feel of a garden, the surrounding terrace is decorated with pretty containers of annuals and tender perennials, plus a number of houseplants summering outside.

A SWIMMING POOL takes up a substantial amount of space in the average suburban backyard, leaving little room for a garden, let alone a spacious shady retreat. In this yard, however, the pool house (1) does double duty. It not only offers a place to change or sit after swimming, but it is also an attractive destination worth visiting anytime, even when the swimming pool is not in use.

Because of the solid roof, the space is suitable for furniture that wouldn't be practical in a more exposed site. Wicker furniture and pieces with thick cushions and pillows work just fine here. The end result is a look that's more reminiscent of an indoor sunroom than an outdoor space. Because of the exposure to moisture and ultraviolet rays, however, the cushions and pillows are covered in fabrics suitable for outdoor furniture.

The pump and related pool equipment is installed on the eastern side of the pool house (2), so this space also has electricity. A ceiling fan keeps the air moving, and lamps make reading possible in the evening. The pool area is also illuminated with decorative, low-voltage lighting. Strings of fairy lights hang from the outside edge of the arbor around the pool house, creating a festive atmosphere at night. A few low-voltage lights also illuminate the path from the house (3) and the plant-

ings alongside the pool house. Finally, a small spotlight shines up into the tree (4) on the western side of the pool to add depth and drama to the nighttime scene.

arbors for shade

Vine-covered arbors (5) extend the eaves of the pool house on three sides, making the space inside even shadier. Many vines would be suitable here for providing extra shade, including wisterias, Dutchman's pipe *(Aristolochia durior),* fiveleaf akebia *(Akebia quinata),* and even climbing roses or clematis.

Privacy is something of an issue here, since the pool house is open on the front and side. Trellises or lattice screens covered with vines could be hung to make the area more private. They would be best along the southeastern side of the building, but should only extend about halfway so the view of the pool remains unobstructed and parents can easily keep an eye on children swimming.

Another option would be to hang lattice screens or lightweight wall panels on sliding tracks so the space could be opened and closed at will. That way, it could be opened up in summer and kept more closed in cooler weather. Screens offer yet another solution and would keep out bugs.

A structure like this one would make a lovely shady retreat even in

N

P O O L

P O O L

H O U S E

7

6

5

1

2

6

3

view-
point

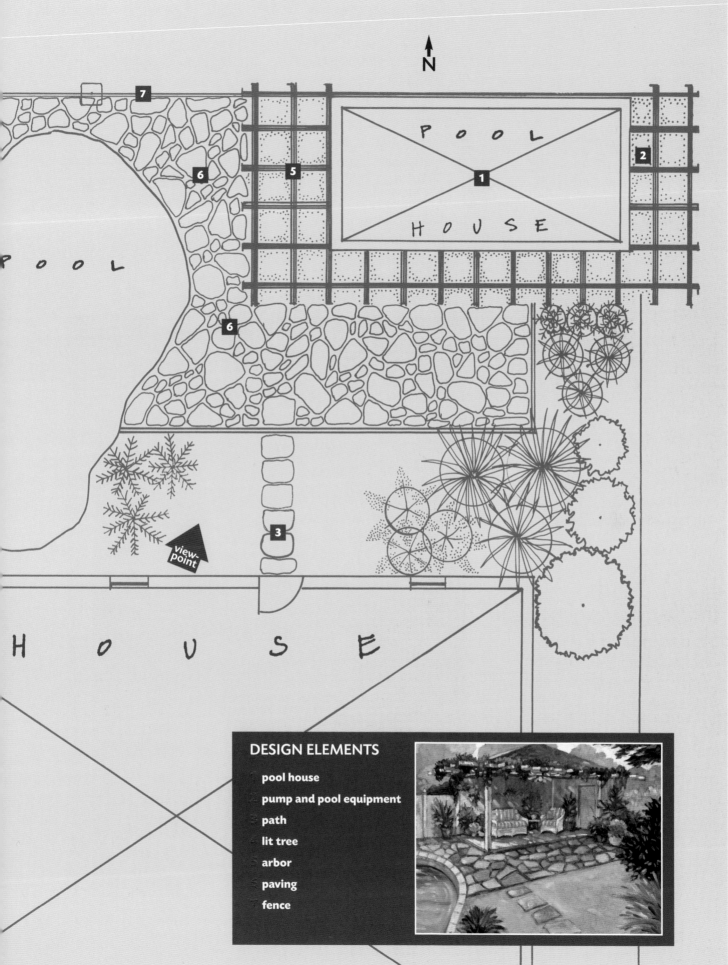

a yard without a pool. Both summerhouses and potting sheds are similar structures with solid roofs and anywhere from one to four walls, making them suitable for use even in rainy weather. And without a pool and the paved area around it (6), it's possible to surround either of these structures with garden beds and screening plants, making them more private and an integral part of the garden.

The wooden fence (7) that surrounds the yard and the back wall of the pool house is decorated with painted trompe l'oeil scenes, a technique that can be used on a wide variety of solid surfaces. On the fence, a painted garden scene makes the yard seem larger than it is. The back of the pool house features a painting of a window with a scene beyond. It, too, makes the pool house seem more spacious.

mix-and-match containers

Plantings around the pool have been kept to a minimum to cut down on debris in the water. Ornamental grasses, lavender, and a variety of low shrubs thrive in the sun. Container gardens provide color from early summer to frost, and a few houseplants spend the summer out in the pool house, thriving in the extra heat and humidity not available indoors.

Each container is planted with a mix of annuals and showy tender perennials selected for colorful foliage or long bloom season. The colors are the same ones used in

the pool house to make a visual link between the two. To create interesting combinations, each container has an upright accent plant (a flag), one or more plants that spill out of the pot or weave around the other plants (trailers/ weavers), one or more plants with small flowers or lacy leaves that fill in between other residents of the

pot (fillers), and a plant with showy flowers or bold foliage (contrast/accent plant).

The tender perennials in Plants to Choose From, page 77, are excellent for containers, but there are many more. To create the most interesting container combinations, mix and match types of plants as described above.

color in the shade

Trompe l'oeil paintings create the illusion that a flat wall is actually three-dimensional. They're a great way to add interest to a garden scene, whether shady or sunny, and also make a small space seem larger. This painting of a gate leading into a garden would add color and charm to any spot.

plants to choose from

BACOPA (*Bacopa* spp.). Trailer/ weaver. The trailing stems of this species are covered with tiny white flowers. There are also cultivars with variegated leaves; 'Blue Showers' features violet blooms.

CURRY PLANT (*Helichrysum italicum* ssp. *serotinum*). Filler. This isn't real culinary curry, but the lacy-textured, silvery leaves smell as spicy as the real thing.

DWARF CANNAS (*Canna* x *generalis* hybrids). Flag. 'Red Futurity' and 'Rose Futurity' feature burgundy leaves and showy flowers; 'Striped Beauty', green-and-yellow-striped leaves and yellow flowers; 'Pink Sunburst', green-and-pink-striped leaves and pale pink flowers.

EGYPTIAN STAR-CLUSTER (*Pentas lanceolata*). Contrast/accent plant. This species bears clusters of tubular flowers in shades from pale to magenta-pink, lilac, or white. The flowers attract hummingbirds.

ORNAMENTAL SWEET POTATOES (*Ipomoea batatas*). Trailer/weaver. Ornamental forms of this vegetable garden resident have colorful foliage on trailing stems. 'Blackie' has lobed, maroon-black leaves; 'Margarita', chartreuse foliage; and 'Pink Frost' features leaves marked in pink, cream, and green.

PURPLE FOUNTAIN GRASS (*Pennisetum setaceum* 'Purpureum'). Flag. This tender ornamental grass produces clumps of red-purple leaves and pinkish red seedheads.

Bacopa sutera **'Blue Showers'**

Canna x *generalis* **'Pink Sunburst'**

Pentas lanceolata

SCENTED GERANIUMS (*Pelargonium* spp.). Filler. These plants feature lacy-textured leaves in a wide variety of fragrances, including rose, peppermint, cinnamon, eucalyptus, coconut, and apple. They also bear small clusters of tiny flowers in a range of colors, such as lilac, salmon, pink, mauve, and white.

ideas for great design

bring the indoors out

The arbors and solid roof of this pool house make it useful in rainy weather and perfect for comforts such as thick cushions and electric lights.

movable privacy

Depending on how you use your retreat, you may want more privacy at some times than others. Containers, especially lightweight polyurethane-foam ones, sliding panels hung on a frame, and curtains are all options that can be moved into place to make a space more enclosed.

decorate with lights

Easy-to-install, low-voltage lighting adds magic to a shady space after dark. It also can make a pathway safer after dusk. Lights with solar panels are also available.

dress up a small space

Painted trompe l'oeil scenes are just one way to decorate a plain wall. Techniques like sponging or stenciling would work, too. Decorative trellises also dress up a wall without taking up space.

ceiling of leaves and sky

Surrounded by beds overflowing with flowers, this arbor would add charm to any garden. Here, it creates a much-needed spot to sit in the shade. The plants surrounding the arbor thrive in full sun for the most part and were selected because they attract butterflies, which provide a never-ending show in summer and early fall. Shade, flowers, and butterflies combine to create an intriguing garden destination in an otherwise featureless backyard. One glimpse of butterflies or roses in June, and visitors are invariably drawn out into the yard to explore, then are compelled to sit and enjoy the garden for a while.

LANDSCAPES that reveal everything in a glance may be pretty pictures to look at, but they're hardly gardens you'll want to spend time in. For that, a yard needs paths to explore, hidden views to discover, and quiet spots to visit. That's a tall order, especially if you're trying to design your own landscape and are starting with an almost blank canvas.

Here, as in many yards, a "what you see is what you get" landscape would have been easy — trees along one side of the yard, a flower bed pushed up against the back lot line, and a swathe of lawn in the center. Instead, this landscape is organized around a single compelling destination: a vine-covered arbor (1). The arbor shelters a terrace and is surrounded by flower beds (2). The end result is a restful space that has all the characteristics of an indoor room, including comfortable furniture, a flagstone floor, flower walls, and a ceiling of leaves and sky. There's also entertainment in the form of butterflies. It is a space that's guaranteed to draw visitors outdoors to explore and enjoy the garden.

A single outdoor room like this one also can be the inspiration for a garden that features a series of rooms, both sunny and shady. In this yard, for example, another shady retreat about the same size would fit under the trees to the west of the arbor (3). Two more

spaces, again about the same size, could be added in the sunny areas on either side of the path (4) and another the east of the arbor (5).

Separate and screen the rooms with hedges, fences, or rows of shrubs and install connecting pathways. To help make the garden more interesting, give each section a theme; in addition to the butterfly garden, there would be room here for a shade garden, herb garden, vegetables, and at least one color-theme garden.

garden over time

This retreat would be easy to install in phases, starting with the structure of the arbor itself. The terrace area underneath could simply be covered in mulch, or left in grass for that matter, until time and money allow for the installation of a terrace. Fast-growing annual vines like scarlet runner beans (*Phaseolus coccineus*) or cup-and-saucer (*Cobaea scandens*) would provide a bit of shade on top of the arbor the first year, until more vigorous perennial vines got established.

The flower beds around the perimeter of the space could be installed gradually, too. Even a 1-foot-wide bed with a single row of sunflowers would provide some privacy the first year. A full-width bed could be filled with giant-size annuals easily started from seed.

N

DESIGN ELEMENTS

1 **arbor and terrace**

2 **flower beds**

3 **trees on west side**

4 **path**

5 **sunny area**

6 **flower beds on west side**

view-
point

Clematis montana 'Rubens'

Rosa spp.

Vitis spp.

CLEMATIS (*Clematis* spp.). Two species are large enough to provide shade for a trellis: *C. montana*, with single, white, dogwoodlike flowers on 15- to 45-foot vines, and vigorous to rampant sweet autumn clematis (*C. terniflora*), which bears fragrant, white, starry flowers on 20-foot vines in fall. 'Rubens' has pink flowers. Smaller hybrids are attractive when trained up the posts of an arbor and will cling to rose canes or small trellises by twining leaf stalks.

GRAPES (*Vitis* spp.). Table grapes and wine grapes are large, vigorous woody vines that will form a thick roof of leaves. Be aware that their ripening fruit is messy and attracts wasps; otherwise, these are excellent vines for covering an arbor. Crimson glory vine *(V. coignetiae)* bears heart-shaped leaves that turn scarlet in fall. All cling to supports by tendrils.

ROSES (*Rosa* spp.). Look for local suggestions when selecting roses for an arbor. Hardiness is a key characteristic, since plants that die to the ground in rough winters won't provide flowers or shade. Also stick to disease-resistant cultivars to ensure a thick covering of leaves overhead. Vigorous, disease-resistant cultivars include 'New Dawn', with fragrant pink flowers; bright pink, extra-hardy 'William Baffin'; and shell pink 'Dorothy Perkins'. There are thornless roses, too, including white-flowered *Rosa banksiae,* which reaches 20 or 30 feet in height but is only hardy to Zones 7 or 8. 'Zépherine Drouhin' is another thornless climber with lightly fragrant pink flowers. Roses cannot cling to supports and must be tied in place with soft string.

TRUMPET VINE (*Campsis* spp.). These vigorous, fast-growing vines bear trumpet-shaped flowers and can reach 30 to 40 feet in height. *C. radicans* bears orange to red flowers from midsummer to fall. 'Flava' has orangish yellow flowers. *C. × tagliabuana* 'Madame Galen' bears orange-red flowers from midsummer to early fall. These plants cling to supports with holdfasts.

VIRGINIA CREEPER, BOSTON IVY, WOODBINE (*Parthenocissus* spp.). These vigorous climbers form a thick roof of lobed leaves that turn brilliant red in fall. Two species are most common: Virginia creeper (*P. quinquefolia*) and Boston ivy (*P. tricuspidata*). Both cling to supports by sucker-like holdfasts.

For instance, try spider flower (*Cleome hassleriana),* sunflowers (*Helianthus annuus),* and Mexican sunflowers *(Tithonia rotundifolia).*

Annual vines trained on strings attached to the arbor are another way to make the space more private without waiting for shrubs or large perennials to become established. What's important is to get started, then experiment with what grows well and looks good. Keep adjusting the design each season, even after the plants mature, to keep it vital and fresh.

blooms and butterflies

Annuals and perennials that attract butterflies fill the beds surrounding this arbor. With the exception of the bed along the western side of the arbor (6),

which is in partial shade, all are in full sun. Perennials include asters, sneezeweed *(Helenium autumnale),* and coreopsis 'Moonbeam' *(Coreopsis verticillata* 'Moonbeam'). Butterfly bush *(Buddleia davidii),* which comes in shades of lavender, pinkish-purple, violet, white, and red-purple, is a must. Deadheading prolongs bloom and helps prevent self-sowing. Annuals that attract butterflies include zinnias, petunias, cosmos, marigolds, and Mexican sunflowers.

While the trees provide some late-day shade for this space, a mix of roses and clematis that bloom at different times provides most of the shade on the arbor overhead. This keeps the space pretty and interesting by extending the bloom season. Plants to Choose From, page 82, features vines vigorous enough to cover an arbor.

Plants to Choose From, page 82, features vines vigorous enough to cover an arbor.

ideas for great design

plant a show
Surrounding a sitting area with flowers that attract butterflies or hummingbirds makes it extra special because of the ever-changing show.

make a room
In a yard that lacks character, a prominent focal point helps organize the rest of the design. Here, the arbor is the center of the garden, with flower beds rolling out from it on all sides.

flexible walls
A shady retreat doesn't always need thick shrubbery. Here, a mix of shrubs, large perennials, and vines provide enough screening. If needed, walls could be screened with lattice, vines, or shrubs to make the space more private.

mix-and-match vines
Combine vines or climbers, such as roses and clematis or annual and perennial vines. It extends bloom time. If one plant has a bad year or succumbs to disease, you'll still have some shade to enjoy.

color in the shade

Place colorful pots of annuals along shady pathways or the front edge of a bed or border. For continuous color all summer long, keep a supply of newly planted containers in a holding area, then move them into the spotlight once they're in full bloom.

arbor and lattice sitting area

This vine-covered arbor offers a cool, shady place to sit overlooking a sunny garden filled with herbs, roses, and vegetables. The arbor creates a retreat that is roomy enough to offer a variety of seating areas, while the table in the center of the space has a good view of the garden beds below the stone retaining wall. Vigorous vines form a solid ceiling of leaves, and a lattice-and-plant screen along the back encloses the space and makes it private. The lattice wall gives the space a feeling of solidity and enclosure, but plants growing behind the arbor make this space really private.

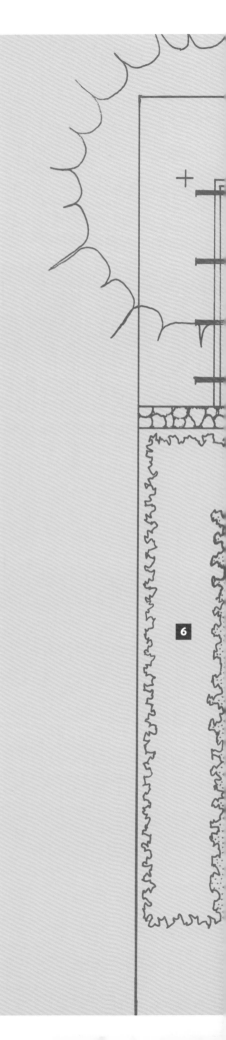

Even the most devoted gardener needs a place to sit down and enjoy the results of his or her labor, and a shady spot is the perfect antidote to time spent working in a sunny herb garden.

Plenty of space and a variety of furniture make this retreat very flexible; it's suitable for everything from entertaining to gardening projects, such as potting up newly divided herbs. There's a terrace (1) under the arbor, which is constructed of pavers set on the diagonal and mortared in place. They form a level floor that makes it easy to move furniture from place to place. A layer of shredded bark mulch would provide a suitable floor, too, and could be installed if the garden was being phased in over several years.

The openwork back of the arbor gives this space a great deal of character. While the lattice (2) creates a solid-looking wall, it allows light to enter the space, and it also ensures good air circulation. Shrubs, ornamental grasses, and perennials planted behind the lattice (3), framed in the slats like a picture, create a soft, living privacy screen.

The contrast between the lattice and the plants causes the hard lines of the lattice to appear to come forward, while at the same time the plants appear to recede. This gives the arbor a feeling of depth, making the space behind it look much larger than it really is.

This design would work anywhere, but it would be especially effective with the back of the arbor facing west, so the plants were backlit by the late afternoon sun.

making level space

This yard originally sloped up to the back lot line and was terraced by a stone wall (4) that crosses the center of the yard and creates the large, level space needed to build this shady retreat. Terracing also allowed plenty of room to dig level garden beds and made the whole yard easier to maintain. All the grass on the upper level has been replaced to avoid having to carry a lawn mower up the steps (5). To reduce trimming below the wall, a row of pavers was installed so they butt against the base of the wall.

Garden beds overflowing with vegetables, herbs, and roses fill the sunny yard surrounding this arbor and provide a large part of its appeal (6). The smell of roses, lavender, thyme, oregano, and basil scent the air. This is clearly a space tailored to the needs of the people who garden here.

An arbor like this would work in a variety of situations. It would make a handsome pool house or it could be the centerpiece of a wild and colorful cottage garden. Surrounded by clipped hedges, with perhaps a large urn on either side of the entrance, it would make a fine retreat for a formal garden.

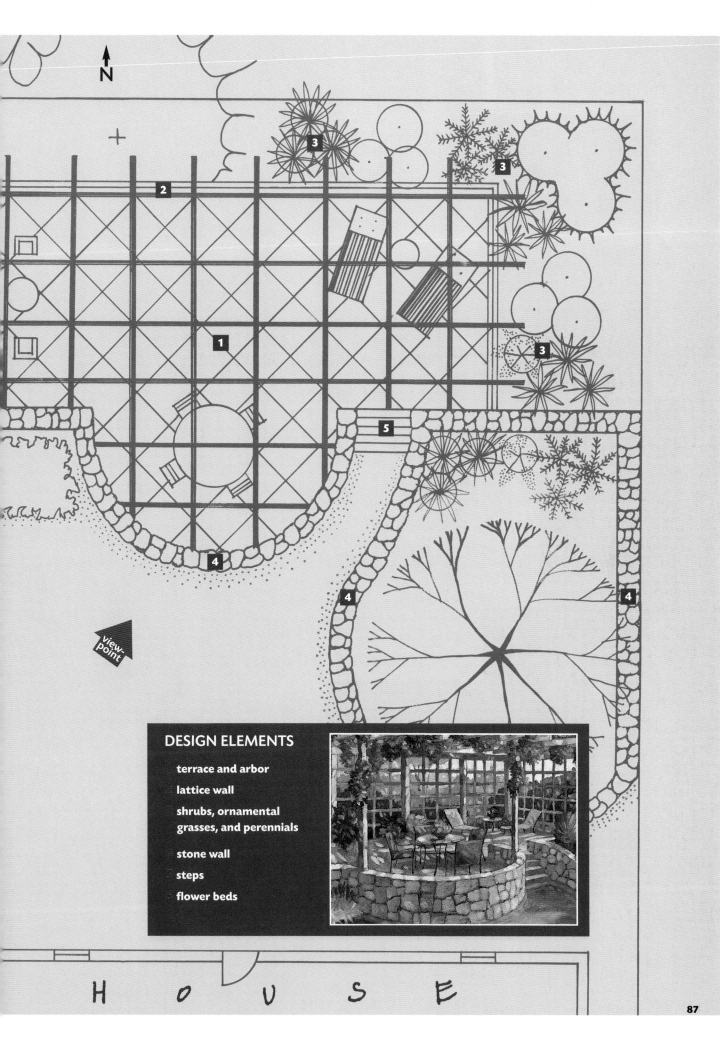

N

+

2

3

3

3

1

5

4

4

4

4

view-point

DESIGN ELEMENTS

terrace and arbor

lattice wall

shrubs, ornamental
grasses, and perennials

stone wall

steps

flower beds

H O U S E

Lavandula angustifolia

Calamintha nepeta

BASIL (*Ocimum basilicum*). Annual. This popular herb comes in a variety of fragrances, from spicy-sweet common basil to lemony, cinnamony, and spicy Thai basil. 'Spicy Globe' is an 8-inch-tall cultivar that can be planted in rows to make a tiny hedge.

CALAMINT (*Calamintha* spp.). Perennial. These mounding plants feature tiny flowers and aromatic, spicy-minty leaves. Greater calamint (*C. grandiflora*) is best in dappled shade, while lesser calamint (*C. nepeta*) grows in sun or part shade.

CATMINT (*Nepeta* spp.). Perennial. Grown for their spikes of lavender-purple flowers and aromatic leaves, catmints are sturdy, easy-to-grow plants for any site in full sun or light shade that has well-drained soil. Shear plants after the main flush of flowers to neaten them up and encourage a second round of bloom.

LAVENDER (*Lavandula angustifolia*). Perennial. Both flowers and foliage of this popular perennial are fragrant. The scent of the silvery leaves can be enjoyed fresh, or cut and dry it, then crush the leaves to release the fragrance. Lavender requires well-drained soil and sun.

OREGANO (*Origanum vulgare*). Perennial. Ordinary culinary oregano has fragrant leaves, but for a garden bed, consider planting golden oregano (*O. vulgare* 'Aureum' or 6-inch-tall 'Compactum').

SALVIA (*Salvia* spp.). Tender perennial. Many salvias have fragrant foliage. *S. elegans* features scarlet flowers in fall and fruity, pineapple-scented leaves all season.

SOUTHERNWOOD (*Artemisia abrotanum*). Perennial. A mounding species that does not spread, southernwood features aromatic, gray-green leaves that are deeply cut and ferny in texture. Cut the plants back in mid-summer to remove the small yellow flowers and keep the clumps looking neat.

THYME (*Thymus* spp.). Perennial. This well-known herb can be used to edge beds and borders, or consider planting some of the creeping forms of wild thyme (*T. serphyllum*) between pavers, so the fragrance is released when the plants are stepped on.

Origanum vulgare 'Aureum'

Thymus serphyllum 'Russetings'

It could also be surrounded by drifts of ornamental grasses and daylilies (*Hemerocallis* spp.) in a modern design.

arbor in a garden

A dense covering of vigorous vines forms the top of this arbor. Grapes, wisteria, Dutchman's-pipe (*Aristolochia durior*), crimson glory vine (*Vitis coignetiae*), or fiveleaf akebia (*Akebia quinata*) would all work here. See Two Shady Spaces for a Small Lot on page 31 and Ceiling of Leaves and Sky on page 78 for more on vigorous vines for arbors.

To add some golden-yellow foliage to the mix and extend the herb-garden theme in the process, golden hops (*Humulus lupulus* 'Aureus') could be planted, too. Or for a quick cover that lasts a year, consider covering an arbor with a planting of gourds. Mini pumpkins like 'Jack Be Little' or 'Baby Boo' would work, too.

Plants with fragrant foliage and flowers make excellent choices for surrounding a shady retreat. Plant fragrant flowers like roses and Oriental lilies (*Lilium* Oriental Hybrids) along with such annuals and tender perennials as four-o'clocks (*Mirabilis jalapa*), heliotrope (*Heliotropium arborescens*), and mignonette (*Reseda odorata*) where their aroma will drift over to the sitting area. Ideally, look for a site protected from wind, however, so the fragrance doesn't just blow away.

Plants with fragrant foliage, such as the ones in Plants to Choose From, page 88, are especially effective when planted along a path so that their fragrance will be released as passersby brush up against them.

color in the shade

Collections add charm to a garden. To brighten up a dark, shady spot, use items that also bring in color — painted birdhouses, mosaic or glazed sculptures, painted wooden whirligigs or folk art, gazing balls, or watering cans. Items can be hung or mounted in groups for a still-life effect or scattered in the garden.

ideas for great design

a sense of self and place

Gardens that express the personality of their owners and highlight the features of the yard, like this one does, are always the most satisfying.

room to move

This shady retreat takes up a large part of the backyard, but the trade-off is worth it: It's a flexible space big enough to accommodate a wide variety of activities.

terraced for easy care

The terraces on this site, which create level spaces for gardening and sitting, also make the yard much easier to maintain.

openwork wall

Combining two elements — lattice and plants — to create a privacy screen for this retreat ensures good air circulation, lets light into the space, adds depth to the design, and makes the space seem spacious and airy.

an inviting place to putter

Sitting and sipping iced tea or reading a book isn't everyone's idea of relaxation. Many people love puttering in their gardens, and this shady potting shed is the perfect place for a range of satisfying activities, from potting plants to drying herbs or sharpening tools. There's ample space for both working and storage, so it's easy to keep necessary tools and equipment at hand. An old armchair and bookshelf in the back corner provides a comfortable spot in which to read. The shed is also conveniently located near the garden, terrace, and house, making it easy to carry projects from one place to another.

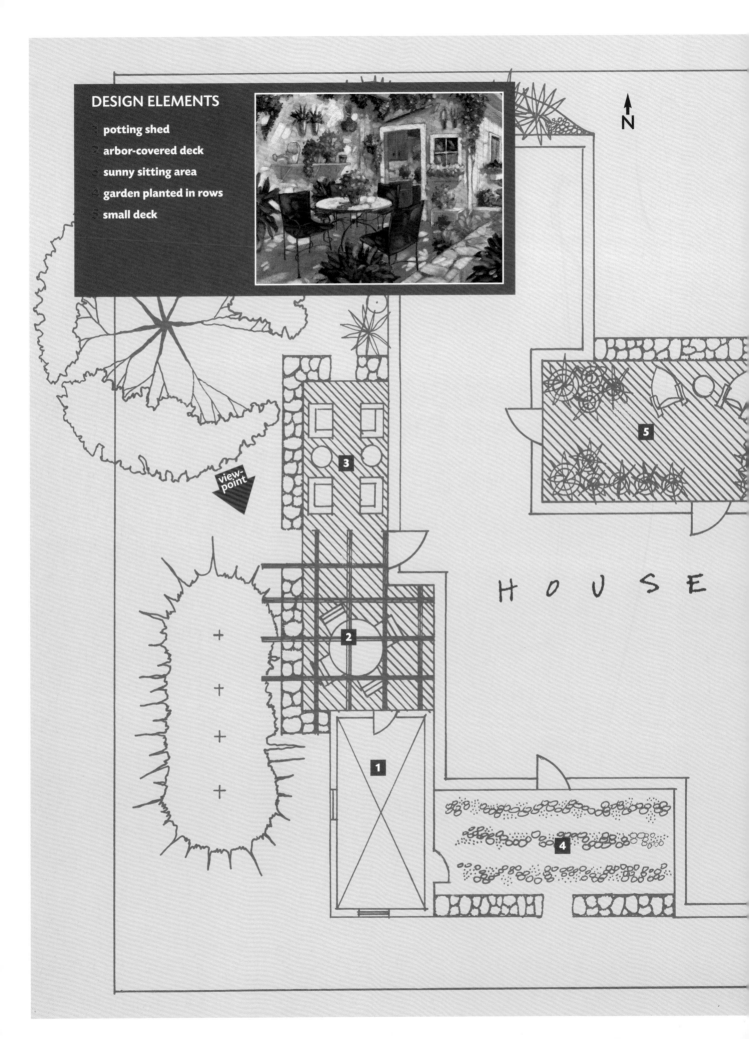

DESIGN ELEMENTS

1. potting shed
2. arbor-covered deck
3. sunny sitting area
4. garden planted in rows
5. small deck

N

view-point

HOUSE

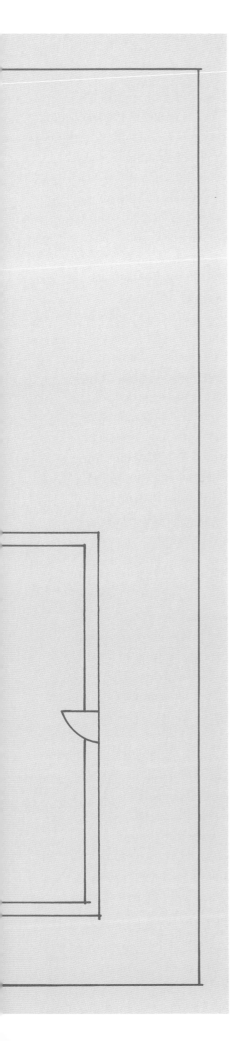

SHADY RETREATS are private, personal spaces, and a potting shed is no exception. Every gardener's shed will be uniquely equipped and decorated. It can range from a strictly utilitarian space to a whimsical garden structure.

The design of this potting shed (1) is very flexible. It offers a secluded place to work or read, yet creates strong connections between indoor and outdoor spaces. The front of the shed opens onto an arbor-covered deck (2) that is large enough to accommodate an array of potted plants. Beyond that is a sunny sitting area (3), which is partially shaded by a tree, for sitting outdoors during times when it isn't too hot.

The back door of the shed opens onto a garden planted in rows (4), with herbs, vegetables, and flowers for drying. The garden also offers ample space for growing newly propagated herbs or perennials until they are large enough to move into a bed. A small private deck on the eastern side of the house (5) is perfect for an afternoon snooze, as the house shades this space from early afternoon on. All the spaces connect, so it's easy to move from garden to kitchen or potting shed and from potting shed to sunny sitting area.

Potting sheds can be attached to a house or garage, but freestanding ones work well, too. They can be located in the garden or in an out-of-the-way service area and still make fine shady retreats. When located in a service area, these structures can be purely practical, with room for hanging hoses and tools, plenty of shelving and workspace, and little in the way of decoration. When located in the garden, the exterior walls of a potting shed (or any flat surface, for that matter) become an opportunity for decorating.

To dress up a plain-looking shed, you can cover it with trellises — even up over the roof — and train vines or climbing roses over it. Containers and birdhouses can be mounted on the walls, too. Or surround the base with garden beds or a collection of potted plants. Find space for a bench outside the door. If your shed doesn't already have a window, consider installing one, then add window boxes. Yet another option is to mount shelves along the outside and use them for displaying potted plants or a collection of knickknacks.

personalize your shed

Prefab sheds are available everywhere and easy to customize and decorate, which makes them much more interesting garden structures. If you're at all handy (or know someone who is), consider one made from salvaged and recycled materials. Old discarded windows, used leftover shingles, pine floor-ing, and any other supplies you can find can be combined with new materials to make a charming, one-of-a-kind shed.

The inside of your potting shed should be set up to suit the activities you want to pursue. Since this shed is next to the house, it has water and electricity. It is equipped with a work sink, hose spigots, lights, and outlets for using power

tools. There are enough supplies stored here to do most garden-related tasks. Recycled kitchen cabinets are a great storage option for a potting shed. Large items like bags of potting soil fit nicely into base cabinets, while the counter-top serves as workspace.

Wall cabinets, or simple open shelving, are useful to store stacks of smaller pots and containers of fertilizer or garden sprays. Draw-

ers are handy for small tools, wire, string, and other items. Pegboard on the walls is another option for storing all manner of tools, stakes, and hoses. You may want to attach a cold frame or small greenhouse to your potting shed. A holding bed, like the small garden next to this shed, is also a handy option for newly propagated cuttings, divisions, and seedlings.

With a bit less equipment and clutter, a potting shed could become more like a summer-house, with space for a few people to sit. It could also be divided into separate spaces and outfitted for two completely different hobbies, or designed with spaces for two completely different gardening interests, such as training topiary and garden railroads, for example.

plants for containers

The collection of container plants under the arbor outside this potting shed makes the deck more colorful and also helps link the potting shed and deck. This is a perfect spot for summering houseplants and containers of coleus, wax begonias, and newly potted sun-lovers are fine here, too.

Shade-loving summer bulbs, such as the ones in Plants to Choose From, page 95, are also good choices. These add color and character to the area all summer long, but they can be dried off gradually in fall and overwintered indoors in a cool, dry spot that stays above freezing.

color in the shade

Mix and match garden ornaments to add a splash of color and create a charming, cottage-garden look. This pretty summer-house features trellised vines, hanging baskets, window boxes, birdhouses, and a wreath on the door.

plants to choose from

ACHIMENES (*Achimenes* hybrids). Related to African violets, achimenes grow from scaly rhizomes and produce showy, trumpet-shaped flowers in shades of pink, purple, red, and white from summer to fall. They're great in containers or hanging baskets and need rich, moist soil and high humidity for best growth.

BEGONIAS (*Begonia* spp. and hybrids). Tuberous begonias (*Begonia* x *tuberhybrida* hybrids) are simply stunning in any shady container garden, and are easy to grow in pots. Or for something a little different, look for *B. sutherlandii*, which bears angel-wing-shaped leaves and masses of orange flowers. Overwinter plants dry or keep them blooming indoors all winter.

CALADIUM (*Caladium bicolor*). These tender bulbs are grown for their showy angel-wing-shaped leaves that come in a wide array of colors. Grow them alone or mix them in containers. 'Candidum' bears white leaves with green veins; 'Fanny Munson' has pink leaves edged and speckled with green. Florida-series cultivars, such as 'Florida Fantasy', come in a range of colors and are more heat- and sun-tolerant than older selections.

OXALIS, WOOD SORREL (*Oxalis* spp.). These tender perennials have pretty foliage with four or more fingerlike leaflets and small flowers with rounded petals. Many species are easy to grow in containers. Look for *O. adenophylla*, with pink

flowers; *O. bowiei*, with pink flowers and green, cloverlike leaves that are green above and purple below; *O. regnellii* var. *triangularis*, with burgundy leaves and pale pink flowers; and *O. tetraphylla* 'Iron Cross', with pink flowers and four-leaflet leaves marked with burgundy.

Achimenes **hybrid**

Oxalis tetraphylla **'Iron Cross'**

Begonia x *tuberhybrida* **hybrid**

ideas for great design

forge your own space

Look at pictures in books and magazines for ideas, but make sure you know how *you* want to use your potting shed. Figure out what you'll need to store and how much workspace you'll want. Don't worry about decorations — just add them over the years as inspiration strikes.

express yourself

One of the best ways to decorate a potting shed or other structure in your garden is to use objects that are meaningful to you. Whether you collect tools or wall plaques, use them to set the theme for your decor.

ventilation

A shed can be a hot place on a summer's day, so install windows and consider outlets for fans if yours isn't shaded by overhead trees.

keep it simple

Inside, don't let decorations and clutter take over everything. Otherwise, you'll have little, if any, workspace.

pergola
for strolling

Sometimes a place to sit just isn't
enough. This shady retreat, which
is sheltered by a pergola, offers
ample space for sitting and dining,
but there's also plenty of room for
stretching exercises, meditation,
yoga, or strolling along admiring
the garden. Flower beds along the
edge of the pergola are planted
with a mix of plants for sun and
shade, while container gardens
add splashes of color underneath.
The shady retreat overlooks a
water garden that sparkles in full
sun and makes a nice, peaceful
view from any angle.

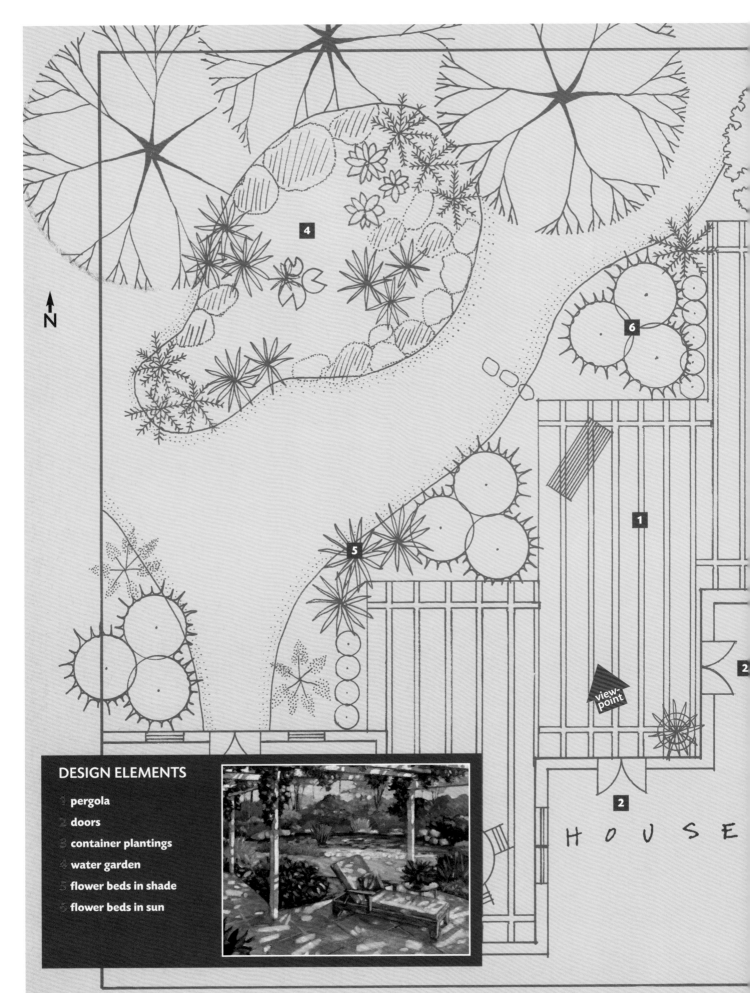

N

DESIGN ELEMENTS

1 pergola
2 doors
3 container plantings
4 water garden
5 flower beds in shade
6 flower beds in sun

4

6

5

1

2

2

view-
point

H O U S E

Once a conventional backyard offering little more than grass and a few trees, this yard has been transformed it into an interesting, multipurpose space. Under the pergola (1), there's room for passive pursuits, like reading or sipping morning coffee, as well as for more active endeavors, such as doing exercises or getting ready for a run. Open the doors (2), and this also makes a nice space for an indoor-outdoor summer party.

This design creates strong links between house and garden; the shape of the house determined the shape of the pergola. From indoors, the yard makes a beautiful picture to look at from any window, and appealing places to sit or walk are visible from every doorway. There's also plenty of room for gardening, from container plantings (3) and flower beds under and along the pergola to the water garden (4) out in the yard.

While hardy kiwis (*Actinidia* spp.) provide the main shade, a mix of annual vines growing on the posts of the pergola add extra color and texture. Planning the flower beds that run along the edge of the pergola took time, since it was important to study the amount of sun and shade each part of the bed receives. Sections of the bed close to the house (5) are shaded until late afternoon, while portions of the bed out toward the center of the yard (6)

are in full sun from midday on. As a result, the bed is filled with plants that withstand a range of conditions.

paving options

A variety of materials could be used to pave the area under the pergola, including bluestone, brick, pea stone gravel, or precast interlocking pavers. The best choice depends on a variety of factors, including style of the house, cost, and how the area will be used. The house often gives very strong clues about what materials will work best in the landscape, since repeating a particular material is a good way to link house and garden. For example, a brick terrace is a perfect choice for a brick house, but sleek bluestone or casual pea stone gravel might work best if the house is ultramodern in style.

Cost is a factor, too, and of these choices bluestone is the most expensive, precast pavers are the cheapest. The flooring also could be upgraded as budget allows — from something as simple as shredded bark to brick or bluestone. Finally, how the area will be used, and by whom, are important factors. Bluestone, brick, and precast pavers are easier to walk on than pea stone is and would certainly be best if the area will be used for formal entertaining (where guests might wear high heels) or if someone in the family uses a wheelchair or walker.

One of the features that makes this shady space so appealing is the water garden glittering in the sunny yard. It provides an ever-changing view to enjoy, whether visitors are sitting and talking or exercising in the shade. The water garden is made from a flexible liner and is designed to give wildlife access to the water. (Rigid fiberglass liners don't allow birds or other creatures safe access to the water, although they can reach it if potted plants are set in the water so the rims are just above the surface.) The front edge of the pool has a gentle slope, much like a beach that ends in a narrow ledge inclining slightly upward. A row of rocks along the ledge, set on top of the liner, hold pea stone gravel on the slope.

Larger rocks set in the pea stone emerge just above the surface to provide creatures with a safe spot to drink. Wildlife from dragonflies, butterflies, and beneficial insects to squirrels and birds visit the water's edge daily to drink, and they provide a source of lively entertainment for anyone looking out over the garden.

plants for a pergola

Container combinations under this pergola change from season to season and year to year. In spring, daffodils, tulips, and other bulbs mix with pansies in the pots, but by summer coleus and other shade-lovers take over. The area also features container water gardens filled with bog plants, including elephant ear (*Colocasia esculenta*), a heat-loving, giant-leaved tender perennial for rich, moist to wet soil. Instead of the all-green species, look for 'Black Magic', which has purple-black leaves, or 'Illustris', which has black leaves with green veins.

To prevent mosquitoes from breeding in the standing water of a container garden, use Mosquito-Dunks monthly. These are small rings of *Bacillus thuringiensis* ssp. *israelensis* that float on the surface of the water and control mosquitoes organically.

Each year in spring or early summer, a mix of annual and tender perennial vines is planted at the base of each post of the pergola. With a little training, they'll climb up the stems of the larger hardy kiwi or the strings put in place for that purpose. Once established, they add flowers all summer long. The species listed in Plants to Choose From, page 101, grow in sun or light shade, although they bloom best in full sun.

color in the shade

Plants with stunning variegated leaves, such as hosta 'Great Expectations', are perfect for bringing color to shady garden beds. Here, the yellow variegation is echoed in the flowers of yellow corydalis (*Corydalis lutea*).

ideas for great design

CUP-AND-SAUCER VINE (*Cobaea scandens*). A vigorous tendril climber that can reach 40 feet, this species features fragrant, bell-shaped flowers, each with a ruffled green saucer (the calyx) at its base. Its flowers open greenish white and fade to purple. 'Alba' has flowers that remain greenish white.

CYPRESS VINE (*Ipomoea quamoclit*). This species bears lacy, deeply cut leaves and, in summer, small scarlet flowers that attract hummingbirds. Plants range from 6 to 20 feet tall.

HYACINTH BEAN (*Lablab purpureus*). This showy vine, which ranges from 6 to 20 feet tall, bears clusters of showy purple flowers, heart-shaped leaves, and glossy, maroon-purple pods.

BALLOON VINE (*Cardiospermum halicacabum*). An old-fashioned, 10- to 12-foot-tall charmer, balloon vine features lacy-textured leaves and insignificant blooms. It is grown for the interesting, balloonlike seedpods that follow the flowers.

MOONFLOWER (*Ipomoea alba*). Heart-shaped leaves and large, very fragrant white flowers that open in early evening make this a must for any shady retreat that's used at night. Vines reach 15 feet in a season.

PURPLE BELL VINE (*Rhodochiton atrosanguineus*). A handsome tender perennial, this species bears

Cobaea scandens 'Alba'

Rhodochiton atrosanguineus

Lablab purpureus

trumpet-shaped, maroon-purple flowers. Each flower has a bell-shaped, mauve-pink calyx at the base. The bell-like calyxes remain on the plant long after the true flowers drop. Plants reach 10 feet in the North but are much taller in warmer climates.

spacious shade
One reason this space is so appealing is its size; there's ample room for both active and passive pursuits.

lawn be gone
Eliminating all the grass in this yard would be a relatively easy task. Low ground covers crisscrossed with stepping-stones would make an ideal lawn substitute.

combined vines
While hardy kiwi provides more than enough shade for this pergola, annual vines make an important contribution, too. They're shorter, so the blooms are visible underneath the pergola. Annuals also make it easy to change the show from year to year.

special scenery
Because of the water garden, the shady area under the pergola becomes a room with a view. There's always something interesting to see, whether it's dragonflies and birds or cloud patterns reflected in the water's surface.

pavilion in a terraced garden

This shady yard has been a garden for many years, but it hasn't always offered a place to sit down and relax. Terraced beds shaded by a number of large trees are filled with all manner of plants — this is a collector's garden featuring wild-flowers, hardy bulbs, choice peren-nials, and dwarf shrubs. Handbuilt stone walls create level beds along the slope, which rises up from the house. The pavilion added on the upper terrace overlooks the whole yard and offers a place to rest and recoup after a gardening session. It's also a perfect perch from which to assess the overall design and look for even more places to add plants!

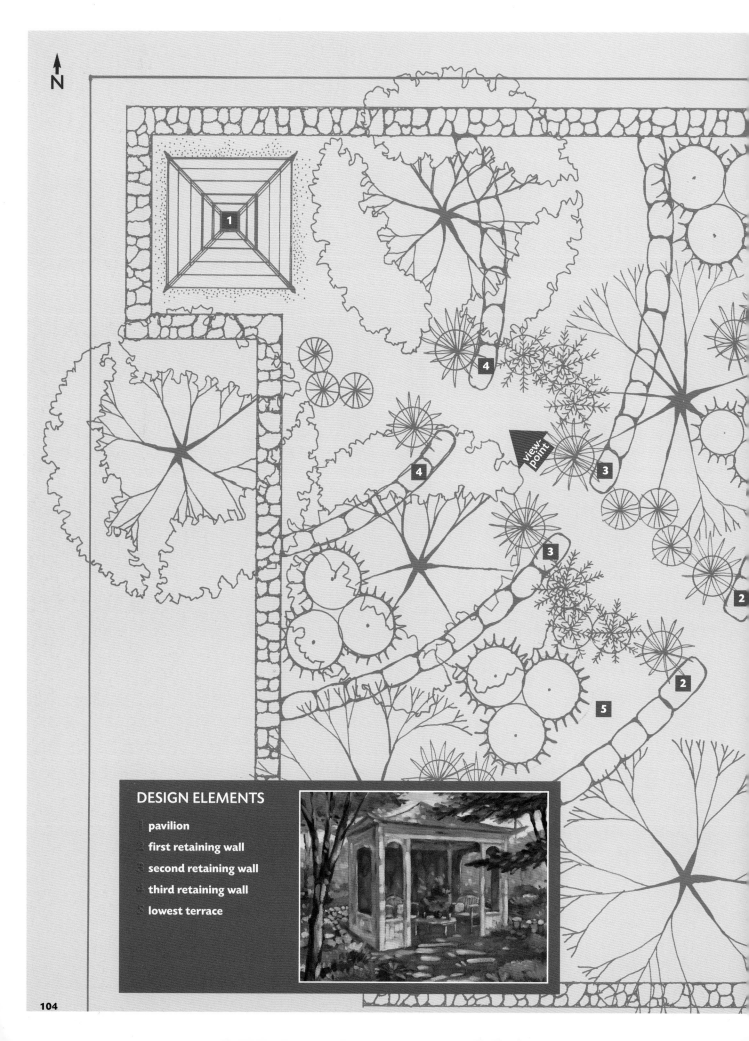

N

view-
point

DESIGN ELEMENTS

1 **pavilion**

2 **first retaining wall**

3 **second retaining wall**

4 **third retaining wall**

5 **lowest terrace**

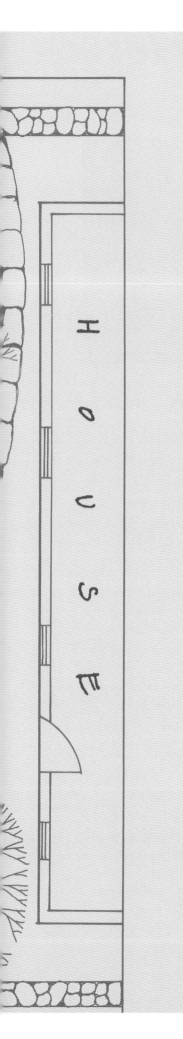

HOME to enthusiastic gardeners, this yard has always offered ample shade, but because of the sloping terrain, it hasn't offered level space for gardening. To create level garden beds, a series of stone walls was built to terrace the slope. The walls, constructed gradually as the garden was developed, were built from the bottom of the slope and upward using the cut-and-fill method. The walls incorporate many rocks that were dug up on site during the process.

The open-sided pavilion at the top of the slope (1) was added to provide a comfortable, shady place to sit and take a break while gardening. It's also a nice spot for drinks or a picnic dinner anytime from spring to fall, because of the view of the garden.

Terracing a slope is a fairly simple, but strenuous, process. Start by building a wall at the bottom of the slope (2), then pull soil downhill to fill in behind that wall, loosening and amending the soil as you go. To add another terrace, build another retaining wall above the first (3), and pull down more soil to create another level planting bed. Build a third retaining wall, if desired (4).

In a site with no trees, all the walls can be identical, but in this case, the height of each wall was determined by the position of the existing trees to help level out the slope but at the same time minimize the grade change and the root disturbance under the trees.

Because water runoff was also a problem, the terraces slope slightly down from northeast to southwest so that they direct water away from the back of the house. As a result, soil in the lowest terrace (5) tends to be much moister than soil higher up on the slope. To help preserve moisture, the garden is kept mulched with chopped leaves, which are raked off the beds in fall, chopped up in the lawnmower on the small lawn next to the house, then replaced. This helps increase organic matter and water retention.

Since beds under mature trees tend to be dry, this garden features many plants that are adapted to dry shade. Soaker hoses hidden by mulch snake through each bed, and are also available for easy, efficient watering during dry spells.

flowers for shade

Many perennials do well in dry shade, especially in soil that is kept mulched and is amended with lots of organic matter. This garden features hostas with variegated leaves along with epimediums, hellebores, and lungworts (*Pulmonaria* spp.). A few clumps of daylilies (*Hemerocallis* spp.) bloom in the brighter spots. See Private Space in a Busy Yard on page 109 for more plants that thrive in dry shade.

Allium moly

Arum italicum 'Marmoratum'

Lilium canadense

AUTUMN CROCUS (*Colchicum* spp.). Fall-bloomers that grow from corms. These bear showy flowers and strap-shaped leaves in spring. They're best planted at the front of informal plantings, since the yellowing leaves are unattractive in early summer and taller perennials will engulf the flowers in the fall. Look for *C. autumnale,* with lavender-pink blooms, or 'Alboplenum', with double white flowers. Hybrids such as 'The Giant', with rose-lilac blooms; 'Waterlily', with double, pinkish lilac flowers; and 'Violet Queen', with violet-purple flowers, are all good choices.

AUTUMN DAFFODIL (*Sternbergia lutea*). The flowers of these fall-blooming bulbs look more like crocuses than daffodils. Plants have narrow, grassy leaves and produce golden yellow, goblet-shaped flowers in fall.

CAMASS, QUAMASH (*Camassia* spp.). These native bulbs produce erect spikes of small, starry flowers in spring or early summer. The blooms are blue, violet-blue, cream, or white. To perform best, they need rich, well-drained soil.

HARDY CYCLAMEN (*Cyclamen* spp.). The hardy members of this genus are diminutive perennials for planting in shady rock gardens or at the front of perennial gardens. They grow from tubers and feature attractive leaves marked with silver and small pink or white blooms that resemble shuttlecocks. Mark where cyclamen are growing in the garden to avoid digging into them by mistake when plants are dormant in summer. Fall-blooming *C. hederifolium* is most common.

HARDY AMARYLLIS (*Lycoris squamigera*). Also called magic lily, this species bears strappy leaves in spring and showy umbels of six to eight fragrant, pink, lilylike flowers in summer.

LILIES (*Lilium* spp.). Several species of lilies will bloom in partial shade, including Canada lily

(*L. canadense),* with yellow-orange flowers spotted with maroon, and Martagon Hybrids, with purple-pink or white flowers with dark spots. Other lilies that tolerate shade include Henry lily (*L. henryi*), leopard lily (*L. pardalinum),* coral lily (*L. pumilum),* and American turk's-cap lily (*L. superbum*).

ORNAMENTAL ONIONS (*Allium* spp.). Although most ornamental onions are plants for full sun, two species will grow in partial shade and flower in early summer. Nodding or wild onion (*A. cernuum*) bears clusters of rose-purple, pink, or white flowers. Lily leek (*A. moly*) bears clusters of starry yellow flowers.

VARIEGATED ITALIAN ARUM (*Arum italicum* 'Marmoratum'). This perennial grows from a tuber and produces handsome arrow-shaped leaves with cream veins over winter. From late summer to fall, spikes of red berries follow the greenish white flowers of early summer.

Planted among the other perennials is an extensive collection of bulbs. Spring bulbs like daffodils, snowdrops (*Galanthus* spp.), and glory-of-the-snow (*Chionodoxa* spp.) all grow well under deciduous trees, since they finish blooming and go dormant not long after leaves emerge. There are also bulbs that bloom from early to midsummer and grow in shade, such as those in Plants to Choose From, page 106. All bloom best in partial shade, so give them the brightest spot your garden has to offer.

color in the shade

Hanging baskets filled with flowers are an easy way to add color to a site under trees or under an arbor. Use baskets planted with a single species, or combine four or five plants with contrasting flowers and foliage. Baskets are most visible when they're hung 4 to 6 feet off the ground; be sure to keep them clear of walkways so they won't pose a hazard to visitors. Also, make sure you can water them easily: In summer, hanging baskets often require daily watering.

ideas for great design

terraced garden beds

Level areas are always easier to plant than slopes. Terracing also helps slow down excess water after a rain, allowing it to percolate into the soil instead of running off.

pop-up plantings

Bulbs are perfect for adding color to any garden and are easy to intersperse among perennials. Once planted, they'll pop up, bloom, then disappear for another year.

root rules

In any garden under trees, avoid disturbing tree roots whenever possible. Don't take away soil or pile it on top of roots. Look for pockets between roots where the soil can be loosened rather than cutting roots to make space for planting.

space to rest

All gardeners need a spot in the shade to sit down and enjoy the fruits of their labors. A pavilion, arbor, or even a table and umbrella would all work equally well.

private space in a busy yard

In a yard where soccer, volleyball, and other sports are the norm, this quiet space remains screened off from all the noise and activity. Surrounded by shrubbery and shaded by trees, and an umbrella, the sitting area is a quiet, private spot that's still close enough to the main yard to keep an eye on things. Shrubs and fences mark the division between this shady retreat and the rest of the property. The beds surrounding it are filled with perennials that thrive in dry shade to keep maintenance to a minimum. To add a bit of white noise, a small fountain splashes onto rocks along the edge of one bed.

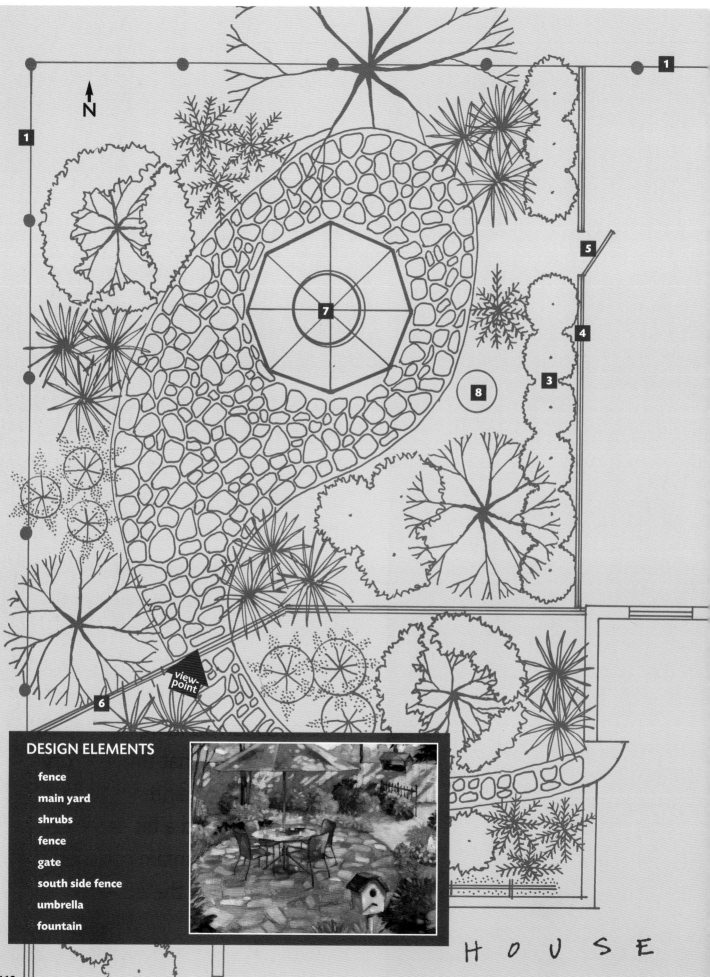

1 N

1

5

4

3

7

8

view-point

6

DESIGN ELEMENTS

- fence
- main yard
- shrubs
- fence
- gate
- south side fence
- umbrella
- fountain

H O U S E

TUCKED NEATLY into the corner of a larger yard, this small space offers a cozy, quiet spot in a yard that's filled with activity. It is a simple retreat that would fit in a side yard or another small underused or forgotten space. A board fence (1) surrounds the entire property, but this shady retreat also is set off from the sunny yard (2) by shrubs (3) and a fence (4) along its eastern edge. A gate (5) connects the lawn to the retreat, so it's easy to get from one place to the other. The south side boundary features a fence (6), too, that divides the space from the garden directly behind the garage.

In both cases, the fences and gates are antique cast iron that have been salvaged and repainted. They separate the spaces and serve as decorative elements. Neither of these barriers are tall or imposing, but they still set this retreat apart from the outside world, reserving it as an area for quiet pursuits.

While the site is fairly well shaded by trees, an umbrella (7) ensures there's always a cool place to sit. A gazebo or small arbor, or even an awning attached to a building, also are effective options for creating shade in a small space. The floor of this outdoor living space is paved with stepping-stones interplanted with low-growing perennials like bugleweed.

In an unmortared terrace like this one, weeds can be a problem.

Instead of using chemical weed killers, douse areas where you don't want *any* plants to grow with a solution of 10 percent vinegar (boil down store-bought vinegar, which is 5 percent, to get the stronger solution) and as much salt as you can dissolve in the mix. The area also could be covered with mulch or crushed gravel.

building a fountain

The small fountain (8) in this retreat adds the appeal of moving water, plus white noise to muffle the sounds of the outside world and make the space seem more removed and private. Called *reservoir features,* they are easy to install, don't require a water garden, and you can have one bubbling away in a weekend.

You'll need a plastic garbage can or large tub for a reservoir, plus a small submersible pump with a flow adjuster, a few bricks, plastic tubing, heavy-duty wire mesh or hardware cloth, a piece of water-garden liner or polyethylene, wire cutters, scissors, and a supply of river rocks.

Dig a hole that's large enough to accommodate the garbage can, and set it with the rim flush with the soil surface. Lay the piece of water-garden liner/polyethylene over the garbage can reservoir; it should extend several feet beyond the edge of the reservoir. Cut a round hole that's 3 or 4 inches *smaller* than the can or tub in the piece of liner over the reservoir. (It directs water from the fountain back into the reservoir and needs to hang over the edges. Build up the soil around it if there's a danger that water will run off rather than into the reservoir.) Attach the plastic tubing to the pump, and place it in the reservoir on a few bricks.

Place one or two layers of wire mesh over the top of the reservoir; these need to be strong enough to support a pile of river rocks. With the wire cutters, cut a hole through the mesh that's large enough for the plastic tubing. String the tubing up through the hole, fill the reservoir with water, and test the pump before cutting off the tubing and covering the area with rocks.

You will have to adjust the stones piled around the tubing until you create a flow for the fountain that's appealing. After seeing how far away the water falls from the fountain, cut off any excess water-garden liner around the edges. Then cover it with rocks or gravel.

The area also is decorated with a collection of birdhouses, which add a touch of whimsy to the space. Quite a few are set on posts installed for just this purpose; others hang from the trees. Most are uninhabited, but wrens and other birds set up housekeeping in their favorites each year. Since an electric line was run out to the site to power the pump, there's also electricity to run fairy lights to illuminate the space in the evening.

plants for dry shade

Plants that grow in dry shade are the main attraction in this garden. A variety of shrubs tolerate these conditions, including evergreens such as English holly *(Ilex aquifolium)*, lawson cypress *(Chamaecyparis lawsoniana)*, and English yew *(Taxus baccata)*, all of which can be shrubs or trees depending on the cultivar you select.

Other evergreen shrubs that grow in dry shade include mahonia or Oregon holly grape *(Mahonia aquifolium)*, Russian arborvitae *(Microbiota decussata)*, dwarf sweet box *(Sarcococca hookeriana var. humilis)*, and mountain laurel *(Kalmia latifolia)*. Deciduous shrubs for a spot in dry shade include Japanese kerria *(Kerria japonica)*, summersweet *(Clethra* spp.*)*, spicebush *(Lindera benzoin)*, black jetbead *(Rhodotypos scandens)*, and blackhaw viburnum *(Viburnum prunifolium)*.

In addition to hostas, hellebores, epimediums, and lungworts *(Pulmonaria* spp.*)*, many other perennials grow in dry shade. Try some Plants to Choose From, page 113.

color in the shade

Combining elements is a very effective way of making a garden more interesting. Although not really colorful, this birdbath and small sculpture add charm to a shady spot, and forget-me-nots provide the color.

plants to choose from

AUTUMN FERN (*Dryopteris ery-throsora*). This evergreen to deciduous species produces clumps of 2-foot-tall fronds that are bronze to copper-red in spring and slowly turn green by summer.

BIGROOT GERANIUM (*Geranium macrorrhizum*). A mounding geranium, this species spreads vigorously via fleshy, deep roots. It features aromatic leaves and pink to purplish pink flowers in spring.

MALE FERN (*Dryopteris filix-mas*). This deciduous fern reaches 3 feet in height; many forms with crested fronds are available. Japanese sword fern (*D. erythrosora*) is a popular relative with coppery pink fronds.

SOLOMON'S SEAL (*Polygonatum* spp.). These sport handsome, arching leaves and bell-shaped flowers in spring. Species to look for are native *P. biflorum*, which ranges from 1½ to 7 feet tall, and variegated, fragrant Solomon's seal (*P. odoratum* 'Variegatum'), a 3-foot-tall selection with leaves that are striped with white.

WOOD SPURGE (*Euphorbia amygdaloides* var. *robbiae*). This species bears greenish yellow flowers in spring or early summer but is grown for its 2-foot-tall mounds of handsome evergreen leaves.

YELLOW CORYDALIS (*Corydalis lutea*). Long-blooming yellow corydalis produces mounds of ferny, blue-green leaves and small yellow flowers from spring to fall.

Polygonatum spp.

Euphorbia amygdaloides

Corydalis lutea

Dryopteris erythrosora

ideas for great design

friendly fences

A fence doesn't have to be tall or solid to do its work. The fences that divide this shady retreat from the rest of the yard may be low, but they still reduce traffic and serve as a barrier.

shady insurance

Having an umbrella or other secondary source of shade is a good idea if trees or other structures don't provide complete protection from the sun.

white noise

The sound of moving water helps block noise from the outside world. Reservoir features, small pools, wall fountains, or freestanding fountains can all be incorporated into even the smallest shady retreat.

match plants to the site

This is a simple rule to garden by, whether you're planting in sun or shade. Plants that grow well in the conditions that exist naturally — dry shade here — will be more vigorous and require less care than ones that have to struggle to survive.

shady seating in a formal garden

The design of this quiet, serene space gives it an austere simplicity that is very compelling. The main view of the garden — from the house across the small pool to the wall fountain against the back wall — becomes a beautiful, living picture from indoors. Take a few steps out into the garden, and two shady sitting areas come into view on either side of the center square. From indoors, these spaces are hidden from sight, but they make this garden an appealing place to spend time. The addition of simple, easy-care plantings makes this an ideal spot for sitting quietly, reading, or meditating.

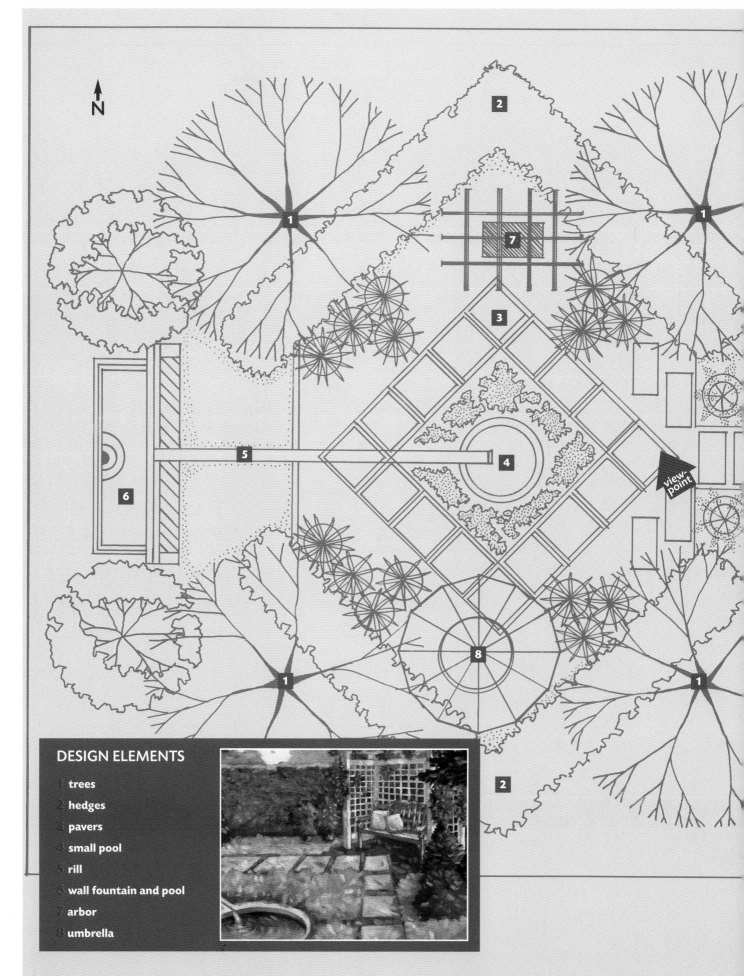

N

2

7

3

4

5

6

view-point

8

1

1

1

1

2

DESIGN ELEMENTS

1 trees
2 hedges
3 pavers
4 small pool
5 rill
6 wall fountain and pool
7 arbor
8 umbrella

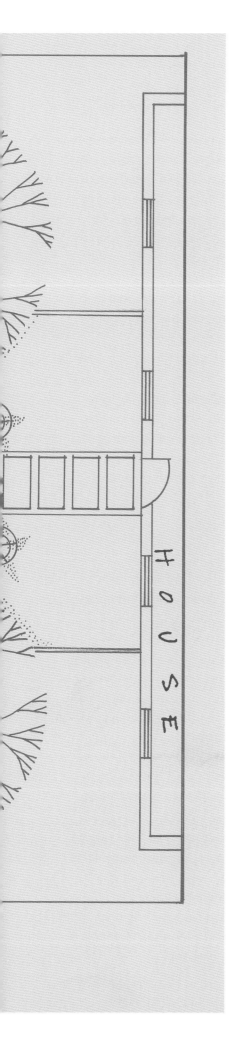

LIKE ANY GARDEN with a formal design, this one features a clear, symmetrical layout with geometric shapes and plants arranged in mirror-image fashion. The largest elements in the design are four trees (1) set at the corners of the space. A pair of clipped hedges (2) frames the central square, which has been rotated to line up with the main view of the garden from the house, across the space, to the back of the yard. Together, the trees and hedges form a solid green wall that blocks sight of the outside world from view.

The long view of the garden looks across a small square of pavers (3) enclosing a bed of ground covers. The pavers surround a small pool (4), and the view continues along a rill or runnel (5), then on to the focal point of the design, a wall fountain spilling into a rectangular pool at its base (6).

This seemingly simple space functions on two levels. From the house, the garden forms a pleasing picture, but once visitors take a few steps out into the yard, they'll discover two cozy, private sitting areas that make it clear there's plenty of room for people in this landscape. The first is a comfortable seat under a small arbor that's shaded with vines (7), and the second is a table shaded by an umbrella (8). Both overlook the pool and rill and are ideal spots

for enjoying the sights and sounds of moving water, along with the quiet serenity of this garden.

formal design basics

In addition to the symmetrical nature of a formal design, a few other characteristics make this a restful, serene space. The limited number of specimens, another characteristic of formal garden designs, means plants are arranged in blocks of all one species. This makes the space look peaceful and gives the eyes a place to rest. Plants in soothing colors, such as this nearly all-green scheme, give a space a relaxing, restful appeal. Or choose soft pastels, such as blues, purples, white, pink, and pale yellow. Finally, the sheer simplicity of the space makes it easy to care for — if you tend to worry about maintenance and other garden responsibilities, keep your shady retreat small and manageable.

The water feature in this garden is fairly complex and probably should be installed by an expert. It's a recirculating system: There's a submersible pump in the pool, which delivers water back to the wall fountain. From there, the water spills into the rectangular pool, then into the rill, which is set in concrete and runs slightly downhill and back into the round pool.

There are simpler options for bringing moving water into a

small space like this one. Perhaps the easiest is to install a water garden with a fountain. A round fiberglass water-garden liner at the center of the garden would work for this. Edge the garden with flat pavers to hide the liner, and install a pump to run the fountain.

Solar pumps that power fountains are available from catalogs and water-garden specialists. These come complete with solar panels and don't require any electricity to run during sunny weather. For a pump that runs at night, an electric outlet with a ground-fault circuit interrupter is required. Another simple option for bringing moving water to a garden like this one would be to install the wall fountain and rectangular pool at the back of the garden and replace the round pool with a container garden or a circle of ground covers in a contrasting color or texture. The round pool also could be replaced with a large container garden.

simple, elegant plants

A variety of ground covers could be used to fill in the center square of this space. Plants that need less than 8 hours of full sun to grow but can stand full sun and heat during the midday hours are the best choices.

Creeping juniper *(Juniperus horizontalis)* or shore juniper *(J. conferta)* are excellent options, as are thymes *(Thymus* spp.), catmints *(Nepeta* spp.), and lavender *(Lavandula angustifolia)*. A mix of low-growing sedums *(Sedum* spp.), hens-and-chicks *(Sempervivum* spp.), thymes, and dwarf conifers arranged in a formal geometric pattern would also work here.

Almost any vine would shade a small arbor or garden seat like this one. Try such perennials as hybrid clematis and goldflame honeysuckle *(Lonicera* x *heckrottii)*, as well as annuals like cup-and-saucer vine *(Cobaea scandens)*.

For the hedges that frame this space, evergreens are the best choice for year-round color that maintains the design even in winter. Possibilities include dwarf alberta spruce *(Picea glauca* var. *albertiana* 'Conica'), common boxwood *(Buxus sempervirens)*, cultivars of sawara false cypress *(Chamaecyparis pisifera)*, sheared hemlocks *(Tsuga* spp.), and white pine *(Pinus strobus* 'Fastigiata', 'Compacta', or 'Nana'). Other excellent hedge selections are included in Plants to Choose From, page 119.

color in the shade

White light reflected from a glass birdbath and the glass chips that fill it illuminate this partly shady spot. White-striped leaves of ribbon grass *(Phalaris arundinacea* 'Picta') echo the effect.

plants to choose from

AMERICAN ARBORVITAE (*Thuja occidentalis*). While this species reaches 60 feet or more at maturity, compact cultivars such as 'Boothii', 'Elegantissima', 'Rheingold', and 'Techny' all make fine evergreen hedges with a minimum of pruning.

HOLLIES (*Ilex* spp.). Several species of hollies can be used as evergreen hedges. All require pruning. Japanese holly (*I. crenata*) and Chinese holly (*I. cornuta*) tolerate severe pruning. Other suitable species include English holly (*I. aquifolium*), American holly (*I. opaca*), Foster's holly (*I. × attenuata* 'Fosteri'), and the blue hollies (*I. × meserveae*).

JUNIPERUS (*Juniperus* spp.). Here, too, choose cultivars that are fastigiate or pyramidal and relatively compact, since the species listed below mature at 40 to 50 feet. A multitude of cultivars of Chinese juniper (*J. chinensis*), Rocky Mountain juniper (*J. scopulorum*), and Eastern red cedar (*J. virginiana*) is available in a range of sizes and shapes. Most are suitable for use as a hedge.

YEWS (*Taxus* spp.). These popular landscape shrubs grow in sun or shade and need moist but well-drained soil. They withstand severe pruning. Look for fastigiate or pyramidal forms, such as Capitata Japanese yew (*T. cuspidata* 'Capitata'), or forms of Anglo-Japanese yew (*Taxus × media*), such as 'Brownii', 'Flushing', 'Kelseyi', 'Hicksii', or 'Viridis'.

Juniperus virginiana **'Blue Arrow'**

Ilex aquifolium

Thuja occidentalis **'Elegantissima'**

ideas for great design

sleek symmetry

A formal design, with mirror-image plantings arranged in geometric patterns, creates a garden that's inherently restful and pleasing to look at.

moving water

Whether you decide on a rill, waterfall, or a simple fountain, try to incorporate moving water into your shady retreat. Splashing water helps block out sounds of the outside world and is absolutely mesmerizing to watch as it sparkles in the sunlight.

comfort before style

Austere stone benches might look elegant, but be sure to choose comfortable benches or chairs if you want a shady retreat you'll really use.

structural strengths

Formal gardens feature a framework that includes paths and terraces made of stone, brick, or crushed gravel. These, together with features such as clipped hedges, make the design visible even in winter, when perennials and annuals may not be.

clearing in the woods

This woodland clearing makes a perfect shady retreat even though it's only a few steps from the house. The rustic arbor, which marks the entrance to the clearing, sets it apart from the rest of the wooded yard. Beyond the arbor, the retreat is outfitted with comfy chairs for sitting and chatting, plus a rustic table and chairs that can be used for picnics or as a craft area. The wild, natural-looking garden surrounding the area is planted with native wildflowers. A rustic, ground-level birdbath invites birds and other wildlife to visit, plus feeders and birdhouses ensure nearly constant activity in the treetops.

DESIGN ELEMENTS

1. clearing
2. seating area
3. table and chairs
4. pavers
5. terrace
6. arbor
7. birdbath

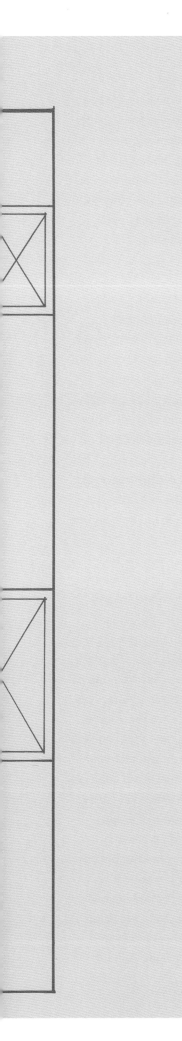

THIS LOT was once a rough woodland filled with a mix of trees, shrubs, and vines. While some of the trees were good native species — oaks (*Quercus* spp.) and hickories (*Carya* spp.), for example — others were weedy and threatened to take over the entire area.

Before starting a garden, the homeowners took time to identify the best plants growing on their property and saved them, even if they were just saplings. Weedy, nonnative trees like Norway maple (*Acer platanoides*) and tree-of-heaven (*Ailanthus altissima*) were removed. Shrubs like amur honeysuckle (*Lonicera maackii*), burning bush (*Euonymus alatus*), and Japanese barberry (*Berberis thunbergii*) were taken out to make room for native spicebush (*Lindera benzoin*), sweetshrub (*Calycanthus floridus*), and silky dogwood (*Cornus amomum*). Nonnative vines such as Japanese honeysuckle (*Lonicera japonica*) and Oriental bittersweet (*Celastris orbiculatus*) also were removed to give the remaining plants more room.

The exact location of this outdoor living space (1) was determined after the site had been cleared, making it easier to see the possibilities. The space is located on a level area where only a few additional saplings had to be removed to make room for the seating area (2) and the rustic table and chairs (3).

For this space, the floor is mulched with shredded bark, and a few pavers (4) lead out from the arbor-covered terrace next to the house (5). The arbor set at the entrance to this shady retreat (6) marks the beginning of a quiet zone, where phones and other electronics aren't taken. It's dedicated to watching wildlife, meditating, or talking quietly.

welcome birds

In addition to hanging birdfeeders and birdhouses, this space features a small, ground-level birdbath (7) that's ideal for attracting birds and other wildlife. It's made by digging a shallow hole with sides that slope very gently. Covered with a square of water-garden liner, the hole is about 1 foot deep at the deepest point and only an inch or two around the edges. Rocks cover the edges of the liner, and a stick is positioned to emerge from the water to give a foothold to any wildlife that happens by.

A ground-level birdbath like this one can be swept out with a broom every few days, cleaned, and refilled. If you opt to leave the water for any length of time, drop a MosquitoDunks ring into the birdbath to prevent mosquitoes from breeding. These are small rings of *Bacillus thuringiensis* ssp. *israelensis* that float on the water's surface and have to be replaced every 30 days. They control mosquitoes organically and are safe for birds and other wildlife.

Moving water is especially attractive to birds, but this space isn't equipped with electricity to power a pump. Instead, a bucket with a tiny hole in the bottom hangs above the water. It has to be refilled daily, but the slow dripping of the water makes the birdbath much more compelling to birds and other animals.

Another wildlife-friendly feature graces this shady retreat. During the clearing process, a dead tree, or snag, was left in place (one that wouldn't fall onto the house). While dead trees might not seem particularly ornamental, they offer important foraging and nesting sites for woodpeckers, brown creepers, and a variety of other wildlife. A snag also makes a fine perch from which owls can hunt.

a wildflower garden

In spring, this wooded yard overflows with spring-blooming wildflowers, including wood anemones (*Anemone quinquefolia*), great merry-bells (*Uvularia grandiflora*), Jack-in-the-pulpit (*Arisaema triphyllum*), Virginia bluebells (*Mertensia pulmonarioides*), wild blue phlox (*Phlox divaricata*), Bowman's root (*Gillenia trifoliata*), creeping Jacob's ladder (*Polemonium reptans*), Solomon's seal (*Polygonatum biflorum*), and Solomon's plume (*Smilacina racemosa*).

Ground covers include heuchera (*Heuchera americana*), Canada wild ginger (*Asarum canadense*), and Allegheny foamflower (*Tiarella cordifolia*). Snakeroot (*Cimicifuga*), hardy ageratum (*Eupatorium coelestinum*), and the bright but poisonous berries of red baneberry (*Actaea rubra*) and doll's eyes (*A. alba*) decorate the space in late summer and fall. Christmas fern (*Polystichum acrostichoides*) contributes evergreen leaves to enliven the area all winter.

The yard also features two other spring wildflowers, toadshade trillium (*Trillium sessile*) and large-flowered trillium (*T. grandiflorum*), found growing here when the lot was cleared. If you grow wildflowers, pay attention to where the plants came from, and avoid wild-collected ones. Ask if the source of native plants offered for sale isn't clear, and take your business elsewhere if you don't get satisfactory answers. Many native wildflowers are available in commerce, but plant sales held by native plant societies and botanical gardens are also good places to shop for them. For more native wildflowers for shade, see Plants to Choose From, page 125, and A Deck in the Woods, page 66.

color in the shade

Spring flowers, such as these forget-me-nots (*Myosotis* spp.), make it easy to light up shady spots in spring. For color that lasts through summer, overplant with impatiens, wax begonias, caladiums, and other shade-lovers.

plants to choose from

AMERICAN TURK'S-CAP LILY (*Lilium superbum*). A stunning lily for a spot with moist soil and partial shade, this species bears clusters of 3-inch-wide orange flowers dotted with maroon in summer.

INDIAN PINK (*Spigelia marilandica*). This clump-forming perennial produces clusters of tubular- to funnel-shaped red flowers with yellow insides from spring to summer.

ORNAMENTAL GRASSES. Commonly thought of as plants for sun, grasses have some shade-loving varieties, including bottlebrush grass (*Hystrix patula*); wild oats (*Chasmanthium latifolium*); and sedges, such as fringed sedge (*Carex crinita*), Pennsylvania sedge (*C. pensylvanica*), Gray's sedge (*C. grayi*), and palm sedge (*C. muskingumensis*).

SPIKENARD (*Aralia racemosa*). A shrubby perennial, spikenard bears large pinnate leaves and clusters of tiny greenish white flowers in early summer. In fall, small purple-black fruit that is attractive to birds follows the flowers.

WHITE WOOD ASTER (*Aster divaricatus*). A clump-forming aster for shade, this species bears an abundance of ½-inch-wide white flowers with brownish yellow centers from midsummer to midfall.

WILD COLUMBINE (*Aquilegia canadensis*). This species bears dainty, fernlike foliage and clusters of nodding, red-and-yellow flowers from spring to midsummer.

Aquilegia canadensis

Lilium superbum

Gaultheria procumbens

WINTERBERRY (*Gaultheria procumbens*). Actually a small shrublet, this 6-inch-tall plant is an evergreen species. The leaves release the scent of wintergreen when crushed. Small white flowers are followed by scarlet berries in fall.

WREATH GOLDENROD (*Solidago caesia*). While goldenrods are best known as perennials for sun, this species bears wands of golden yellow flowers in late summer to fall.

ideas for great design

clear carefully

When clearing a wooded lot, use a field guide to identify weedy, nonnative species. Then save the native trees, even if they are still small.

simple says it all

This space feels like a woodland clearing, but it still has all the features of an outdoor living space. Mulch serves as flooring, shade-loving shrubs form the walls, arching tree branches create a ceiling, and comfortable furnishings make visitors feel welcome.

two spaces, one yard

Why not have two shady retreats? This design features a shady terrace attached to the house along with a shady retreat out in the woods.

shop with care

Trilliums (*Trillium* spp.) and native orchids (*Cypripedium* spp.) are among the species that are still wild-collected. Nursery owners who sell propagated plants will be proud of that fact and will highlight the source of their plants in sales materials.

old-fashioned front porch

Usually, a front porch is a very public space, open to the street and completely visible to passersby. Here, however, vines and hanging baskets, plus a front-yard cottage garden, transform this old-fashioned porch into a wonderful private retreat only a few steps from the sidewalk. While the vines shade this space and give it privacy, they don't close it off entirely, so it's easy to get a glimpse out to the street when sitting on the glider or in one of the armchairs. A dining table tucked away in the corner makes this a handy, but secluded, spot for a meal or just coffee or drinks.

DESIGN ELEMENTS

1 glider
2 armchairs
3 table and chairs
4 shrubs and perennials
5 container plantings

N

H O U S E

5

3

5

2 1

2

5 5 5 5

4

4 4

view-point

IT'S POSSIBLE to have a shady retreat even on a small lot where most of the open space is in the front yard. Once a public area with little appeal, this old-fashioned porch came into its own once vines were added to screen it. Now, it's a full-fledged outdoor living space with privacy, cool shade, and comfortable spaces to curl up with a book, play board games, or sit and chat.

In addition to a comfortable glider (1) and armchairs (2), there's also a table and chairs (3) suitable for an outdoor supper or sharing a cup of coffee with a friend. Ceiling fans on the porch roof help move the air around on days when there isn't a breeze. In the front yard, perennials and flowering shrubs (4) replaced dull foundation plantings and lawn.

All the vines that shade the porch lose their leaves in winter or die back to the ground. This makes the porch shady and private in summer and also keeps the house cooler. In winter, it lets sunlight into the front of the house when the extra warmth is appreciated.

There are several options for training vines across a porch like this one. For annuals and tender perennials, the easiest is to attach strings at the top of the porch and stake them to the ground in the bed below. For a thicker screen of vines, weave some strings at a diagonal so they can grow across,

not just up. Cut down the strings and vines in fall for composting.

Wires affixed in a similar fashion will support heavier, hardy vines. Lightweight wood lath trellises also can be cut and fitted along the front of a porch. A wire framework works for training any kind of vines. In fact, the pipe armatures for porch awnings can be strung with wire and covered with vines such as Dutchman's pipe (*Aristolochia macrophylla*) to replace the canvas. However you train your vines, plan on leaving some openings to create a view from the porch.

front-porch garden

This is a cottage garden planted with a wide variety of annuals, perennials, shrubs, trees, and vines. Fragrant flowers play a prominent role, both in the garden and in pots on the porch (5). The porch also is a great place to give houseplants a summer vacation, since it's shady and they're easy to keep watered here.

Spring flowers are easy, but there are fewer selections for summer-flowering shrubs and trees. Two lilacs with fragrant trusses of flowers are great choices for a front-yard garden. 'Miss Kim' lilac (*Syringa pubescens* ssp. *patula* 'Miss Kim') is a shrubby, 8-foot-tall species that bears pale lilac flowers in early summer.

Passiflora caerulea

Clematis 'Perle d'Azure'

Humulus lupulus 'Aureus'

CROSSVINE (*Bignonia capreolata*). This native vine, which climbs by tendrils to about 30 feet, bears fragrant, red-brown flowers in spring that are yellow-orange inside.

PASSIONFLOWER (*Passiflora* spp.). Most of these handsome flowering vines are tender perennials, but two commonly grown species are hardy to at least Zone 6. Blue passionflower (*P. caerulea*) bears white-and-blue flowers from summer to fall on vines that can reach 30 feet. 'Constance Elliott' bears fragrant flowers. *P. edulis* bears white-and-purple blooms on 15-foot vines in summer. 'Incense' features fragrant flowers. Grow tender species in containers.

CAROLINA JESSAMINE (*Gelsemium sempervirens*). This twining, evergreen vine, hardy to Zone 6, bears small, fragrant yellow flowers in spring and summer. 'Pride of Augusta' features abundant crops of double flowers.

GOLDEN HOPS (*Humulus lupulus* 'Aureus'). Grown for its foliage rather than its flowers, this twining vine adds bright color in the form of chartreuse leaves all summer. The 20-foot vines die to the ground in winter in the North.

HYBRID CLEMATIS (*Clematis* spp.). A stunning addition to any garden, clematis can be trained up a trellis or grown on the stems of a climbing rose, such as 'New Dawn'. For the longest season of bloom, plant hybrids from more than one hybrid group. Early-blooming, large-flowered hybrids include violet-blue 'General Sikorski', white 'Henryi', red 'Niobe', and pink-and-white 'Nelly Moser'. Late-flowering hybrids include violet-purple 'Jackmanii' and 'Perle d'Azure', mauve-pink 'Comtesse de Bouchaud', magenta-pink 'Ernest Markham', and blue-purple 'Polish Spirit'. 'Betty Corning' features pale lavender, bell-shaped flowers.

MANDEVILLA (*Mandevilla* x *amoena* 'Alice du Pont'). This tender perennial, also called Chilean jasmine, bears showy, pink, funnel-shaped flowers in summer. Plants can reach 20 feet; in the North, they are commonly grown as annuals or as tender perennials that are kept in pots and brought indoors during cool weather.

POTATO VINE (*Solanum jasminoides*). Despite the less-than-alluring common name, this tender perennial bears clusters of small, fragrant, bluish-white flowers in summer and fall. Plants can reach 20 feet.

Mandevilla x amoena 'Alice du Pont'

Japanese tree lilac *(S. reticulata)* is a small, 30-foot tree that produces fluffy, creamy white, astilbe-like trusses early to midsummer. Sweet bay magnolia *(Magnolia virginiana)* offers fragrant, creamy white flowers in early summer and intermittently through the summer to fall. This tree reaches about 20 feet in the North, where it is deciduous to semievergreen, and 60 feet in the South, where it is evergreen.

Few shrubs can surpass roses for fragrant summer flowers. Rugosa roses, such as pink 'Apart', white 'Blanc Double de Coubert', crimson 'Roseraie de l'Häy', and pink 'Sarah van Fleet', are good choices, but there are many others, including disease-resistant shrub rose 'Carefree Beauty'. Other summer-blooming shrubs with fragrant flowers include Virginia sweetspire *(Itea virginica)*, sweetshrub or Carolina allspice *(Calycanthus floridus)*, and

summersweet clethra *(Clethra alnifolia)*.

The garden also includes the fragrant-flowered Trumpet and Aurelian Hybrid lilies, such as 'Black Dragon' and 'African Queen', along with Oriental Hybrids, such as 'Casa Blanca' and 'Black Beauty'. Perennials include lavender *(Lavandula angustifolia)*, lemon lilies *(Hemerocallis lilioasphodelus)*, August lilies *(Hosta plantaginea)*, and pinks *(Dianthus* spp.). The garden also features fragrant-flowered annuals and tender perennials, such as petunias and heliotropes *(Heliotropium arborescens)*.

While annual vines, including morning glories *(Ipomoea nil* and *I. purpurea)* and purple bell vine *(Rhodochiton atrosanguineus)* would do a fine job of screening this porch, consider some of the less-common choices in Plants to Choose From, page 130.

less-common choices in Plants to Choose From, page 130.

color in the shade

Decorations can run the gamut on a covered porch. Here, white wicker furniture, summering houseplants, and a pair of colorful glazed containers used as end tables create a bright, welcoming spot in the shade. Shutters along one end of the porch ensure privacy.

ideas for great design

a private, public space

Even a front porch can have a cozy, private feel. Vines do most of the screening here, but a front-yard garden overflowing with fragrant plants also helps screen this old-fashioned porch.

summer shade, winter sun

Vines that lose their leaves over winter, whether they're simply deciduous or are annuals or tender perennials, are a good choice for shading areas directly attached to a house because they allow the winter sun to reach inside.

fragrant flowers

Strongly scented flowers can envelope a shady retreat and help give it a special character all its own. A still night and a location protected from the wind are best for enjoying fragrant flowers.

trellis windows

Leave openings in the vines that shelter a porch to ensure that it is a relaxed and comfortable space but not claustrophobic.

a perch in the trees

This shady retreat offers all the magic of a tree house but isn't actually built in a tree. Constructed at treetop level in the middle of a tree and shrub border, it's a freestanding building made of a platform set on posts. While the trees around it will one day provide deep shade, for now a solid roof decorated with vines provides ample protection from sun and rain. The base of the structure is engulfed in a garden designed to attract hummingbirds. It also features many plants with large, tropical-looking foliage to give this retreat an exotic appeal.

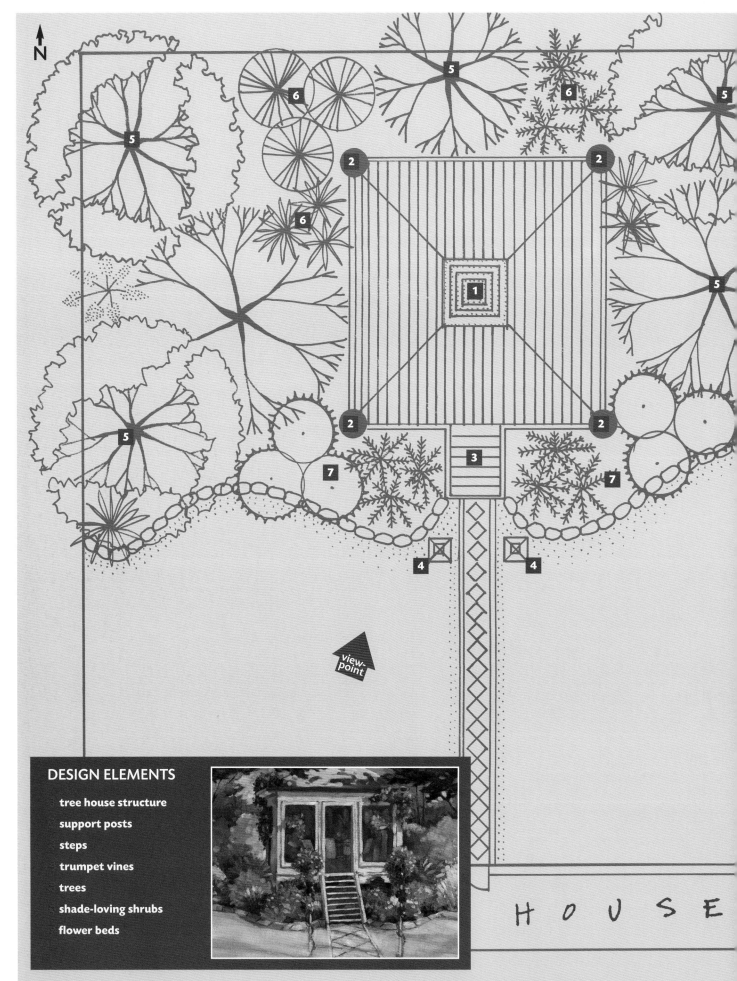

N

DESIGN ELEMENTS

1. tree house structure
2. support posts
3. steps
4. trumpet vines
5. trees
6. shade-loving shrubs
7. flower beds

view-point

H O U S E

MOST YARDS don't offer trees large enough to support a full-size tree house, and that's the appeal of this whimsical structure (1): It could be erected nearly anywhere. Although it sits at treetop level, it's actually a structure built on posts set in the ground (2). Ladderlike steps lead up to the entrance (3).

Unlike a true tree house, which needs to be custom-made to fit the tree (and also harms it by nailing or bolting wood into branches and trunks), this one simply started out as a platform on posts; it could be built from one to several feet off the ground.

Solid sides and a roof enclose the space, but for a more open-sided effect, arbor supports could be added over the platform and covered with vines. If you use solid walls, be sure to leave ample openings for windows on all sides so the space offers views in every direction. Screens or mosquito netting could be added to the structure, if necessary.

While a shady retreat like this one would be perfect on a wooded site — and trees would certainly help underscore the central illusion of a treetop perch — this tree house would work anywhere. Use it as a surprise in an out-of-the-way corner of the yard, or clear space for a tree house in an existing shrub border. Or construct a tree house right in the lawn and plant a new shrub and perennial

border around it. A structure like this could also do double duty: Build it for your kids, then retrofit it for yourself once they're grown.

One of the reasons this private perch is so compelling is that it reflects archetypal spaces, meaning spaces that have an instinctual and universal appeal related to our earliest memories and favorite childhood places. In this case, the tree house has a cavelike feeling where visitors are surrounded on all sides but have a safe view out into the world. It's also a high point that overlooks the surrounding area, creating a feeling of excitement and exploration.

When planning a shady retreat, get in touch with memories of cherished places from your childhood. If you haven't thought about them for a while, jot down reminiscences, then think about how you can use them in your design. Whether you settle on a rose-covered arbor set against a wall or a secret hideout in a wooded corner, retreats inspired by personal recollection and inspiration will be the most satisfying.

tree house in the tropics

This hot-colored garden has a tropical flair that appeals to hummingbirds and gardeners alike. Two posts in front of the tree house support a pair of trumpet vines (4)

(Campsis radicans), which produce from summer to fall plentiful orange to red blooms that attract hummingbirds like magnets.

Yellow trumpet vine *(C. radicans* forma. *flava)* is another option here, as is *C.* x *tagliabuana* 'Madame Galen', with orange-red blooms. Each year in late winter, the vines are pruned hard to keep them in bounds. Trumpet vines could be used to cover a tree house structure, provided it isn't one that needs painting, since they stick tightly to supports with aerial roots. A pair of coppiced purple smoke trees *(Cotinus coggygria* 'Velvet Cloak' or 'Royal Purple') complements the vines.

Although this tree house has a conventional roof, vines growing over the top of the structure give it a sense of enclosure and make it feel wild and remote. Vines suitable for growing over a roof include climbing roses *(Clematis montana)*, sweet autumn clematis *(C. terniflora)*, grapes *(Vitis* spp.), or crimson glory vine *(V. coignetiae)*, and wisteria *(Wisteria* spp.). String wires or use large-mesh hardware cloth over the roof to give these vines something to cling to.

color in the shade

Bold containers make it easy to brighten up a shady spot. This beautiful stained-glass container is planted with purple heart (*Tradescantia pallida* 'Purpurea'), pansies, and other annuals. To prevent soil moisture from damaging an unusual container, plant in a conventional pot, then set it in the container.

welcome hummingbirds

While trees (5) and shade-loving shrubs (6) surround the back of the tree house, the bed in front (7) features a riot of plants in hot, tropical colors with large leaves and/or trumpet-shaped blooms that attract hummingbirds. Cannas *(Canna* x *generalis)* add flowers and lush foliage. Cultivars include 'Pretoria', with orange-yellow blooms and yellow-striped leaves; 'Australia', with orange-red flowers and burgundy-black leaves; and 'Durban' with red flowers and leaves striped with orange, yellow, and red. All reach 5 to 6 feet in a single summer. Three annual or tender perennial vines that attract hummers celebrate this red-and-orange color scheme: cypress vine *(Ipomoea quamoclit)*, Chilean glory vine *(Eccremocarpus scaber)*, and scarlet runner beans *(Phaseolus coccineus)*.

In addition to those in Plants to Choose From, page 137, hummingbirds visit petunias, phlox, hostas, columbines *(Aquilegia* spp.), beard-tongues *(Penstemon* spp.), lilies *(Lilium* spp.), daylilies *(Hemerocallis* spp.), snapdragons *(Antirrhinum majus)*, and hollyhocks *(Alcea rosea)*.

plants to choose from

BEE BALM (*Monarda didyma*). Grown for its fragrant leaves and ragged clusters of scarlet or pink flowers, this perennial also attracts butterflies. Red-flowered 'Jacob Cline', pink 'Marshall's Delight', and purple 'Prairie Night' are mildew-resistant.

FLOWERING TOBACCO (*Nicotiana* spp.). This long-blooming annual comes in shades of red, pink, purple-pink, and white. The trumpet-shaped blooms attract hummers along with butterflies and moths.

FOUR-O'CLOCK (*Mirabilis jalapa*). This tender perennial bears trumpet-shaped flowers that open in the afternoon. It comes in shades of red, magenta-pink, pink, yellow, and white and attracts night-flying moths as well as hummingbirds.

HIBISCUS, ROSE MALLOW (*Hibiscus* spp.). Dinner-plate-size blooms make hardy hibiscus a fine addition to a garden with a tropical theme. Scarlet rose mallow (*H. coccineus*) bears dark red flowers, while common rose mallow (*H. moscheutos*) blooms in shades of red, pink, or white.

SALVIA (*Salvia* spp.). This garden favorite bears two-lipped flowers in shades of violet, purple, lilac, blue, scarlet, pink, and white. Perhaps the best-known is annual scarlet sage (*S. splendens*), which blooms from summer to frost. *S. coccinea* is another good annual for hummingbirds. Look for scarlet 'Lady in Red'

Salvia coccinea

Monarda didyma

Hibiscus moscheutos

or pink 'Coral Nymph'. Gregg sage (*S. greggii*) is a tender perennial that blooms in shades of red, purple, violet, pink, or yellow.

STAR CLUSTER (*Pentas lanceolata*). This tender perennial bears rounded clusters of small, trumpet-shaped flowers in shades of pale pink, mauve, magenta, purple-red, lilac, or white.

ideas for great design

take a new view
From its high vantage point, this treetop perch provides an immediate, away-from-it-all feel. A garden filled with tropical foliage and hot-colored flowers also adds to the illusion of an exotic retreat.

a retreat for any site
Like a potting shed or summerhouse, a treeless tree house could be built nearly anywhere. Even in a yard with mature trees, you could build this type of structure without harming vegetation.

too hot to handle
If you've never tried a hot-colored garden, annuals and tender perennials are a good place to start. Grow them for a season, then return to softer hues if you don't like all the excitement.

symmetrical statement
Although this design is far from formal, the pair of trumpet vines in front of the retreat is a formal element that marks the entrance and adds order to the setting.

private gathering place

Adjoining spaces make this shady retreat especially flexible. A vine-covered pergola flanked with flower borders links the house to a Chinese arbor (also covered with vines) that functions as a shady spot for gathering. Beyond that lies a fire cauldron set in a circle of grass; this represents a traditional tribal gathering place and is perfect for family get-togethers. This yard can be used during the day, but it really shines in the early evening and at night, when candles on the table and a fire in the cauldron light the space. In keeping with the nighttime theme, the gardens feature white flowers, which glow in the moonlight.

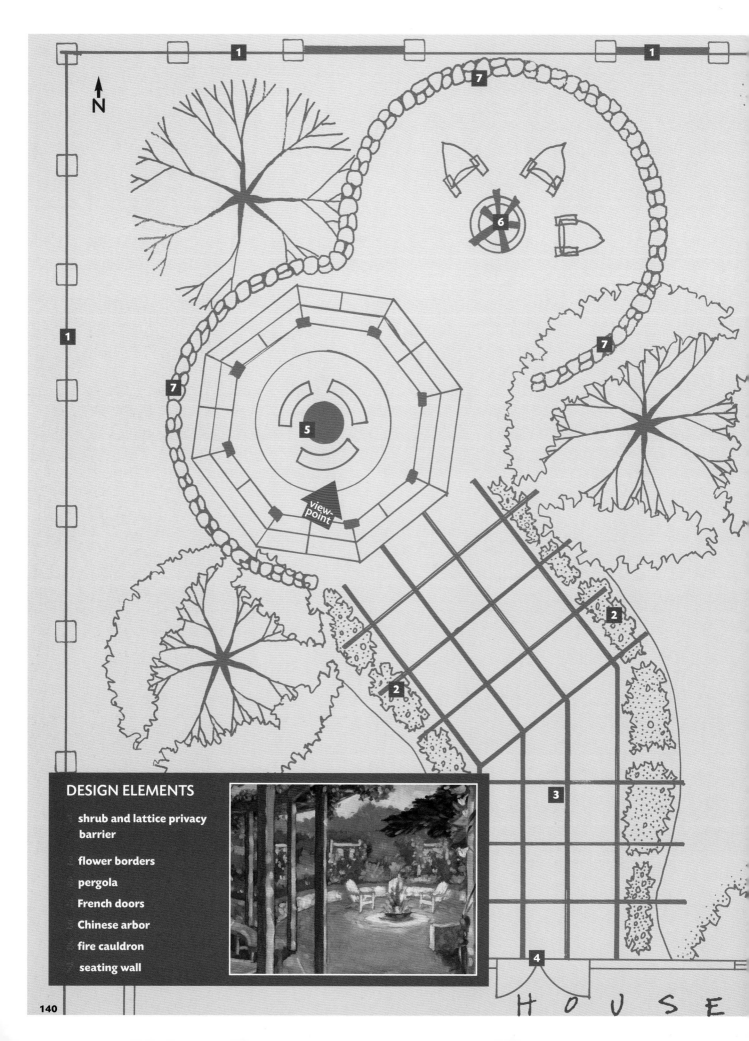

N

1

7

7

6

5

view-point

7

2

2

3

4

DESIGN ELEMENTS

1 shrub and lattice privacy barrier

2 flower borders

3 pergola

4 French doors

5 Chinese arbor

6 fire cauldron

7 seating wall

140

H O U S E

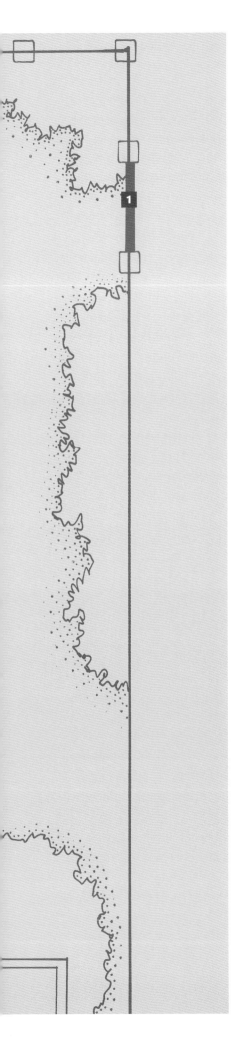

LIKE MANY BACKYARDS, this one started out as a nearly empty canvas, with lots of grass and three trees that provided a little bit of shade. The yard overlooks a golf course, so the design highlights the view yet still provides plenty of private space for family activities.

Instead of a solid fence or hedge, shrubs interspersed with freestanding panels of lattice (1) provide a privacy barrier along the lot lines. (Privacy fence panels would work here, too.) The shrubs and fence panels don't form a solid line, however. Openings along the back lot line, as well as toward the corners of the side lot lines, take advantage of the view. This kind of barrier would be effective on suburban lots that overlook golf courses, parkland, or large nearby lots, because it provides privacy yet takes advantage of nearby views.

One of the keys to this design is that it features connecting spaces that can be used separately or together. The design begins at the back door, where flower borders (2) along the sides of a pergola (3) frame a view that's especially nice from inside the French doors (4).

A stroll along the pea stone gravel walkway under the pergola leads to a circular space covered by a Chinese arbor (5). The arbor area is connected to a second circular space that contains a fire cauldron (6) surrounded by con-centric rings of crushed gravel and lawn. A low seating wall (7) curves around both areas, linking them together.

While the arbor and fire cauldron areas can be used concurrently for parties and large family gatherings, either area also is perfect for using separately, whether that means a family supper under the arbor or a bonfire on a late summer evening. The level path under the pergola makes access easy. It is lit by low-voltage, ground-level fixtures designed to light the path without illuminating the rest of the area — candles and fire are the light sources of choice farther out in this retreat.

cultural attractions

One of the features that makes this backyard unique is that it uses elements from other cultures as inspiration. The eight-sided Chinese arbor, painted a traditional red, is a strong organizing influence. The shape of the arbor duplicates an important symbol in the Chinese *I-Ching* — the *ba gua*, or eight trigrams, which represents the five elements of earth, fire, water, metal, and wood. The *ba gua* forms an octagon around a central circle that symbolizes yin and yang. *Ba gua* mirrors also take this shape and are used in feng shui.

The arbor also establishes a circular motif for the design. It shelters a round table surrounded by a circle of curved benches; the fire cauldron also is round, as is the seating wall in both areas. The circle has meaning in many cultures, including that of eternity, cosmic order, wholeness, unity, and relation. Using a circular theme brings a reminder of that rich cultural heritage into this garden.

Elements from other cultures don't have to be large and imposing to inspire a design, however. Even small items like statues, stone lanterns, rock cairns, or bowls of water that reflect the sky all can impart meaning and make a shady retreat special. The key is to identify cultures and traditions that are meaningful to you, then use influences from those cultures to decorate and enrich the spaces in your outdoor garden room.

a moon garden

Because of the fire cauldron, this space is especially wonderful at night. To highlight the evening magic, the borders along the pergola are filled with plants that feature white flowers, which glow late into the evening and through the night when the moon is full. (For ideas, see Plants to Choose From, page 143.) White-flowered vines, including fragrant annual moonflowers *(Ipomoea alba)* and wisteria *(W. sinensis* 'Alba' or *W. floribunda* 'Alba'), climb the posts of the arbor and pergola. In areas with cool summers, annual sweet peas *(Lathyrus odoratus)* would work just as well. White-flowered perennial pea *(Lathyrus latifolius* 'White Pearl') is another good choice.

In the rough-cut grass outside the fire circle, ox-eye daisies *(Leucanthemum vulgare)* and Queen Anne's lace *(Daucus carota)* twinkle in the moonlight. The flower beds along the pergola are filled with drifts of white-flowered annuals and perennials.

Here, drifts of white petunias and dahlias are planted with cleome *(Cleome hassleriana* 'Helen Campbell'), cosmos *(Cosmos bipinnatus* 'Sonata White'), lavatera or mallow *(Lavatera trimestris* 'Mont Blanc'), flowering tobacco *(Nicotiana sylvestris),* Angel's trumpets *(Brugmansia* spp. and *Datura* spp.), and even Italian white sunflowers *(Helianthus debilis* ssp. *cucumerifolius* 'Italian White'). All thrive quite happily alongside perennials.

Collecting white-flowered plants can become a fun and satisfying obsession, but pale yellow, soft pink, and light lavender flowers also show up well after dark.

color in the shade

With a little creativity, you can brighten up nearly any part of a shady retreat. Here, flooring adds interest in the form of a circular mosaic on the ground. It's made from tiles in various sizes interspersed with stones and pebbles to add both texture and color to this pathway.

plants to choose from

ARTEMISIA (*Artemisia* spp.). These bring silvery white foliage to the mix. Look for beach wormwood or perennial dusty miller (*Artemisia stelleriana*), wormwood (*A. absinthium* 'Lambrook Silver'), white sage (*A. ludoviciana* 'Silver King' or 'Silver Queen'), and *A.* 'Powis Castle'. Annual dusty miller (*Senecio cineraria* 'Silver Dust' or 'Silver Queen') also would bring silver-white foliage to the garden.

AUGUST LILY (*Hosta plantaginea*). This is just one of the white-flowered hostas that would be ideal for shady spots under a pergola. Plants produce mounds of green leaves and fragrant white flowers in summer.

BUTTERFLY BUSH (*Buddleia davidii*). 'White Bouquet' and 'White Profusion' are two good choices. Where hardy, these are shrubs, but for best results, cut it to the ground in late winter and it will fill the garden with white trusses of flowers on 10-foot-tall plants in late summer.

GARDEN PHLOX (*Phlox paniculata*). Rounded clusters of fragrant flowers are the hallmark of this garden favorite. For best results, look for mildew-resistant cultivars, such as white-flowered 'David'.

LILY (*Lilium* spp.). These bring to the garden glowing white blooms that glisten in moonlight. Many lilies also feature fragrant flowers, including Oriental lily 'Casa Blanca', Madonna lily (*Lilium candidum*), and *Lilium formosanum*.

SHASTA DAISY (*Leucanthemum* x *superbum*). This plant features simple daisy-shaped blooms with a ring of petals surrounding a yellow center, but semidouble and double Shasta daisies are available, too. All are lovely at night as well as during the day.

Buddleia 'White Bouquet'

Lilium 'Casa Blanca'

Artemisia 'Powis Castle'

ideas for great design

connected spaces

A design with spaces that can be used separately or together is especially flexible, since it can be comfortable for one or many people to use.

cultural inspiration

Symbols, structures, or icons from other cultures can provide powerful inspiration for a shady retreat. You can also use mementos from a vacation or a special place to inspire your design.

let there be light

In this garden, the path under the pergola is illuminated with low-level lighting to make access safe and easy. Beyond the pergola, candles and fire are used to illuminate the space in the evening to make the area seem far away from the everyday world.

open screening

The view beyond a yard often features both views you'd like to reveal and others you want to hide. Here, shrubs, free-standing lattice panels, and openings reveal the best and hide the rest.

PART 3

favorite
shade plants

Whether you're a fanatic plant collector or just want a handful of tough ground covers to fill a shady spot, you'll find a wealth of good candidates in the encyclopedia that follows. Plants are organized into three sections: Perennials; Annuals, Biennials, and Tender Perennials; and Shrubs, Small Trees, and Vines. Each entry provides information on the best species and cultivars, including a description of the most important ornamental features, such as flowers and foliage. There are also suggestions on how to use each plant in the garden. Since I couldn't fit all of my own favorite shade plants here, you'll find lists with additional plants to consider. Plants are also featured with each of the garden designs in part 2, where you'll find lists of specimens for wet soil and shade, plants for dry shade, and summer bulbs for shade, to name a few.

To find even more plants for your shade garden, visit arboretums and other gardens — both public and private — in your area. Local garden clubs and plant societies often sponsor garden tours, which can be great sources of ideas and inspiration. Members of these organizations frequently have plants to share, too. Well-stocked garden centers and nurseries that have display gardens also can be good places to look for new and exciting plants. And remember: If the main source of shade in your shady retreat is a structure like a gazebo, you may very well be looking for plants that like partial shade to full sun.

Rodgersia podophylla

perennials

For color in the shade that lasts all season long, concentrate on choosing perennials that feature handsome foliage. Flowers are a bonus, of course, but perennials with colorful variegated leaves contribute bright hues during the season, whether or not they're in bloom. To create the most interesting plantings, look for leaves in a range of greens, too — from chartreuse through dark black-green, gray-green, and blue-green. Also, mix up leaf sizes and textures. Combine lacy ferns with bold-leaved hostas, for example. The plants listed here are some of the best choices for shade. You'll find additional ideas in the plant lists that accompany the garden designs in part 2. Perennials that can be used as **ground covers** are marked with a leaf (🍃).

Aconitum spp.
ACONITE, MONKSHOOD
Stunning hooded flowers in shades of rich blues and purples are the hallmark of these long-lived perennials. Plants flower from midsummer to fall and are carried in erect clusters above clumps of handsome, deeply cut leaves. Be aware that all parts of the plant — leaves, roots, flowers, and seeds — are quite poisonous.

Grower's Choice: For blooms in mid- to late summer, plant bicolor monkshood *(A.* x *cammarum)* or common monkshood *(A. napellus).* Both bear violet-blue to bluish purple flowers on 3- to 4-foot plants. Azure monkshood, also violet-blue, blooms from late summer into fall and ranges from 2 or 3 feet to as tall as 5 feet. All are hardy in Zones 3–7; common monkshood *(A. napellus)* can withstand Zone 8's summer heat.

Special Uses: Plant monkshood to add rich, late-season color to shade gardens and clearings with bright, dappled shade. Plant them toward the middle or back of perennial beds, and stake the clumps so their flowers show to best advantage. They resent transplanting, so pick a permanent spot.

Aegopodium podagraria
BISHOP'S WEED
Think long and hard before you plant this fast-spreading perennial with its attractive three-leaflet foliage and white flowers in summer. Plants thrive in any soil and make fine ground covers in the right spot, but established plants spread quickly and are hard to eradicate.

Grower's Choice: 'Variegata' features attractive leaves with creamy white margins. It is grown more often than the all-green species and is somewhat less invasive. Dig up and discard any plants that revert to green. Zones 4–9.

Special Uses: Use bishop's weed as a ground cover in a spot with poor, dry soil where little else will grow. Plants also easily compete with tree roots and can be used as a ground cover under shrubs. Select a spot where it cannot spread into other flower beds or wild areas; it will overwhelm less vigorous plants.

Ajuga spp.
AJUGA, BUGLEWEED
photo on page 47

Grown for their colorful leaves and showy spikes of colorful, spring to early-summer flowers, ajugas make a great addition to the shade garden. They are low-growing plants forming ground-hugging clumps of spinachlike leaves. Most, but not all, are fast spreaders that are vigorous enough to invade lawn.

Grower's Choice: Blue bugleweed *(A. genevensis)* spreads gradually and bears indigo-blue flowers in spring; 'Pink Beauty' has pink blooms. Zones 4–8. Pyramid bugleweed *(A. pyramidalis)* is another fairly restrained spreader; 'Metallica Crispa' produces handsome, crinkled, dark green leaves flushed with metallic bronze-purple. Zones 3–8. Common, or carpet, bugleweed *(A. reptans)* is the fastest-spreading species; 'Catlin's Giant' and 'Jungle Beauty' are especially vigorous, while

variegated cultivars, such as Burgundy Glow' and 'Multicolor', spread less quickly. Zones 3–9.

Special Uses: Plant fast-spreading bugleweeds as ground covers under trees and shrubs. Grow forms with colorful or variegated leaves in drifts as specimen plants toward the front of flower beds or around the edges of a sitting area.

Alchemilla spp.
ALCHEMILLA, LADY'S MANTLE
This perennial is grown for its handsome mounds of rounded leaves as much as for its frothy-textured chartreuse flowers. Plants form good-size drifts in rich, moist soil and grow into 1- to 2-foot-tall mounds of softly hairy, rounded and pleated leaves that are topped by clusters of frothy, somewhat sprawling, chartreuse flowers from late spring to early summer. Zones 4–7.

Special Uses: Plant drifts of lady's mantle toward the front of flower beds or around the edges of a sitting area. If leaves become tattered-looking by midsummer, cut the plants to the ground and water deeply, and new leaves will appear in fall.

Anemone spp.
ANEMONE, WINDFLOWER
Two spring-blooming species of anemones make attractive additions to shade gardens. The fall-blooming species will bloom in partial or bright shade, although not as abundantly as they do in full sun. All produce saucer- to cup-shaped flowers with a cluster of showy yellow stamens in the center.

Grower's Choice: Meadow anemone *(A. canadensis)* is a very vigorous native plant that bears single white flowers on 6- to 8-inch-tall plants from late spring into early summer. Zones 3–7. Snowdrop anemone *(A. sylvestris),* another vigorous species, reaches 1 to 1½ feet in height and produces single white flowers in spring. Zones 3–8. Chinese anemone *(A. hupehensis),* Japanese, or hybrid, anemones *(A. x hybrida),* and grape-leaved anemone *(A. tomentosa)* are all similar fall-blooming species ranging from 3 to 5 feet tall and bearing clusters of pink, purple-pink, or white flowers in late summer. Zones 4–8.

Special Uses: Plant the spring-blooming species as ground covers in moist, rich soil. Combine them with other vigorous perennials, or plant them under shrubs in an area where they can spread. Both are vigorous to invasive plants and will spread far and wide. Snowdrop anemones go dormant in summer after blooming, so combine this species with hostas or overplant them with impatiens or other annuals. Plant the fall bloomers in beds and borders, and give them as bright a spot as possible for the best bloom.

Aquilegia spp.
COLUMBINE

photo on page 125

These plants bear loose clusters of showy, spurred flowers above pretty mounds of lacy-textured leaves. While plants bloom best in sun, they will bloom in partial or bright, dappled shade.

Grower's Choice: Many species are available, with flowers in nearly all colors including true blue. Wild columbine *(A. canadensis)* is a native wildflower with red-and-yellow blooms. Zones 3–8. Golden columbine *(A. chrysantha),* a Southwest native, tolerates heat and does especially well in shade. Zones 3–9. Hybrid columbines are quite colorful, especially long-spurred selections, such as the McKana Hybrids and the Song Bird Series. Zones 3–9. European columbine *(A. vulgaris)* bears short-spurred, violet-blue flowers. Zones 3–8.

Special Uses: Grow columbines to add spots of bright color to shady beds and borders. They grow from taproots and resent being moved, so plant them in a permanent spot. Cut foliage to the ground if it becomes tattered-looking by midsummer; new plants will sprout once cool weather arrives. Plants self-sow, and seedlings are easy to move.

Aruncus spp.
GOAT'S BEARD

These native American wildflowers are grown for their airy clusters of tiny, creamy white flowers above mounds of deeply cut, fernlike leaves.

Grower's Choice: Dwarf goat's beard *(A. aethusifolius)* forms 8- to 12-inch-tall clumps of leaves. Zones 4–8. *A. dioicus* is shrub size, from 3 to 6 feet in height. Zones 3–7. Both species bloom from early to midsummer.

Special Uses: Goat's beards do best in rich, moist soil and will spread to form broad, handsome clumps.

Plant them along a stream or pond or in a spot with rich, moist to damp soil.

Asarum spp.
ASARUM, WILD GINGER

Handsome, low-growing perennials, asarums make attractive ground covers in any shady spot. Plants are grown for their kidney-shaped leaves rather than their inconspicuous flowers, which are borne in spring under the foliage next to the ground. They spread slowly but steadily by rhizomes.

Growers Choice: Canada wild ginger *(A. canadense)* is a native woodland wildflower with deciduous leaves. Zones 4–8. European wild ginger *(A. europaeum)* forms handsome mounds of glossy evergreen leaves. Zones 3–8. Both *A. hartwegii* and *A. shuttleworthii* feature evergreen leaves marked with silver. Zones 5–9.

Special Uses: Evergreen species make attractive mounds of foliage and are perfect for mixing with drifts of other ground covers. Or use them as edgings. Plant Canada wild ginger, which is more vigorous, in a woodland garden.

Aster spp.
ASTER

While asters are primarily plants for sun, a few species grow nicely in shade and are well worth searching out at local wildflower sales or in catalogs specializing in native plants. All will brighten partially shaded spots with clusters of daisylike flowers.

Grower's Choice: Blue wood aster *(A. cordifolius)* bears pale lavender or white flowers from late summer to fall on 2- to 5-foot-tall plants. White wood aster (*A. divaricatus*) produces small white daisies from midsummer through fall on 1- to 1½-foot-tall plants. Large-leaved aster (*A. macrophyllus*) features flat clusters of white to pale lavender flowers from late summer to fall on 1- to 2-foot-tall plants. Both *A. divaricatus* and *A. macrophyllus* grow in full shade, although they bloom best in light to partial shade. Both also tolerate dry shade once established. All three species are hardy in Zones 4–8.

Special Uses: Add shade-loving asters to wildflower gardens and shady beds and borders, where they'll add late-season color and foliage texture.

Astilbe spp.
ASTILBE
These popular perennials are perfect for decorating flower beds in a shady retreat, where their fernlike leaves and feathery plumes add lacy color and texture. Blooms come in white and shades of pink, ruby-red to crimson, and rosy purple.

Grower's Choice: Hybrid astilbes are most commonly available and are great choices for any garden. The plants are 2 to 3 feet tall, bloom in late spring to early summer, and come in the full range of astilbe colors. Chinese astilbe (*A. chinensis*) is a vigorous species with pinkish white flowers in late summer. Star astilbe (*A. simplicifolia*) is a dwarf, 1- to 1½-foot-tall species with glossy leaves and flowers in mid- to late summer. 'Sprite' sports handsome pale pink flowers.

Hardy in Zones 4–8; to Zone 3 with winter protection.

Special Uses: Astilbes are lovely in shady beds and borders, provided they have rich, constantly moist soil that is well drained. A site with sun in the morning and shade in the afternoon is ideal for best bloom. In addition, consider astilbes for shady sites along ponds and streams.

Begonia grandis ssp. *evansiana*
HARDY BEGONIA
Although the best-known begonias are tender, this is a hardy species that makes an attractive addition to shady garden beds and borders. The plants produce handsome, wing-shaped leaves topped by arching sprays of pink or white flowers that appear from late summer to early fall.

Grower's Choice: Hardy begonias range from 2 to 2½ feet in height and produce large leaves that are dark green on top and usually red underneath. They bear pink flowers from late summer into fall; the variety *alba* bears white flowers. Zones 6–10; hardy to Zone 5 with winter protection.

Special Uses: Add hardy begonias to any spot that offers rich, moist soil. Plants produce tiny tubers in the leaf axils in late summer or fall; plant them outdoors where you'd like new plants to grow, or bring them indoors and sow them like seeds.

Bergenia spp.
BERGENIA
Grown more for their foliage than for their flowers, bergenias bear

large, handsome leathery leaves that range from 8 to 12 inches long. The leaves turn bronze-purple or red in fall and usually are evergreen, although they're fairly tattered by spring. Clusters of small, funnel-shaped flowers appear in spring in white or shades of pink.

Grower's Choice: Most bergenias grown today are hybrids that were selected either for fall foliage color or for flowers. 'Bressingham Ruby' has maroon leaves in fall and maroon-red flowers in spring; 'Sunningdale' turns coppery red in fall. Zones 3–8.

Special Uses: Plant bergenias in beds and borders where the soil remains evenly moist. Use them as ground covers or edging plants, too. In the right site, they are long-lived and undemanding. Cut off the old foliage in spring.

Brunnera macrophylla
BRUNNERA, SIBERIAN BUGLOSS
Spring-blooming brunneras produce handsome, 1-foot-tall mounds of hairy, heart-shaped, 6- to 8-inch-long leaves. Clusters of ½-inch-wide purple-blue flowers are borne in dainty panicles above the leaves in mid- to late spring.

Grower's Choice: 'Dawson's White' has white-edged leaves; the foliage of 'Langtrees' is silver-spotted. Zones 3–8.

Special Uses: Plant brunneras in beds and borders. Moist, rich soil yields the largest leaves, but they tolerate fairly dry soil, although they go dormant during droughts.

Campanula spp.
BELLFLOWER, CAMPANULA
Although they are not plants for deep shade, some bellflowers are suitable for the shade garden. Give them a spot that receives dappled all-day shade but good light, or plant them along the edge of a shade garden where they'll receive morning sun but afternoon shade, and thus protection from the mid-day heat.

Grower's Choice: Carpathian harebell *(C. carpatica),* an 8- to 12-inch-tall selection, bears cup-shaped blue, violet, or white flowers from late spring through summer. Look for its cultivars 'Blue Clips' and 'White Clips'. Zones 3–8. Clustered bellflower *(C. glomerata),* which grows to 2 feet tall, is a spreader that produces rounded clusters of lovely violet-purple flowers from early to midsummer. Zones 3–8. Peach-leaved bellflower *(C. persicifolia),* which reaches up to 3 feet tall, bears showy clusters of bell-shaped blooms in pale blue, violet-blue, or white from early to midsummer. Zones 3–7. Dalmatian bellflower *(C. portenschla-giana)* is a mounding, 6-inch-tall selection with clusters of violet-purple flowers from late spring to early summer. Zones 4–8. Creeping bellflower *(C. rapunculoides)* is a very invasive, 2- to 4-foot-tall species that produces violet-purple bells in summer. Zones 3–7. Bluebell or harebell *(C. rotundifolia)* is a native wildflower ranging from 5 to 12 inches tall that bears pretty, nodding bells in pale violet, violet-blue, or white in summer. Zones 2–7.

Special Uses: Plant clustered and Dalmatian bellflowers with other ground covers. If you decide to plant creeping bellflower, put it in a wild part of the garden or combine it with other very vigorous ground covers, because it is difficult to eradicate once established. Plant other species in beds and borders. The more sun they receive, the more they'll bloom.

Chelidonium majus
GREATER CELANDINE
This species is a biennial or short-lived perennial that is related to poppies. Greater celandine bears deeply lobed leaves and bright yellow, ¾- to 1-inch-wide flowers on 2-foot-tall plants in summer. Zones 5–8.

Special Uses: Greater celandines are useful for adding bright color

more perennials for partial shade

You can never have too many flowers, especially in a shady spot. All of the perennials listed here will appreciate a home on the edge of a woodland, in a bed or border that receives half sun and half shade, or in an area that receives dappled shade, but bright light, all day. For more shade perennials, see the designs in part 2.

Acanthus spinosus, spiny bear's breech

Adenophora confusa, common ladybells

Anthriscus sylvestris, anthriscus, cow parsley

Astrantia major, greater masterwort

Clematis integrifolia, clematis

Coreopsis rosea, pink coreopsis

Digitalis grandiflora, yellow foxglove

Digitalis x *mertonensis,* strawberry foxglove

Gaultheria procumbens, winter-berry, checkerberry

Hemerocallis spp., daylily

Lamium orvala, lamium

Lychnis x *arkwrightii,* Arkwright's campion

Lychnis coronaria, rose campion

Lysimachia clethroides, gooseneck loosestrife

Lysimachia nummularia, creeping Jenny

Lysimachia punctata, yellow loosestrife, whorled loosestrife

Mazus repens, mazus

Omphalodes verna, blue-eyed Mary

Physostegia virginiana, obedient plant

Polemonium caeruleum, Jacob's ladder

Primula elatior, oxlip, primrose

Primula veris, cowslip, primrose

Primula vulgaris, English or common primrose

Ranunculus acris, tall or meadow buttercup

Ranunculus repens 'Pleniflorus', double-flowered creeping buttercup

Stachys macrantha, betony

to a summer shade garden. They self-sow with enthusiasm and can become weedy. Fortunately, the seedlings are easy to pull. Plants have brittle stems with orange-yellow sap that may cause skin irritation, so wear gloves when pulling them.

Chrysogonum virginianum ✿
GREEN-AND-GOLD, GOLDENSTAR
A native woodland wildflower, green-and-gold is a creeping, 6- to 8-inch-tall perennial that features heart-shaped leaves and small, starry yellow flowers that appear from spring to early summer. Zones 5–8.

Special Uses: Use green-and-gold as a ground cover, either alone or mixed with other low-growing plants, such as ajugas. Or use them to edge shady beds and borders. Plants bloom best in partial shade, but they will tolerate nearly full shade.

Cimicifuga spp.
SNAKEROOT, BUGBANE
photo on page 71

Large and eye-catching, cimicifugas are must-have perennials for any shade garden with rich, moist soil. The plants produce large mounds of deeply cut, fernlike leaves topped by spikes of graceful, bottlebrush-like wands of tiny white flowers from midsummer through fall.

Grower's Choice: American bugbane (*C. americana*) is a 2- to 8-foot-tall species with 2-foot-long racemes of creamy white flowers from late summer to fall. Zones 3–8. Black snakeroot, or black cohosh (*C. racemosa*),

another native wildflower, ranges from 4 to 7 feet tall when in bloom and sports fluffy, branched clusters of white flowers in mid-summer. Zones 3–8. Kamchatka bugbane, or autumn snakeroot (*C. simplex*), is a 3- to 4-foot-tall species that bears arching, 3- to 12-inch-long clusters of fragrant flowers in fall. Its cultivars 'Atro-purpurea' and 'Brunette' feature interesting purplish tinted foliage. Zones 4–8.

Special Uses: Plant cimicifugas toward the back of shady borders or use them as specimen plants. Plants are slow to establish, so be patient. With time, clumps will reach 2 to 4 feet across. Once planted, they are happiest when left undisturbed.

Convallaria spp. ✿
LILY OF THE VALLEY
Grown for its arching clusters of small, nodding, sweetly scented bells, this tough perennial forms dense mats of rounded leaves. Lily of the valley ranges from 6 to 9 inches tall and produces white flowers in late spring, followed by red berries. Zones 2–8.

Special Uses: Plant lily of the valley as a ground cover under shrubs and trees. Established clumps tolerate dry shade.

Corydalis spp.
CORYDALIS
photo on page 113

At first glance, corydalis looks like it's related to bleeding heart (*Dicentra* spp.), but its dainty flowers have one spur at the back rather than two. The flowers are carried above mounds of lacy-textured, fernlike foliage.

Grower's Choice: Yellow corydalis (*C. lutea*) is a garden standout. Its blue-green leaves stay attractive from spring to late fall and its golden yellow flowers are abundant from mid-spring to early fall. Zones 5–8. Blue corydalis (*C. flexuosa*) is grown for its bright blue flowers. Although commonly available, it is difficult to grow unless you have a site with rich soil that stays evenly moist. Zones 6–8. *C. ochroleuca* produces white flowers with yellow throats above ferny foliage from spring to summer. Zones 6–8.

Special Uses: Plant corydalis toward the front of beds and borders; they bloom best in light to partial shade. Plants self-sow where happy.

Dicentra spp.
BLEEDING HEART
Old-fashioned bleeding hearts have been popular shade-garden choices for generations. They feature deeply cut leaves and flowers that resemble hearts. Blossoms come in shades of pink, white, yellow, and purple.

Grower's Choice: Fringed bleeding heart (*D. eximia*), a native wildflower, is the best choice for a shade garden because of its long bloom season. Plants produce ferny, blue-green foliage topped by clusters of pendant, heart-shaped pink flowers from spring to fall, provided the soil remains moist. Look for cultivars of this species, including rose-red 'Bountiful', cherry-red 'Luxuriant', and white 'Langtrees'. Zones 3–9. Western bleeding heart (*D. formosa*), another native wildflower, bears pink flowers from late spring to early summer and spreads by rhizomes. Zones 3–9. Common bleeding heart (*D. spectabilis*) produces showy, arching clusters of pink or white blooms in spring, but the plants go dormant shortly after blooming. Zones 2–9.

Special Uses: Fringed and western bleeding hearts can be used in mass plantings in shady flower beds and borders. When common bleeding heart begins to die back in early summer, plant begonias and impatiens around the clump to help fill in the space during the rest of the growing season. Always handle bleeding heart plants very carefully to avoid breaking their brittle roots.

Disporum spp.
FAIRY BELLS

Native wildflowers, fairy bells are grown for their small, spring-borne flowers and their attractive, rounded leaves. In fall, clusters of fleshy black berries follow the flowers of both species listed here.

Grower's Choice: *D. flavens* is a 2½-foot-tall species that bears pale yellow flowers in early spring followed by black berries in fall. Zones 4–9. *D. sessile,* which reaches 1 foot tall, bears clusters of creamy white, pale yellow, or greenish flowers in late spring and early summer. Zones 4–9.

Special Uses: Plant fairy bells in shady garden beds and borders with rich soil that remains moist and cool.

Epimedium spp. ❧
EPIMEDIUM, BARRENWORT,
BISHOP'S CAP

Tough, easy-to-grow perennials, epimediums bring to the garden sprays of dainty spring flowers and 8- to 12-inch-tall mounds of handsome leaves. Flowers come in white, rose, red, yellow, and bicolored, and most bloom before the wiry-stemmed leaves emerge. Each leaf consists of several heart-shaped or somewhat triangular leaflets. The leaves remain attractive from early spring into late fall or early winter; some species are evergreen or semievergreen.

Grower's Choice: Long-spurred epimedium (*E. grandiflorum*) is a deciduous species with flowers in white, yellow, pink, or purple. Look for its cultivars 'Crimson Beauty', with coppery red blooms; 'Rose Queen'; and 'White Queen'. Zones 4–8. *E.* x *perralchicum* is a vigorous, 12- to 16-inch-tall hybrid with evergreen or semi-evergreen leaves and bright yellow flowers. Zones 5–8. Red-flowered epimedium (*E.* x *rubrum*) has deciduous leaves and red and pale yellow flowers. Zones 4–8. Bicolor epimedium (*E.* x *versicolor*) is a vigorous species with evergreen to semievergreen leaves and flowers that are pinkish red and yellow. Its cultivar 'Sulfureum' features long-spurred, dark yellow flowers. Zones 4–8. Warley epimedium (*E.* x *warleyense*) is a vigorous species featuring evergreen to semievergreen leaves and orange-red flowers. Zones 4–8. Young's epimedium (*E.* x *youngianum*) is a compact, 8-inch-tall species that forms 1-foot-wide clumps. You'll find them with white ('Niveum') or pink ('Roseum') flowers. Zones 4–8.

Special Uses: Plant epimediums anywhere in the shade garden. Their leaf texture contrasts nicely with those of hostas, hellebores, and ferns. Plants tolerate dry shade and can compete with tree roots; water them regularly until they are established. Plants described above as being vigorous are the best choices for use as ground covers. They spread steadily but slowly. Be sure to cut down the old foliage in late winter so it does not hide the emerging spring flowers.

Eupatorium spp.
EUPATORIUM, BONESET,
JOE-PYE WEED

photo on page 71

In summer and fall, these handsome native perennials feature rounded clusters of fuzzy flowers that are very attractive to butterflies, bees, and other insects.

Grower's Choice: Hardy ageratum, or mistflower (*E. coelestinum*), is a 2- to 3-foot-tall plant with fluffy, flat-topped clusters of lilac-blue flowers from late summer through fall. Zones 5–9. White snakeroot (*E. rugosum*), which ranges from 5 to 6 feet tall, produces white flowers from midsummer through fall. Look for its cultivar 'Chocolate', which has purple-brown leaves. Zones 3–7.

Special Uses: Eupatoriums provide valuable late-summer flowers to any shade garden, so use them in beds, borders, and wildflower plantings. Divide hardy ageratum every 3 or 4 years. Both species self-sow.

Euphorbia spp. ❧
EUPHORBIA, SPURGE

photo on page 113

The most popular euphorbias are plants for full sun, but two species make great additions to any shady retreat. Like all euphorbias, they bear clusters of very small flowers surrounded by showy, petal-like bracts. The stems contain milky sap that may irritate the skin.

Grower's Choice: Wood spurge (*E. amygdaloides* var. *robbiae*) is a 1½- to 2-foot-tall species that forms mounds of handsome evergreen leaves and bears greenish yellow flowers from mid-spring to early summer. Zones 6–9. *E. dulcis* 'Chameleon' is a 1-foot-tall cultivar that features purple-maroon foliage and yellow-green flowers. Zones 4–9.

Special Uses: Wood spurge makes an excellent ground cover and will spread vigorously by rhizomes. It can become invasive. Plants prefer rich, moist soil but tolerate dry shade. *E. dulcis* 'Chameleon' makes a handsome addition to shady beds and borders and self-sows politely.

FERNS ❦

photos on pages 29, 41, and 113

No shade garden should be without a few ferns. Their lush foliage adds elegance to any planting and is especially eye-catching when combined with bold-leaved plants. In general, ferns thrive in partial to full shade, but for best growth they need good light. In the wild, they are found growing along the edges of woods and in clearings in bright, indirect light.

Grower's Choice: Maidenhair ferns (*Adiantum* spp.) need evenly moist to damp, well-drained soil. They have delicate fronds with black stems. Look for northern maidenhair (*A. pedatum*) or west-ern maidenhair (*A. paleuticum*). Zones 2–8. If you live in the South, try evergreen southern maidenhair (*A. capillus-veneris*). Zones 7–10.

Lady ferns (*Athyrium* spp.) are easy to grow and widely available at garden centers. European lady fern (*A. filixfemina*) reaches from 2 to 3 feet tall and looks its best when divided every few years. Zones 4–8.

Japanese painted fern (*A. nipponicum* 'Pictum') is a vigorous 1- to 1½-foot-tall spreader with fronds marked by splashes of maroon and silver. Zones 4–9.

Wood ferns (*Dryopteris* spp.) form handsome clumps of leathery fronds. Look for male fern (*D. filix-mas*), a native species that is best divided regularly to keep clumps vigorous. Zones 4–8. Autumn fern (*D. erythrosora*) bears handsome evergreen to semievergreen fronds that are bronze when they emerge in spring. Zones 5–8.

Ostrich fern (*Matteuccia struthiopteris*) is a bold, vigorous fern that ranges from 2 to 6 feet tall — abundant soil moisture is the key to growing large plants. A native species, it produces vase-shaped clumps of fronds and spreads by underground stolons. Zones 2–6.

Sensitive fern (*Onoclea sensibilis*) is a vigorous spreader with coarse-looking fronds. It will grow in constantly wet to fairly dry soil; plants need dividing every 2 to 3 years to keep them in bounds. Zones 2–10.

Flowering ferns (*Osmunda* spp.) have large, featherlike fronds and grow in soil that ranges from moist and well drained to wet. Look for cinnamon fern (*O. cinnamomea*) and royal fern (*O. regalis*), both of which are hardy in Zones 2–10, along with interrupted fern (*O. claytoniana*), which will tolerate dry soil; Zones 2–8.

Shield, or sword, ferns (*Polystichum* spp.) bear leathery, often evergreen leaves. Best known is Christmas fern (*P. acrostichoides*), a native species that grows in moist to dry soil and thrives even on rocky woodland slopes. Zones 3–9. Gardeners in the Northwest should grow western sword fern (*P. munitum*), another native evergreen species, instead of Christmas fern. Zones 6–9.

Maiden fern (*Thelypteris* spp.) is a large genus containing both native and nonnative ferns. Look for Japanese beech fern (*T. decursive-pinnata*), which has bright green, erect fronds. Zones 4–10. Two native species are ideal for large gardens, but they need to be divided every few years to contain their spread: broad beech fern (*T. hexagonoptera*), which tolerates drier soil than many of the other ferns and is hardy in Zones 5–9, and New York fern (*T. noveboracensis*), which is hardy in Zones 4–8.

Special Uses: Plant ferns in beds and borders and add them to woodland gardens. For an attractive contrast in texture, combine them with hostas or hellebores. Large ferns also can be used with shrubs or as specimen plantings. Several species make handsome large drifts and are good ground covers for shade; these include lady ferns (*Athyrium* spp.), Japanese painted fern *(A. nipponicum),* wood ferns *(Dryopteris* spp.), ostrich fern *(Matteuccia struthiopteris),* sensitive fern *(Onoclea sensibilis),* flowering ferns *(Osmunda* spp.), shield ferns *(Polystichum* spp.), and maiden ferns *(Thelypteris* spp.).

Galium odoratum 🌿
SWEET WOODRUFF

Primarily grown as a ground cover in shade, sweet woodruff is a creeping plant that spreads at a moderate rate. This 6- to 8-inch-tall species bears whorls of narrow leaves topped by clusters of tiny, fragrant white flowers from late spring to summer. Zones 4–8.
Special Uses: Plant sweet woodruff in partial to full shade as a ground cover, or grow it in drifts as an edging plant.

Geranium spp.
HARDY GERANIUM, CRANESBILL

Although geraniums are best known as plants for full sun, several species make nice additions to shady beds and borders. Along with their loose clusters of showy flowers, most feature handsome foliage. Blooms come in shades of pink and magenta, as well as white, purple, and violet-blue. Several hardy geraniums are evergreen to semievergreen in mild climates.
Grower's Choice: Dalmatian cranesbill *(G. dalmaticum)* is a mounding or trailing species that produces soft pink flowers in late spring and early summer and features good red-orange foliage in fall. Zones 4–8. Bigroot geranium *(G. macrorrhizum)* is a vigorous, 1½-foot-tall species that spreads by deep, fleshy roots. It sports aromatic leaves and pink to purplish pink flowers in spring. Zones 3–8. Wild cranesbill, or spotted geranium *(G. maculatum),* is a native wildflower with pink blossoms from spring to midsummer. Zones 4–8. Dusky cranesbill, or mourning widow *(G. phaeum),* forms 1½- to 2½-foot-tall clumps topped by black-purple, maroon, violet, or white flowers from late spring to early summer. Zones 5–7. Bloody cranesbill *(G. sanguineum)* is a low-growing species forming mounds of deeply cut, lacy leaves that turn bright red in fall. Plants are topped by bright pink flowers from spring into summer. The cultivar 'Shepherd's Warning' is only 4 to 6 inches tall, while *G. sanguineum* var. *striatum* bears pale pink flowers, also on 4- to 6-inch-tall plants. Zones 3–8. Wood cranesbill *(G. sylvaticum)* is a bushy, 2½-foot-tall species with deeply cut leaves and violet-blue flowers in spring. Zones 3–8.
Special Uses: Plant vigorous bigroot geraniums as a ground cover in shade. Use all of the species listed here in shady beds and borders. Low-growing selections, such as bloody cranesbill, make nice additions to shaded rock gardens or can be used as edging plants.

Helleborus spp. 🌿
HELLEBORES

photo on page 29

These evergreen charmers are perfect, hardworking shade-garden residents. Plants bloom in winter or early spring and produce handsome clumps of glossy, dark green, evergreen leaves that remain quite attractive even into the following winter.

Grower's Choice: Lenten rose *(H. x hybridus,* often listed as *H. orientalis)* bears loose clusters of cup-shaped flowers in late winter or early spring and comes in shades of creamy white (often speckled with maroon) through mauve, mauve-purple, maroon, and maroon-black. To show the flowers to best advantage, cut down the leaves in midwinter. Zones 4–9. Stinking hellebore *(H. foetidus)* is a shrubby species bearing clusters of small chartreuse-green flowers from midwinter to spring. The narrow, deeply cut leaves have an unpleasant scent when crushed. Blooming stems are biennial; cut them to the base of the plant after flowering to make room for next year's blossoms. Zones 6–9; to Zone 5 with winter protection.
Special Uses: Grow hellebores in drifts as ground covers or feature them as specimen plants. The plants self-sow, and the seedlings are easy to dig up around the parent plant in summer and move to a new site.

Heuchera spp.
HEUCHERA, CORALBELLS

These native wildflowers were once grown only for their sprays of tiny, bell-shaped flowers, but new hybrids are planted for their colorful foliage. All heucheras bear clusters of tiny, sometimes petal-less flowers over mounds of heart-shaped leaves.
Grower's Choice: Heucheras are hybrids produced by crossing *H. americana* and *H. micrantha* and are prized for their 1-foot-tall mounds of patterned leaves. Many gardeners remove the panicles of

tiny white or greenish white flowers. Leaves come in many patterns, including green with silver blotches and veins, purple-brown with metallic mottling, rose-burgundy with silver overtones and purple veins, and green with purple-red mottling. New leaves, which are the most colorful, are produced all season long. Look for cultivars such as 'Chocolate Veil', 'Dale's Strain', 'Garnet', 'Persian Carpet', 'Ruby Ruffles', and 'Velvet Knight'. Zones 4–8. Coralbells (*H. x brizoides* and *H. sanguinea*) are grown for their airy clusters of tiny flowers borne over lobed and scalloped evergreen leaves. Look for cultivars such as rose-pink 'Chatterbox', red 'Firefly', white 'June Bride', red 'Mt. St. Helens', and coral 'Rosamundi'.

Special Uses: Use heucheras as edging plants along a walkway, or arrange them in drifts at the front of shady beds and borders. Plants take a season or two to settle in, so be patient. Water regularly during dry weather, and mulch plants to keep the soil moist.

Hosta spp. 🌱
HOSTAS

photo on page 41

Classic perennials for shade, hostas can add bold foliage color to the garden all summer long. Plants spread steadily to form large clumps, but some cultivars spread faster than others. The biggest hostas form clumps from 4 to 6 feet or even more across. Foliage ranges from enormous heart-shaped leaves that can exceed 1 foot in length down to tiny lance-shaped ones that stay under 2 inches. Many hostas have attractive flowers as well. Plants bloom from early to late summer, depending on the cultivar.

Grower's Choice: There are hundreds of hosta cultivars from which to choose. The best way to select them is first to look at them in a public or private garden or in a garden center with demonstration plantings. Plants in nursery pots never grow as large or as well as ones in the ground. For lists of suggested cultivars, see the plant lists on pages 29 and 41.

Special Uses: Plant hostas in drifts, use them as edging plants, or arrange them as a ground cover. They also make fine plants for large perennial containers. When selecting hostas, mix various leaf sizes, shapes, and variegation patterns for best effect. For example, combine a large-leaved cultivar that has yellow in the center of the leaf with a smaller one that has yellow-edged leaves. Plants in evenly moist, rich soil grow the largest. Underplant them with daffodils or other spring bulbs to provide an extra season of color.

Kirengeshoma palmata
KIRENGESHOMA, YELLOW WAX BELLS

A Japanese native, kirengeshoma is a 3- to 4-foot-tall species that forms large, 2- to 4-foot-wide clumps. Plants bear maplelike leaves and nodding, pale yellow flowers in late summer and early fall. Zones 5–8.

Special Uses: Plant kirengeshomas in beds and borders, or use them as specimen plants. Give them a spot with rich, evenly moist soil with an acidic pH. Clumps are best left undisturbed, so try to pick a permanent site.

Lamium spp. 🌱
LAMIUM, DEADNETTLE

These low-growing perennials bear small clusters of two-lipped flowers in summer, but their foliage is definitely their greatest attraction. Many cultivars feature attractive variegated leaves. Be aware that lamiums are spreaders, especially in rich, moist soil. Keep the really vigorous ones away from slower-growing, more delicate perennials.

Grower's Choice: Many cultivars of spotted lamium (*L. maculatum*) are available, including 'Beacon's Silver', with silver, green-edged leaves and pink flowers; 'Beedham's White', with chartreuse leaves and white flowers; and 'White Nancy', with silver, green-edged leaves and white flowers. Zones 3–8. Yellow archangel (*L. galeobdolon*) has green leaves and yellow flowers and is extremely vigorous. Its cultivar 'Hermann's Pride', which features leaves streaked with silver, is also quite vigorous but is more suitable for gardens. Zones 4–8.

Special Uses: Lamiums make excellent ground covers. Plant spotted lamiums in drifts with other perennials for foliage contrast. They also can be used in large perennial containers.

Liriope spp. 🌱
LIRIOPE, LILYTURF

Liriopes are tough perennials grown for their dense clumps of narrow, arching leaves that are either evergreen or semievergreen. Plants range from 1 to 1½ feet tall and bear spikes of tiny, pale purple or white flowers that are followed by black berries.

Grower's Choice: 'Big Blue' lily-turf (*L. muscari*) is an evergreen species that spreads fairly slowly and blooms in fall. Plant the green-leaved species or look for cultivars with variegated leaves, such as 'John Burch' and 'Variegata'. Zones 6–9. *L. spicata* is semi-evergreen and a fairly fast spreader. Zones 5–10.

Special Uses: Use liriopes as ground covers. Variegated forms, which spread more slowly than do the species, make nice accent plants toward the front of beds or around shady sitting areas. They also can be used in large perennial containers. Plants tolerate heat, humidity, drought, competition from tree roots, and heavy shade but are slower to spread under tough conditions. Cut leaves to the ground in late winter to make room for fresh foliage.

Ophiopogon spp. ☙
OPHIOPOGON, MONDO GRASS
Like liriopes, which ophiopogons resemble, these grassy-leaved perennials spread steadily to form handsome clumps of evergreen foliage. The clumps are topped by clusters of small flowers and followed by blue or black berries.

Grower's Choice: Mondo grass (*O. japonicus*) is an 8- to 12-foot-tall species with green leaves, but 'Compactus' is only 2 inches tall and 'Variegatus' features white-striped leaves. Zones 7–10. *O. planiscapus* reaches 8 inches tall and has dark green leaves. For a dramatic touch, look for its cultivar 'Nigrescens' (also sold as 'Black Dragon' and 'Ebony Knight'), which has nearly black leaves. Zones 6–10.

Special Uses: Plant these tough perennials as ground covers or as edging plants along walkways, sitting areas, shady beds, or borders. Mondo grass is quite drought-tolerant once it is well established.

ORNAMENTAL GRASSES AND SEDGES
photos on pages 41 and 71

Ornamental grasses are best known as plants for full sun, but some varieties make stunning shade plants as well. Like their sun-loving cousins, they add texture and color to the garden, along with movement and sound as they rustle in the breeze.

Grower's Choice: Northern sea oats (*Chasmanthium latifolium*) is a native species that forms 2- to 3-foot-tall clumps of bamboolike leaves and showy, drooping seed heads in midsummer. Seed heads emerge green and ripen to brown, and leaves turn brown in fall. This species self-sows with enthusiasm. Zones 5–9.

Hakone grass (*Hakonechloa macra*) produces handsome, 1½- to 2-foot-tall mounds of arching green leaves. Its cultivar 'Aureola', more commonly grown than the species, bears stunning green-and-yellow-striped leaves. Plants spread, but never fast enough for most gardeners, and require evenly moist soil. Zones 5–9.

Sedges (*Carex* spp.) aren't true grasses, but they are great grasslike plants for shady spots. All are primarily foliage plants, and many variegated forms are available. Give all the species here a spot in evenly moist, well-drained soil.

C. conica 'Marginata' forms 6-inch-tall clumps of evergreen leaves edged in white. Zones 5–9. *C. morrowii* 'Variegata', also evergreen, forms 1½- to 2-foot-tall clumps of silver-edged leaves. Zones 5–9. *C. siderosticha* 'Variegata', which is deciduous, forms handsome, low clumps of green-and-white-striped leaves. Zones 6–9; to Zone 5 with winter protection.

Greater woodrush (*Luzula sylvatica*) isn't a true grass either, but it makes an ideal grasslike plant for shady garden beds. The plants form broad mats of glossy, 1-foot-long, ¾-inch-wide leaves and bear brown flowers on 2-foot-tall stalks in spring and early summer. The leaves are semievergreen to about Zone 6. In addition to the species, look for cultivars 'Aurea', which sports yellow leaves, and 'Marginata', which has dark green leaves edged in creamy white. This species tolerates drought but will perform best in moist soil. Zones 4–9.

Special Uses: Use low-growing grasses — especially variegated types — as accent plants toward the front of shady beds and borders. Plant them in drifts as ground covers. Taller species, including northern sea oats, are suitable for the back of borders and wildflower plantings. Variegated hakone grass (*Hakonechloa macra* 'Aureola') is especially striking in a container.

Pachysandra spp. ☙
PACHYSANDRA, SPURGE
photo on page 47

Classic ground covers, pachysandras are either evergreen or deciduous plants with handsome leaves and spikes of small, petalless flowers that appear in spring or early summer.

Grower's Choice: Allegheny spurge (*P. procumbens*), a native wildflower, is a deciduous 1-foot-tall species with semievergreen leaves that emerge green and are marked with maroon-brown later in the season. Plants bear white flowers in spring and spread slowly to form drifts. Zones 5–9. Japanese spurge (*P. terminalis*), the best known of the pachysandras, is an evergreen species that spreads quickly to form a broad carpet. Its cultivar 'Variegata' has leaves marked with white and spreads slowly. Zones 4–9.

Special Uses: Use Allegheny spurge in beds and borders with other shade-loving perennials. Use Japanese spurge alone or with other very vigorous ground covers. Variegated Japanese spurge can be planted with other perennials or used as a ground cover.

Phlox spp.
PHLOX
There are phlox for both sunny and shady gardens, and the two best-known species for shade are native wildflowers that bloom in spring. Both bear clusters of showy, trumpet-shaped flowers.

Grower's Choice: Wild blue phlox (*P. divaricata*), which is about 1 foot tall, sports clusters of fragrant lavender, pale violet, or white flowers in spring. Zones 3–9. Creeping phlox (*P. stolonifera*), which reaches only 6 inches tall, features clusters of pink, lilac-blue, or white flowers in spring. Look for its cultivars 'Blue Ridge', 'Bruce's White', and 'Pink Ridge'. Zones 3–8.

Special Uses: Both species listed here thrive in rich, moist, well-drained soil. Wild blue phlox forms nice-size clumps and self-sows, while creeping phlox spreads more quickly and widely, although it doesn't crowd out

other perennials. Use them in shady beds and borders to add bright spring color.

Polygonatum spp.
SOLOMON'S SEAL
photos on pages 113 and 157

These shade-loving plants are grown primarily for their hand-some foliage. All are rhizomatous perennials that spread slowly but steadily. Their erect or arching, unbranched stems with narrow to rounded leaves create a plumelike effect in the garden. Small bell-shaped or tubular flowers dangle beneath the leaves in spring. The flowers, which are creamy white or white with green markings, are followed later in the season by round black berries.

Grower's Choice: Solomon's seal (*P. biflorum*) is a native wildflower ranging from 1½ to 7 feet tall and forms broad clumps with time. The tallest forms (4 to 7 feet) are commonly called great Solomon's

hardy bulbs for shade

Spring bulbs, such as daffodils (*Narcissus* spp.), snowdrops (*Galanthus* spp.), and glory-of-the-snow (*Chionodoxa* spp.), all grow well in the shade of deciduous trees, as they finish blooming and go dormant not long after leaves emerge. Most of the following bulbs flower from early to midsummer — species marked with an asterisk (*) bloom late summer to fall — and will add splashes of color to any shady retreat. For best bloom, give them a site in partial shade. All are hardy to at least Zone 6.

Allium cernuum, nodding or wild onion

Allium moly, lily leek

Arum italicum 'Marmoratum', variegated Italian arum

Begonia grandis ssp. *evansiana*, hardy begonia

Camassia spp., camass or quamash

Colchicum spp., autumn crocus*

Cyclamen hederifolium, c. coum, hardy cyclamen*

Dichelostemma ida-maia, fire-cracker plant

Lilium canadense, Canada lily

Lilium Martagon Hybrids, Martagon lily

Lilium henryi, Henry lily

Lilium pardalinum, leopard lily

Lilium pumilum, coral lily

Lilium speciosum, Japanese lily

Lilium superbum, American turk's-cap lily

Lycoris squamigera, hardy amaryllis, magic lily

Ranunculus ficaria, lesser celandine

Sternbergia lutea, autumn daffodil*

Triteleia laxa, grass nut

* Blooms late summer to fall

seal and are often listed as *P. commutatum*. Zones 3–9. Dwarf Solomon's seal (*P. humile*) is an 8-inch-tall species that forms loose clumps. Zones 5–8. Variegated fragrant Solomon's seal (*P. odoratum* var. *thunbergii* 'Variegatum'), a 2½- to 3-foot-tall species, features white-striped leaves. Zones 4–8.

Special Uses: Let the taller Solomon's seals spread to form bold clumps in woodland gardens, beds, and borders. They can be used as ground covers, too. Plant dwarf Solomon's seal along the front edge of beds or other shady plantings, or combine it with very low ground covers, where its leaves will poke up to add interesting contrast. The plants prefer moist, well-drained soil but will tolerate dry soil.

Pulmonaria spp.
PULMONARIA, LUNGWORT
Treasured for their elegantly marked leaves, pulmonarias also bring early-spring flowers to shade gardens. Dainty, bell-shaped blooms appear in late winter to late spring. The most popular pulmonarias feature green leaves splashed or patterned with silver. The foliage remains attractive through the season and until early winter. In mild climates, some pulmonarias are evergreen. Most pulmonarias have flowers that open pink and fade to blue. The leaves emerge after the flowers have finished or while the plants are still in bloom.

Grower's Choice: Hybrids are the most popular. Look for cultivars 'Janet Fisk', with white-splashed leaves, Zones 3–8; 'Spilled Milk',

with silver-white leaves, Zones 5–8; and 'Roy Davidson', with green leaves blotched with silver and sky-blue flowers, Zones 5–8. Longleaf lungwort (*P. longifolia*) features wide mounds of 1½-foot-long leaves spotted with silver and purple-blue flowers. Plants spread by rhizomes to form broad clumps. Zones 4–8. Bethelehem sage (*P. saccharata*) is an 8- to 12-inch-tall perennial with silver-spotted leaves. 'Mrs. Moon' is the most commonly available cultivar; 'Pierre's Pure Pink' has shell pink flowers. Zones 3–8.

Special Uses: Plant pulmonarias to add a splash of silver to shady spots. They are attractive in beds and borders when combined with hostas, hellebores, and other shade-loving species. Plants self-sow.

Rodgersia spp.
RODGERSIA
These astilbe relatives are planted for their bold, attractive foliage and fluffy, branched clusters of tiny flowers. The handsome leaves are compound, with leaflets arranged like fingers (palmate) or in a featherlike fashion (pinnate). With time, the plants will form broad mounds that reach from 2 to 6 feet across.

Grower's Choice: *R. aesculifolia* features 4-foot-tall mounds of crinkled, leathery, palmate leaves that look like buckeyes or horse chestnuts (*Aesculus* spp.). Plants produce 2-foot-long clusters of white flowers in mid- to late summer and are up to 6 feet tall when in bloom. Zones 5–8. *R. pinnata* produces 2- to 3-foot-tall mounds of rough-textured, pinnate leaves

topped by 1- to 2-foot-long clusters of yellowish white, pink, or red flowers in mid- to late summer. Its cultivar 'Superba' features leaves that are a stunning bronze-purple when young as well as rose-pink flowers. Zones 5–8. Bronze-leaved rodgersia (*R. podophylla*) forms 4-foot-tall mounds of foliage topped by 1-foot-tall clusters of creamy white flowers in mid- to late summer, and the leaves turn bronze-red in fall. Zones 5–8.

Special Uses: Grow these shrub-size perennials in a spot that has rich, moist soil. Although they will tolerate dry conditions, they grow best in wet soil. Give rodgersias plenty of space, as they are most attractive — and happiest — when allowed to form broad mounds.

Rohdea japonica
ROHDEA, SACRED LILY
This little-known perennial brings evergreen foliage to the shade garden. The narrow, strappy leaves are glossy, dark green, and leathery and reach a length of about 1 foot. Plants form 1-foot-tall clumps that spread to 2 feet or more. Bell-shaped, greenish white spring flowers are followed by red berries in fall.

Grower's Choice: Start with the green-leaved species, but look for variegated cultivars at specialty nurseries, too. These have leaves edged or splashed with white; most originate from Japan. Zones 6–10.

Special Uses: Grow rohdeas as you would hostas — just evergreen ones. They thrive in either moist or dry soil and, once established, are quite tough. Plant them at the base of trees, along walkways, or anywhere else that a bright spot of green would liven up the winter garden.

Smilacina racemosa
SOLOMON'S PLUME, FALSE SOLOMON'S SEAL

A native wildflower, Solomon's plume is a 1½- to 3-foot-tall perennial that produces erect or arching, unbranched stems with oval leaves that end in clusters of starry, creamy white flowers, which appear in spring. Red berries appear in late summer or fall. Zones 4–9.

Special Uses: Add this species to wildflower gardens or shady beds and borders. The plants spread steadily but are not invasive, and they will form nice-size drifts with time.

Spigelia marilandica
SPIGELIA, INDIAN PINK, MARYLAND PINKROOT

Not seen often enough in gardens, spigelia is a native wildflower grown for its showy red flowers. Look for it at nurseries that specialize in native or rare plants. This perennial forms 2-foot-tall clumps of rounded leaves topped by tubular red flowers from spring to summer. Zones 6–9.

Special Uses: Give spigelia a spot with rich, moist, well-drained soil. Plants make a handsome addition to wildflower gardens, as well as to shady beds and borders.

Stylophorum diphyllum
CELANDINE POPPY

Grown for its deeply cut leaves and clusters of four-petaled, golden yellow, poppylike flowers from spring to summer, this perennial resembles greater celandine *(Chelidonium majus)*, with which it shares a common name. Zones 4–8.

Special Uses: Let the bright flowers of this plant light up shady spots wherever seedlings appear. In gardens with dry soil, the foliage dies back by summertime, but in a moist spot leaves persist until fall. Where happy, plants self-sow easily.

Thalictrum spp.
THALICTRUM, MEADOW RUE

photo on page 65

These delicate-looking perennials produce lacy-textured, blue-green leaves topped by clusters of tiny flowers. Although the flowers lack petals, most feature showy stamens, and they are borne in large, branched clusters above the attractive foliage.

Grower's Choice: Columbine meadow rue *(T. aquilegifolium)* features fuzzy-looking clusters of tiny flowers that are pinkish purple, purple, or white, as well as 2- to 3-foot-tall mounds of leaves that look like those of columbine *(Aquilegia* spp.). Zones 4–8. Yunan meadow rue *(T. delavayi)* is 2 to 4 feet tall and bears fluffy clusters of purple flowers from summer to fall. Zones 4–9. Yellow meadow rue *(T. flavum),* which spreads vigorously to form large clumps, reaches 3 feet in height and bears yellow flowers in summer. Zones 5–9. *T. rochebrunianum* 'Lavender Mist' ranges from 3 to 5 feet tall and bears loose clusters of lilac-pink flowers with yellow stamens in summer. Zones 4–7.

Special Uses: Plant thalictrums in beds and borders. They require rich, moist soil to grow well and will thrive for years without needing to be divided.

Tiarella spp. ❧
TIARELLA, FOAMFLOWER

Woodland wildflowers native to North America and eastern Asia, tiarellas are grown for their low mounds of attractive leaves and spikes of small, starry flowers in spring.

Grower's Choice: Allegheny foamflower *(T. cordifolia)* is a vigorous, low-growing perennial with maplelike leaves and fluffy spikes of white flowers in spring. Several cultivars are available, including 'Eco Red Heart', featuring leaves with a reddish central blotch; 'Slickrock', with deeply cut, dark green leaves; and 'Tiger Stripe', with red-veined leaves and a prominent central stripe. Zones 3–8. Wherry's foamflower *(T. wherryi),* a slower spreader than Allegheny foamflower, also has maplelike leaves and fluffy spikes of starry white or pink flowers that appear in spring. Look for its cultivars 'Dunvegan', which has deeply lobed leaves and pink flowers, and 'Oakleaf', with oakleaf-shaped leaves and pink flowers. Zones 3–8.

Special Uses: Allegheny foamflower is a vigorous spreader that easily forms a 1- to 2-foot-wide clump. Use it as a ground cover, or combine it with a mix of other shade-loving perennials. Wherry's foamflower is also a perfect complement for smaller perennials toward the front of shady beds and borders.

Tradescantia spp.
TRADESCANTIA, SPIDERWORT

Both hardy and tender perennials belong to this genus. All bear three-petaled, saucer-shaped flowers that each last half a day. Because the flowers are carried in clusters, plants bloom over a long season. The hardy perennial species have long, strap-shaped leaves.

Grower's Choice: Most tradescantias grown in gardens are hybrids. Plants reach 1½ to 2 feet tall and spread from 2 to 3 feet. They bloom from early to midsummer and come in shades of violet, lavender-blue, pink, rose-red, and white. Older hybrids include 'Iris Pritchard', bearing white flowers shaded with pale lavender-blue; violet-purple 'Purple Dome'; rose-red 'Red Cloud'; and white 'Snowcap'. Newer cultivars tend to be more compact (15 to 18 inches) and feature especially handsome, narrow leaves. These include purple-blue 'Concord Grape', which blooms all summer; pale lilac 'Lilac Frost'; and bright purple 'Purple Profusion'. Zones 4–9; to Zone 3 with winter protection.

Special Uses: Plant tradescantias in shady beds and borders and in wildflower gardens. Their leaves make an attractive textural contrast with those of hostas. Cut plants to the ground after the main flush of flowers to encourage rebloom, keep plants looking neat, and discourage reseeding (they self-sow with enthusiasm, but hybrids don't come true from seed).

Tricyrtis spp.
TRICYRTIS, TOAD LILY

Perennials that bloom from late summer into fall are valuable in sunny gardens, but in shade they're simply indispensable. These tough perennials produce upright stems with leaves that clasp the stem. Unusual, waxy-textured flowers appear either in the leaf axils or at the stem tips.

Grower's Choice: Formosa toad lily (*T. formosana*), a 1- to 2-foot-tall perennial that spreads to about 2 feet, sports glossy dark green leaves spotted with purple-green and small starry white, pinkish white, or pinkish purple flowers dappled with red-purple from late summer into fall. Zones 4–9. Toad lily (*T. hirta*), a 2- to 3-foot-tall perennial, sports white flowers spotted with purple in late summer and fall. Look for its cultivar 'Variegata', which has yellow-margined leaves. Zones 4–9.

Special Uses: Plant tricyrtis in shady beds and borders. Ideally, select a site where their subtle, late-season flowers will show to best advantage.

Uvularia spp.
MERRY-BELLS, BELLWORT

These lovely spring-blooming wildflowers bear showy clusters of dangling, bell-shaped blossoms that appear in spring. The flowers are carried at the tips of the stems, which are clothed with attractive rounded leaves. The leaves are unusual in that the leaf bases are perfoliate, meaning they surround the stems.

Grower's Choice: Large, or great, merry-bells (*U. grandiflora*) forms 1- to 1½-foot-tall clumps with yellow to orange-yellow, 2-inch-long flowers that are carried either singly or in pairs at the stem tips in mid- to late spring. Zones 3–9. Perfoliate bellwort (*U. perfoliata*), which ranges from 1 to 2 feet in height, bears pale yellow flowers in spring. Zones 4–8.

Special Uses: Add merry-bells to plantings of wildflowers, or use them in shady flower beds and borders. The foliage contrasts nicely with that of hellebores, large-leaved hostas, and ferns.

Vancouveria hexandra ❧
VANCOUVERIA, AMERICAN BARRENWORT

This native woodland wildflower from the West is closely related to *Epimedium* spp. The plant ranges from 10 to 14 inches tall and slowly spreads by rhizomes to form 2-foot-wide clumps. It bears white spring flowers and forms handsome, low mounds of fernlike leaves with rounded, lobed leaflets. Zones 5–7.

Special Uses: Plant this perennial as a ground cover or combine it with hellebores, smaller hostas, and lungworts toward the front of shady beds and borders. It also makes a nice edging plant along walkways and around shady sitting areas.

Veratrum viride
VERATRUM, FALSE HELLEBORE, INDIAN POKE

A bold, vigorous native wildflower, veratrum brings attractive clumps of rounded, pleated leaves to the shade garden. This species ranges from 2 to 6 feet tall and bears starry, green to greenish yellow flowers from early to midsummer.

Zones 3–8. *Note:* All parts of this plant are poisonous.

Special Uses: Plant veratrum as a bold accent toward the back of beds and borders. This plant needs deeply dug soil that is very rich and moist but well drained.

Vinca minor ❧
VINCA, COMMON MYRTLE, LESSER PERIWINKLE

photo on page 29

Vigorous, fast-spreading plants, vincas form 4- to 6-inch-tall mats, have rounded leaves, and in spring produce five-lobed flowers in shades of lavender-blue, pale lavender, or white. Their wide-spreading stems root at the leaf axils anywhere they touch the ground. Zones 4–9.

Grower's Choice: Cultivars with variegated leaves, such as 'Alba Variegata', are especially attractive in shady gardens.

Special Uses: Plant vinca as a ground cover. It is particularly effective under shrubs and trees. The plants are quite vigorous, so keep them away from all but the largest, most vigorous perennials, or they'll engulf other plants.

Selections with variegated leaves are less vigorous than are the green-leaved ones.

Viola spp.
VIOLET, VIOLA

No woodland garden would be complete without a few violets, and there are plenty to choose from within the more than 500 species in the genus. All feature five-petaled flowers with flat, pansylike faces (pansies are perennial violets grown as annuals) and a spur that points out the back.

Grower's Choice: Most gardeners are likely to have a few native violets in their gardens already. Native Canada violet (*V. canadensis*) bears white flowers from spring to early summer. Zones 3–8. Common, or woolly blue, violet (*V. sororaria*, formerly *V. papilionacea*) blooms in spring to early summer, producing violet-blue flowers or white flowers speckled or streaked with blue. Zones 4–8. Labrador violet (*V. labradorica*), another native plant, produces pale purple flowers from spring into summer. Zones 2–8. Sweet, or English, violet (*V. odorata*) has

heart-shaped leaves and sports lavender-blue or white flowers in spring. Zones 6–8.

Special Uses: Plant violets along walkways and in wild gardens. Most native species self-sow and can crowd out less vigorous perennials.

Waldsteinia fragarioides ❧
WALDSTEINIA, BARREN STRAWBERRY

This rose family relative features ground-hugging three-leaflet foliage topped by saucer-shaped golden yellow flowers in spring and summer. The flowers are followed by small, dry, inedible fruits. Zones 3–8.

Special Uses: Plant waldsteinia as a ground cover along walkways or around shady sitting areas. Plants tolerate dry shade. Although this is a vigorous ground cover, do not confuse it with mock strawberry (*Duchesnea indica*), which is a closely related species that spreads quickly by runners and is very invasive. Mock strawberry also has yellow flowers, but its fruits are larger and fleshier than those of waldsteinia.

tender bulbs for shade

Add summer color or a tropical flair to any shady retreat with some of these tender bulbs. In areas where they are not hardy, all can be dug up and overwintered indoors. Or keep them in containers year-round; sink the pots in the soil outdoors in summer and bring them indoors in winter.

Alocasia hybrids and *A. macrorrhiza*, giant taro

Amorphophallus spp., Voodoo lily

Begonia sutherlandii, Sutherland begonia

Begonia Tuberhybrida Hybrids, tuberous begonias

Caladium bicolor, caladium, angel wings

Colocasia esculenta, elephant's ear, taro, dasheen

Curcuma spp., pinecone ginger

Hedychium Coronarium, ginger lily, butterfly ginger

Hymenocallis spp., Peruvian daffodil, spider lily

Oxalis spp., wood sorrel or oxalis

Stenanthium gramineum, featherfleece

Zantedeschia spp., calla lily

Plectranthus argentatus

annuals, biennials, and tender perennials

These hardworking plants are invaluable for adding summerlong color to shade gardens, because of either long bloom seasons or colorful foliage. In addition to using them in beds and borders, combine them in containers to brighten up shady sitting areas or to mark the entrance to your shady retreat.

Begonia semperflorens
WAX BEGONIA

Popular for full sun, wax begonias are actually much happier in shade. Plants produce mounds of fleshy, somewhat brittle leaves in green or bronze topped by clusters of pink, white, or red flowers. Wax begonia (*B. semper-florens*), by far the best known, ranges from 8 to 12 inches tall and flowers abundantly from spring to frost. Both single- and double-flowered forms are available.

Grower's Choice: Other begonias include *B.* 'Richmondensis Alba', with white or pale pink flowers and angel-wing-shaped leaves. Sutherland begonia (*B. suther-landii*) is a tuberous species with pale orange flowers and angel-wing-shaped leaves; it is hardy to Zone 8. Also consider tuberous begonias, which are tender perennials or warm-weather annuals;

they come in red, orange, pink, cream, yellow, and white.

Special Uses: Plant wax begonias to edge along walkways or around sitting areas. All the selections here will enhance any bed or border and are stunning in containers.

Browallia spp.
BROWALLIA, BUSH VIOLET

These charming annuals bear trumpet-shaped blooms in shades of purple, blue-violet, and white.

Grower's Choice: Two species make nice additions to shady gardens: *B. americana* and *B. speciosa*. Both bloom from early summer to frost and range from 1 to 2 feet in height, although tender perennial *B. speciosa* reaches up to 5 feet in the tropics. Warm-weather annuals.

Special Uses: Add browallias to shady garden beds and borders. Although plants will self-sow, start some indoors for the earliest

flowers. Just press the seeds onto the soil surface, as light is required for germination.

Hypoestes phyllostachya
POLKA-DOT PLANT, FRECKLE FACE

Known for its brightly colored leaves, polka-dot plants are grown as houseplants or as bedding plants outdoors. They grow to about 1 foot and bear leaves heavily dotted with pale to deep rose-pink or white. The tiny pink to lilac flowers, borne from summer to fall, are insignificant. Tender perennial or warm-weather annual.

Special Uses: Add polka-dot plants to shady beds and borders, or use them to edge around sitting areas or along walkways. These plants make a great addition to containers, too. They are easy to grow from both seeds and cuttings.

annuals and biennials for bright shade

If you're into annuals, you'll want to try some plants that are usually grown in sun. Although all bloom best in full sun, they will bloom in shadier areas provided they receive good light. Look for a spot in dappled shade under high trees or one that receives several hours of direct sun daily. A few are actually tender perennials usually grown as annuals. Plants marked with an asterisk (*) are biennials.

Alternanthera ficoidea, Joseph's coat, parrot leaf

Borago officinalis, borage

Catharanthus roseus, rose periwinkle

Coriandrum sativum, cilantro, coriander

Cuphea ignea, cigar flower, fire-cracker plant

Cynoglossum amabile, Chinese forget-me-not

Digitalis purpurea,* foxglove

Erysimum cheiri, wallflower

Exacum affine, Persian violet

Hesperis matronalis,* dame's rocket

Limnanthes douglasii, fried eggs, meadow foam

Lobularia maritima, sweet alyssum

Lychnis coronaria, rose campion

Nemophila maculata, five-spot

Nemophila menziesii, baby blue eyes

Nicotiana spp., flowering tobacco

Persicaria capitata, persicaria

Persicaria orientale, prince's feather

Reseda odorata, mignonette

Salvia spp., salvia, sage

Scaevola aemula, fan flower

Silene armeria, Sweet William catchfly

Trachelium caeruleum, blue throatwort

Viola tricolor,* Johnny-jump-up

Viola x *wittrockiana,* pansy

Impatiens spp.
IMPATIENS, BUSY LIZZIE

Classic annuals for shade, common impatiens are available everywhere once the warm weather arrives. Although other impatiens species make fine shade plants, New Guinea impatiens are best grown in full sun.

Grower's Choice: Garden impatiens, busy Lizzie, and patience plant (*I. walleriana*) are brittle-stemmed annuals or tender perennials that form 6-inch- to 2-foot-tall mounds covered with showy, flat-faced flowers from early summer to frost. Many cultivars are available in a wide range of single or double flowers with both solid-color and bicolor blooms. Impatiens come in shades of pink, lavender, rose, white, salmon, red, and orange-red. Garden balsam (*I. balsamina*), a warm-weather annual that grows from 1 to 2½ feet tall, bears spikes of single or double flowers along the main stem in the leaf axils from summer to early fall. Flowers come in shades of pink, white, red, and purple.

Special Uses: Plant drifts of impatiens to add splashes of color to any shady spot. They also can be used as a temporary ground cover. Dwarf forms, such as 'Super Elfin', make fine edging plants along walkways or around sitting areas. Add garden balsam to flower beds and borders.

Lobelia erinus
EDGING LOBELIA

A popular annual for shade, edging lobelia features narrow leaves that are sometimes flushed with maroon-bronze. Plants range from 4 to 9 inches tall and produce an abundance of blue, purple, violet, pink, cherry red, or white flowers from early summer to frost.

Grower's Choice: Many cultivars of edging lobelia are available. Plants in the Cascade Mixed Series are 8-inch-tall trailers that are perfect for containers; those in the Rainbow Series are dwarf, 5-inch-tall plants ideal for edging. Warm-weather annual.

Special Uses: As their common name implies, edging lobelias are ideal for edging shady flower beds, borders, walkways, and sitting areas. Also use them as filler plants among other low-growing annuals and perennials. Edging lobelias make attractive additions to containers, too.

Lunaria annua
LUNARIA, MONEY PLANT, HONESTY

A biennial that self-sows and thus behaves more like a perennial, lunaria features 1-foot-tall mounds of large, heart-shaped, evergreen leaves the first year, and then tall clusters of showy purple flowers from late spring to summer the second year. The attractive flowers are followed by sprays of round, flat seedpods that split open to reveal silvery, papery partitions that make these plants important additions to dried flower arrangements.

Grower's Choice: Look for the cultivar 'Variegata', which has white-edged leaves and comes true from seed. Biennial; Zones 5–9.

Special Uses: Add lunarias to beds and borders with perennials such as hostas and hellebores. They also can be planted around shrubs.

Plants self-sow reliably. Pull up seedlings that appear where they're not wanted, or move them to an empty spot in the garden.

Plectranthus spp.
PLECTRANTHUS, MEXICAN MINT

These plants are grown primarily for their handsome foliage, although some produce attractive spikes of flowers as well. Plectranthus have somewhat fleshy stems that are either erect or trailing, and the leaves range from heart-shaped to rounded with scalloped, toothed, or wavy margins. The trailing types are 10 to 12 inches tall and spread to about 3 feet. Many species feature strongly aromatic leaves.

Grower's Choice: Mexican mint, Cuban oregano, Indian borage, or Spanish thyme (*P. amboinicus*) is a trailer bearing aromatic, spicy-flavored leaves that can be used in cooking; its cultivar 'Variegatus' features white-edged leaves. *P. argentatus*, which reaches 2 to 3 feet in height, features attractive gray-green leaves and 1-foot-long spikes of tiny bluish white flowers.

P. forsteri, another trailer, features rounded, scalloped-edged leaves and short spikes of tiny pale pink or white flowers. Its cultivar 'Marginatus', also sold under the name 'Iboza', has white-edged leaves; another cultivar, 'Green-on-Green', bears green leaves edged in chartreuse.

Mintleaf (*P. madagascariensis*) is another trailer that features rounded, scalloped-edged leaves that have a minty aroma when they are crushed. The plant bears short spikes of tiny pale lavender or white blossoms; the cultivar 'Variegated Mintleaf' features white-edged leaves. Tender perennials grown as warm-weather annuals.

Special Uses: Plant plectranthus in beds and borders. Types with variegated leaves are especially useful for brightening up shady spots. They also make handsome container plants. Root some cuttings in fall and overwinter them indoors.

Solenostemon scutellarioides
COLEUS

Best known by their former botanical name, *Coleus*, these plants are grown for their foliage — most gardeners choose to remove the spikes of tiny flowers. These bushy, brittle-stemmed plants range from 1 to 3 feet tall. Coleus leaves come in a truly amazing array of shapes and patterns, and their color combinations include green, cream, chartreuse, maroon, red, purple-black, orange, and pink. It's easy to find shade gardeners with large collections of coleus cultivars that they overwinter indoors each year.

Grower's Choice: Choose seed-grown cultivars, such as dwarf Wizard Mixed, or look for 'Alabama Crimson', 'Ella Cinders', 'India Frills', 'Inky Fingers', and 'The Line'. (Start collecting, and you'll want to have them all!) Tender perennial grown as a warm-weather annual.

Special Uses: Add coleus to any shady planting that features moist, rich, and well-drained soil. The plants do best in locations protected from wind. Coleus make stunning container plants. Root cuttings in fall and overwinter them indoors.

Torenia spp.
TORENIA, WISHBONE FLOWER

These unusual-looking plants are grown for their clusters of tubular flowers that come in shades of violet, purple, pink, white, and yellow. The plants are approximately 1 foot tall and bear rounded to lance-shaped leaves.

Grower's Choice: Wishbone flower (*T. fournieri*) bears purple flowers with darker violet lobes on their sides and yellow throats. Look for the Clown Mix Series, which features lavender and white, violet and purple, and pink and white flowers with yellow throats. Yellow wishbone flower (*T. flava*) bears golden yellow flowers with dark purple-red throats. Warm-weather annuals.

Special Uses: Add torenias to shady beds and borders or use them in container gardens.

tender perennials for shade

All of the following plants bloom in partial shade. Grow them as annuals or bring them inside for overwintering, then return them to the garden the following year. To overwinter, dig up and pot the plants, or take cuttings in late summer for rooting. To overwinter four-o'clocks (*Mirabilis jalapa*), dig up the woody tubers and store them in barely damp vermiculite in a cool, dry place.

Abutilon spp., abutilon, flowering maple

Begonia semperflorens, wax begonia

Fuchsia x *hybrida,* fuchsia hybrids

Fuchsia magellanica, hardy fuchsia

Heliotropium arborescens, heliotrope

Hypoestes phyllostachya, polka-dot plant, freckle face

Impatiens walleriana, garden impatiens, busy Lizzie, patience plant

Mirabilis jalapa, four-o'clock

Plectranthus spp., plectranthus

Salvia spp., salvia, sage

Solenostemon scutellarioides, coleus

Strobilanthes dyerianus, Persian shield

Tradescantia pallida 'Purpurea', purple heart

Hypoestes phyllostachya spp.

Rhododendron schlippenbachii

shrubs, small trees, and vines

Use the following plants to create shrub borders on shaded sites, to thicken up privacy barriers under trees, over arbors and trellises, or simply to add flowers to a shady spot. Many of the plants listed also can be used as hedges, specimen plants, and accents. Keep in mind that plants grown primarily for their flowers will bloom best with good light, so look for a spot that receives a half day of sun or bright, dappled shade all day long.

Abelia x grandiflora
GLOSSY ABELIA

Handsome foliage and flowers that appear over a long season make this shrub an excellent choice for shade. This species features shiny leaves that are dark green in summer and bronze-green to reddish in fall and early winter. Small, white to pale pink flowers appear from spring through summer.

Grower's Choice: The species ranges from 3 to 6 feet tall, but smaller cultivars include 'Compacta', which grows to 4 feet, and 'Dwarf Purple', which grows to 2½ feet. Zones 6–9; to Zone 5 with winter protection.

Special Uses: Plant glossy abelias as a screen, in mixed borders, or in low hedges. Plants bloom best in partial, or half-day, shade and will be somewhat lankier and less dense in deeper shade.

Acer spp.
MAPLE

Several smaller maples grow in light to partial shade and are valuable for adding height to plantings of shrubs that screen a shady retreat.

Grower's Choice: Paperbark maple (A. griseum), which grows from 30 to 50 feet tall, features dark green leaves that turn red in fall and gorgeous red-brown to cinnamon-brown exfoliating bark on trunk and branches. Although happiest in sun, it tolerates partial shade. Zones 5–7. Japanese maple (A. palmatum) is a much loved, 15- to 25-foot-tall species with deeply cut green or red leaves and attractive gray bark. Leaves of some forms stay red all summer; foliage turns yellow, reddish, or bronze in fall. Hundreds of cultivars are available. Zones 5–8. Striped maple, or moosewood (A. pensylvanicum), is a native woodland tree that reaches 15 to 20 feet in height. It bears rounded, three-lobed leaves that turn yellow in fall and greenish bark striped with creamy green. Zones 3–7. Two other native maples that grow naturally in wooded areas are suitable for shade: Oregon vine maple (A. circinatum) and mountain maple (A. spicatum).

Special Uses: Feature paperbark and Japanese maples as specimen plants, add them to shrub borders, or use them in front of screening shrubs that will highlight their ornamental features. Use the other maples to thicken understory growth in cool, shady woodland gardens.

Aesculus parviflora
BOTTLEBRUSH BUCKEYE

This showy, multistemmed shrub features plumelike clusters of white flowers from early to midsummer and large, compound leaves that turn yellow in fall. The 8- to 12-inch-long flower clusters are showy and come at a time when few other shrubs are flowering. Plants range from 8 to 12 feet tall and spread by suckers to form rounded mounds as large as 15 feet across. Zones 5–9.

Special Uses: Feature bottlebrush buckeyes in shrub borders, in mass plantings, or as specimen plants. They tolerate considerable shade but bloom best with good light. Plants prefer acidic soil but will also accept slightly alkaline conditions and may be slow to establish.

Aronia arbutifolia
RED CHOKEBERRY

Bright red berries, bright red fall color, and clusters of spring flowers make this a handsome shrub that adds three-season interest to the garden. This species reaches 6 to 10 feet in height and spreads by suckers to form clumps 5 feet or more across. White spring flowers are followed by bitter-tasting berries. Zones 4–9.

Special Uses: Add red chokeberries to shrub borders or any screen plantings. They are most effective when planted in masses and bloom best in partial shade.

Calycanthus floridus
SWEETSHRUB,
CAROLINA ALLSPICE

This native shrub has many more common names that refer to its fragrant flowers, including strawberry shrub, sweet bubby, and spicebush. Plants are found growing wild in woodlands and make attractive additions to any shady retreat. Sweetshrub grows from 6 to 9 feet tall and spreads from 6 to 12 feet across. Plants have dark green leaves and, from late spring to midsummer, bear red-brown, 2-inch-wide flowers that have a rich, sweet, fruity aroma.

Grower's Choice: Not all plants are fragrant and some have a sour smell, so buy plants of named cultivars or ones propagated from a sweet-smelling parent. 'Edith Wilder' is an excellent cultivar. Zones 4–9.

Special Uses: Add sweetshrubs to shrub borders or plant them near a shady sitting area, where the fragrance of the flowers can be enjoyed in the evening.

Carpinus caroliniana
AMERICAN HORNBEAM

Also called blue beech, ironwood, and musclewood, this small tree thrives in woodlands. It has handsome gray bark with sinewy, musclelike ridges. Ranging from 20 to 30 feet tall at maturity, this species has dark green leaves that turn yellow or orange-red in fall. Plants grow in acidic or alkaline soil and tolerate sites that are flooded periodically. Zones 3–9.

Special Uses: Plant this small tree toward the back of shrub borders, or use it to thicken up the understory growth on a wooded site.

Cephalotaxus harringtonia
CEPHALOTAXUS,
JAPANESE PLUM YEW

A lovely evergreen for shade, this shrub or small tree is still not commonly planted in the United States. In addition to growing in shade, it abides sun and is extremely heat-tolerant. As a shrub, this species ranges from 5 to 10 feet tall but reaches 20 to 30 feet as a small tree. The plants have dark green evergreen needles and resemble yews (*Taxus* spp.).

Grower's Choice: Dwarf cultivars, including 3- to 4-foot-tall 'Duke Gardens', are available. Zones 6–9; to Zone 5 in a protected spot.

Special Uses: Use cephalotaxus in shady shrub borders, as a screening plant, or as a hedge. In the South, it is an excellent substitute for yew.

Cercis canadensis
EASTERN REDBUD

This native tree features early-spring flowers; heart-shaped leaves; and attractive, smooth gray-black bark. Redbuds are native to woodlands, river bottoms, stream banks, and forest edges, and they make handsome additions to shady gardens. A small, spreading tree, redbud reaches 20 to 30 feet tall and up to 35 feet wide at maturity. Specimens often have multiple trunks. Clusters of small, deep pink flowers are borne in spring before the leaves appear along the branches and even on the trunk. The flowers are followed by brown pods. The leaves turn yellow-green to yellow in fall. Plants are relatively short-lived.

Grower's Choice: 'Forest Pansy' features purple leaves; 'Alba', white flowers. Zones 5–9.

Special Uses: Include redbuds in mixed borders and shrub borders, or use them as specimen plants. They also are ideal for planting along woodland edges or as understory plants. Redbuds grow in full shade but bloom less there than they do when planted in sun.

more shrubs and small trees for partial shade

A surprising number of shrubs and small trees can grow in partial shade. Most will have a looser growth habit than they would in sun, however. All will bloom best with good light, so plant them in a spot that receives a half day of sun or is under high trees and in light, dappled shade. Plants marked with an asterisk (*) will grow in partial to full shade.

Amelanchier arborea, downy serviceberry

Asimina triloba, papaw, custard apple

Chimonanthus praecox, fragrant wintersweet

Chionanthus virginicus, white fringe tree

Daphne spp., including *D. x burkwoodii*, *D. mezereum*, and *D. odora*, winter daphne

Davidia involucrata, dove tree

Disanthus cercidifolius, disanthus

Enkianthus campanulatus, red-vein enkianthus

Forsythia spp., forsythia

Gaylussacia brachycera, box huckleberry

Ilex spp. hollies, including *I. aquifolium*, *I. crenata*, *I. glabra*, *I. opaca*, *I. pedunculosa*, and *I. verticillata*, holly

*Illicium floridanum**, Florida anise tree

*Kerria japonica**, Japanese kerria

*Leucothoe fontanesiana**, drooping leucothoe

Loropetalum chinense, Chinese fringe flower

Myrica pensylvanica, northern bayberry

Nandina domestica, nandina, heavenly bamboo

Paxistima canbyi, Canby paxistima

Photinia serratifolia, Chinese photinia

Pieris japonica, Japanese pieris

Rhodotypos scandens, black jetbead

Rubus odoratus, flowering raspberry

Sambucus nigra, European elder

*Sasa veitchii**, sasa bamboo

*Skimmia japonica**, Japanese skimmia

*Symphoricarpos albu**, common snowberry

Clethra alnifolia
CLETHRA, SUMMERSWEET, SWEET PEPPERBUSH

With clusters of fragrant flowers, clethra is a pretty, 4- to 8-foot-tall shrub that spreads by suckers to form clumps that are usually wider than they are tall. In midsummer, the plant sports narrow clusters of fragrant white flowers that range from 2 to 12 inches long and are set off by shiny, dark green leaves that turn yellow to golden brown in fall.

Grower's Choice: 'Hummingbird' is a dwarf form, ranging from 2½ to 3½ feet tall, that blooms in early to midsummer. 'Ruby Spice' bears rose-pink blooms. Zones 4–9.

Special Uses: Plant clethra near sitting areas or along walkways so you can enjoy its fragrant flowers, or use in shrub and mixed borders. It does best in moist, rich soil.

Cornus spp.
DOGWOOD

photo on page 41

Popular dogwoods range from mid-size shrubs to trees and, in addition to spring flowers, many feature handsome bark, showy fruit that attracts birds, and good fall color.

Grower's Choice: Pagoda dogwood (C. alternifolia), a large shrub or small tree ranging from 15 to 25 feet tall, bears clusters of small, yellow-white flowers that are almost sickeningly sweet. Zones 3–7. Silky dogwood (C. amomum) is a 6- to 10-foot-tall shrub with yellow-white late-spring flowers; it is native to eastern woodlands and thrives in moist to wet soil. Zones 4 to 8. Flowering dogwood (C. florida) is a well-known native tree; it grows from 20 to 40 feet tall and bears attractive scaly bark, showy white or pink flowers in spring, and brilliant red foliage and bright red berries in fall. Many cultivars are available. Zones 5–9. Cornelian cherry (C. mas) is a large shrub or small multistemmed tree that grows from 20 to 25 feet tall, bearing clusters of small yellow flowers in very early spring before the leaves appear. Zones 4–7 or 8.

Special Uses: Plant dogwoods in shrub borders and mix them with other shrubs as hedge plants. They are attractive in woodlands and other naturalized areas. In general, dogwoods thrive in partial shade with moist, cool soil; they tolerate full shade but bloom less.

Decumaria barbara
WOOD VAMP, CLIMBING HYDRANGEA

This vining hydrangea relative deserves to be more commonly grown in gardens because of its fragrant white flowers borne in late spring or early summer and dark green leaves that turn creamy yellow in fall. Climbing by aerial rootlets, this species reaches 10 to 20 feet or even more. Zones 5–9.

Special Uses: Train this vine up walls, trees, or trellises. Plants thrive in partial shade and grow best in moist soil.

Eleutherococcus sieboldianus
FIVE-LEAF ARALIA

This species, formerly called Acanthopanax sieboldianus, is a little-known shrub that is terrific for shade gardens. The plant features arching branches with bright green leaves. It reaches 8 to 10 feet tall and spreads by suckers to form a handsome 8- to 10-foot-wide clump. The yellow-green flowers are insignificant. Zones 4–8.

Grower's Choice: A handsome variegated form, 'Variegatus', has leaves edged in creamy white.

Special Uses: Five-leaf aralia is a tough shrub for tough sites. Plants tolerate full shade, dry soil (sandy to clayey), pollution, and heavy pruning. Use this species as a screen plant, in shrub borders, or in an informal hedge.

Euonymus fortunei
WINTERCREEPER EUONYMUS

Used as a ground cover or a climbing vine, wintercreeper euonymus is a vigorous evergreen grown for its leaves, which can be dark blue-green or variegated. When used as a ground cover, this species is about 1 foot tall, but it attaches itself to walls or trees by clinging rootlets and can climb to 70 feet.

Grower's Choice: Many cultivars with variegated leaves are available. Habits vary, and there are dwarf shrubby types along with climbers. Zones 5–9.

Special Uses: Plant this species as a tough ground cover for difficult spots. It tolerates most soils except wet ones and also grows in very heavy shade. Keep it away from less vigorous plants. When using wintercreeper euonymus as a climber, select locations carefully because it will engulf small shrubs and climb trees.

Fothergilla spp.
FOTHERGILLA

Fragrant flowers and spectacular fall foliage are the two main traits that make these multistemmed shrubs great garden plants. Clusters of white, honey-scented flowers are borne in spring; the dark green to blue-green leaves turn yellow, orange, and scarlet in fall.

Grower's Choice: Dwarf fothergilla (*F. gardenii*), which grows from 2 to 3 feet tall and just as wide, bears 1- to 2-inch-long clusters of flowers. Zones 5–9. Large fothergilla (*F. major*), which reaches from 6 to 10 feet both tall and wide, bears 1- to 2-inch-long clusters of flowers slightly later than dwarf fothergilla. Zones 4–8.

Special Uses: Plant fothergillas in shrub borders, use them around sitting areas, or mass them in mixed plantings. For best results, give them partial to bright, dappled shade and rich, acidic soil. Fall color is brightest in full sun.

Hamamelis spp.
WITCH HAZEL
photo on page 58

These large shrubs or small, multistemmed trees are grown for their aromatic flowers and spectacular fall foliage.

vines to avoid

Fast-growing vines that engulf the garden are nothing more than a headache. Avoid the plants listed here.

Celastris orbiculatus, Oriental bittersweet

Fallopia aubertii (formerly *Polygonum aubertii*), silver lace vine, mile-a-minute plant

Lonicera japonica, Japanese honeysuckle

Pueraria lobata, kudzu

Grower's Choice: Common witch hazel (*H. virginiana*) reaches from 20 to 30 feet tall and spreads to about 20 feet. The plant has rounded leaves that turn yellow in fall and bears fragrant yellow flowers in mid- to late fall. Zones 3–8. Hybrid witch hazels (*H. x intermedia*) offer the largest choice of cultivars and are the plants to grow for fragrant spring flowers. Plants range from 15 to 20 feet tall. Cultivars include 'Arnold Promise', with yellow blooms, and 'Jelena', with coppery red blooms. Zones 5–9.

Special Uses: Plant witch hazels in shrub borders, as screening plants, or along the edge of a naturalized woodland. They do best in rich, moist soil.

Hedera helix
ENGLISH IVY

This vigorous evergreen vine is well known to gardeners and nongardeners alike. Tough, tolerant, and easy to grow, English ivy can also become an invasive weed and thus should be used with care. Plants form a 6- to 8-inch-tall ground cover or can attach themselves to walls and trees via clinging rootlets and then climb to 90 feet. The species has lobed, dark green leaves, but many cultivars exist.

Grower's Choice: Use variegated forms to add an attractive splash of color in shady areas; English ivy types with deeply cut or unusual leaves can add interesting texture. Hardiness of cultivars varies greatly, and most cultivars are less hardy than the species. Zones 5–9; to Zone 4 in a protected site.

Special Uses: Plant English ivy as a ground cover or train it over walls to provide color, texture, and sound insulation. Cultivars, especially the variegated ones, are less invasive than the species.

Hydrangea spp.
HYDRANGEA
photo on page 52

The best-known hydrangeas are multistemmed shrubs that need bright light all day or a half a day of sun for best bloom.

Grower's Choice: Smooth hydrangea (*H. arborescens*), which grows from 3 to 5 feet tall and similarly wide, bears rounded clusters of greenish white to white flowers from midsummer to fall. 'Annabelle' features 12-inch-wide flower clusters. Zones 4–9. Bigleaf hydrangea (*H. macrophylla*), which grows from 3 to 6 feet tall, produces showy clusters of pink or blue flowers that are either flattened or nearly round. Many cultivars are available, including 'Blue Wave'; 'Nikko Blue'; and 3-foot-tall 'Pia', which has pink blooms. 'Variegata' features white-edged leaves and blue flowers. Zones 6–9. Oakleaf hydrangea (*H. quercifolia*), which grows from 4 to 6 feet tall and spreads to 10 feet or more by suckers, features white summer flowers, brilliant red to orange-brown fall foliage, and cinnamon-colored bark. 'Snow Queen' bears dense, upright clusters of flowers; 'Snowflake' sports showy double flowers. Zones 5–9.

Special Uses: Plant shrubby hydrangeas in shrub borders and screen plantings. Smooth hydrangea blooms on new wood, meaning growth of the current year; cut plants to the ground in late winter for best bloom. Bigleaf and oakleaf hydrangeas bloom on old wood, meaning growth of the previous season, so unusually cold temperatures in winter or spring can kill the flower buds. Prune them immediately *after* flowering.

Climbing hydrangea (*H. petiolaris)* is a stunning vine that brings attractive flowers, handsome foliage, and ornamental bark to the shade garden. The plants climb by rootlike holdfasts. Formerly listed as *H. anomala* var. *petiolaris,* this species can reach from 60 to 80 feet. In early to midsummer, climbing hydrangea features showy, flat-topped, 6- to 10-inch-wide clusters of white flowers that stand out against dark green, glossy leaves. Older stems have shaggy exfoliating cinnamon-brown bark. Zones 4–8 or 9.

Special Uses: Train climbing hydrangea up walls — the height of the vine will be determined by the height of the wall. It also will grow up trees or can be used somewhat as a ground cover to train over rough, rocky areas or low walls. Plants are slow to establish and require rich, moist, well-drained soil.

Itea virginica
VIRGINIA SWEETSPIRE

This 3- to 5-foot-tall native shrub usually forms clumps that are broader than they are tall. Narrow clusters of white, slightly fragrant flowers appear in early summer, and the plants are clad in brilliant foliage in fall. The leaves are evergreen or semievergreen where temperatures stay above 15 to 20°F in winter.

Grower's Choice: 'Henry's Garnet' features 6-inch-tall flower clusters and red-purple fall foliage. Zones 5–9.

Special Uses: Plant this shrub in naturalized areas, along the edge of a woodland, or anywhere in the shade garden. Plants do best in sites with moist to wet soil but will tolerate drought. Flowers appear on old wood (wood from the previous year), so prune immediately *after* flowering.

Kalmia latifolia
MOUNTAIN LAUREL, KALMIA, CALICO BUSH

photo on page 58

Beautiful flowers and glossy evergreen leaves make these native shrubs all winners. Mountain laurel features clusters of small, broadly bell-shaped flowers in white or pink that are marked or dotted with dark pink to purple-pink. Buds are often darker than the flowers, imparting a two-toned effect, and the plant blooms from late spring to early summer. This slow grower reaches 4 to 8 feet tall and was once widely collected in the wild. Fortunately, many new cultivars are available, and purchasing cultivars does not harm wild populations.

Grower's Choice: Cultivars include 'Bullseye', 'Carousel', 'Olympic Fire', 'Pink Charm', 'Silver Dollar', and dwarf 'Tinkerbell', which reaches about 2½ feet. Zones 4–9.

Special Uses: Plant mountain laurels as specimens, around sitting areas, or in shady beds and borders, shrub plantings, or naturalized areas. Plants tolerate heavy shade but bloom best in partial shade or good light all day. In addition to

an acidic pH, they need cool, moist, well-drained soil.

Lindera benzoin
SPICEBUSH

The extra-early flowers of spicebush are a sure sign of spring, and this native shrub also offers attractive leaves that turn a rich yellow in fall. Spicebush ranges from 6 to 12 feet tall and spreads as far. Plants bear an abundance of tiny yellow flowers in early spring before the leaves appear. Glossy scarlet fruits follow the flowers, but only on female plants. Leaves give off a spicy scent when crushed. Zones 4–9.

Special Uses: Plant spicebushes in shrub borders or naturalized areas. They tolerate full shade but do best in partial shade or a spot with dappled, bright shade all day long.

Magnolia virginiana
SWEET BAY MAGNOLIA

Depending on where you grow this native plant, it is a small, multistemmed deciduous shrub or a large semievergreen or evergreen tree. Plants range from 10 to 20 feet tall in colder zones but can grow to 60 feet in the South. Fragrant, 2- to 3-inch-wide, creamy white flowers appear from spring intermittently through early fall and are followed by handsome seed capsules containing bright red seeds. The leaves are dark green on top and silvery underneath. A number of cultivars are available, including several with reliably evergreen leaves into the colder zones. Zones 5–9.

Special Uses: Plant sweet bay magnolias in shrub borders, in screen plantings, or as specimens in a shady sitting area, where the fragrant flowers will be easy to enjoy. Plants require acidic soil and grow in moist, well-drained soil but will thrive in wet conditions.

Mahonia aquifolium
MAHONIA, OREGON HOLLY GRAPE, OREGON GRAPE HOLLY

This lovely evergreen shrub is grown for its flowers, foliage, and fruits. It spreads by suckers and forms a broad clump with time. Ranging from 3 to 6 feet tall, plants bear clusters of yellow flowers at the tops of the stems in spring, followed by blue-black, grapelike berries in late summer to fall. The glossy, spiny, hollylike leaflets are arranged in a feather-like fashion on 6- to 12-inch-long stems. Zones 5–9.

Special Uses: Plant mahonias in shady shrub borders or as part of a shrub planting designed to screen a sitting area. Select a spot with moist, acidic soil that is protected from wind, which damages the foliage in winter.

Rhododendron spp.
RHODODENDRON AND AZALEA

photo on page 52

Known to gardeners and non-gardeners alike, rhododendrons and azaleas are beloved for their spectacular spring flowers, borne in clusters called trusses. Blooms usually are bell- or funnel-shaped and 2 to 3 inches wide. Plants usually range from 1 to 20 feet tall and leaves can be deciduous or evergreen. There is a multitude of plants to choose from — the genus contains 500 to 900 species and thousands of cultivars. Gar-

deners in the Pacific Northwest have the widest choice; their cool, moist summers and mild winters are ideal for these plants. In the central United States, alkaline soil, winter cold, summer heat, and drought make growing these plants difficult.

Grower's Choice: The best way to choose rhododendrons and azaleas is to visit a local botanical garden, arboretum, or well-stocked garden center to find out which ones grow best in your area. Because the plants often survive colder winter temperatures better than do the flower buds, look for plants whose flower buds will pull through the minimum winter low temperature in your area.

Azalea hybrids can be deciduous or evergreen, and many groups exist. Hardiness varies from cultivar to cultivar, even within individual groups, so ask for local recommendations. (Hybrids sold by florists are typically hardy only to Zone 8.) Exbury and Knap Hill azaleas, deciduous shrubs from 8 to 12 feet tall, bear clusters of flowers in mid-spring in shades of orange, red, yellow, cream, and pink. They also feature red, orange, or yellow fall foliage color. Zones 5–8. Gable Hybrids, which grow from 2 to 4 feet tall, are evergreens with clusters of single or double flowers in shades of pink, red, red-orange, and white. Zones 5 or 6–8. Girard Hybrids, which can be deciduous or evergreen, are suitable for Zones 5 or 6–8, and the Glenn Dale azaleas, which are evergreen, are suitable for Zones 6 or 7–8. Gumpo and North Tisbury Hybrids both make fine 12- to 15-inch-tall ground covers.

Gumpo cultivars include 'Gumpo Pink' and 'Gumpo Red'; North Tisbury cultivars include 'Joseph Hill' and 'Pink Pancake'. Zones 6–8. Northern Lights cultivars are good choices for gardeners in Zones 3 and 4. Developed by the University of Minnesota, they produce clusters of fragrant flowers on 6- to 7-foot-tall plants and are generally hardy to −40°F. Cultivars include 'Golden Lights' and 'Spicy Lights'.

Species azaleas are less showy than the hybrids but are charming shrubs for any shade garden. Unless otherwise noted, all of the following are native to North America and bloom in spring. (For information on summer-blooming azaleas, see Gazebo at a Forest's Edge on page 60 and A Deck in the Woods on page 66.) Sweet azalea (*R. arborescens*) bears white to pale pink flowers in late spring to early summer on 8- to 20-foot-tall plants. Zones 5–9. Flame azalea (*R. calendulaceum*) produces yellow, orange, or red flowers on 4- to 8-foot plants. Zones 6–8. Pinxterbloom azalea (*R. periclymenoides*) sports lightly fragrant pink, white, or violet-purple flowers on 4- to 6-foot-tall plants. Zones 4–9. Roseshell azalea (*R. prinophyllum*) bears very fragrant pink flowers on 2- to 8-foot-tall plants. Zones 4–8. Royal azalea (*R. schlippenbachii*) features fragrant pink flowers on 6- to 8-foot-tall plants, has good yellow to red fall color, and tolerates neutral soil pH. Zones 5–8. Pinkshell azalea (*R. vaseyi*) has pale pink to rose flowers on 5- to 10-foot-tall plants. Zones 5–8.

Hybrid rhododendrons also are best chosen based on local recommendations. In the South, heat tolerance is an important factor; gardeners in the North will want to consider hardiness, which varies from cultivar to cultivar and is generally given as a minimum low temperature rather than a zone. Red-flowered 'Nova Zembla', for example, is a good choice for midwestern gardens because it is heat-resistant and tolerates temperatures to −25°F. Evergreen Dexter Hybrid rhododendrons are the best known and are hardy to about −10°F. Cultivars include pink-flowered 'Scintillation'. Popular 'PJM' bears lavender-pink blooms and is hardy to Zone 4.

Species rhododendrons are often overlooked in favor of hybrids, but they make charming additions to shade gardens. Plants bloom in spring. Carolina rhododendron (*R. carolinianum*) is a native evergreen species with pale rose-purple, pale pink, or white blooms on 3- to 5-foot-tall plants. Zones 5–8. Catawba rhododendron (*R. catawbiense*), another native plant, bears lilac-purple or pinkish flowers with spotted throats and evergreen leaves on 6- to 10-foot-tall plants. Zones 5–8; to Zone 4 in a protected location. Korean rhododendron (*R. mucronulatum*) bears rose-purple flowers and deciduous leaves that turn yellow, bronze, or red in fall on 4- to 8-foot-tall plants. Zones 4–7. Yako rhododendron (*R. yakushimanum*), which ranges from 3 to 5 feet tall, features rose-pink buds, white flowers, and dark green leaves that are silvery and woolly underneath. Zones 5–9.
Special Uses: Plant rhododendrons and azaleas in shrub bor-

ders, in informal hedges, and as specimens. Although they all tolerate considerable shade (and require it in the South, where summer heat is a problem), they bloom best in a spot with good light — in partial shade, in half-day shade, or under high trees. These plants also require acidic soil (pH between 4.5 and 6.5) that is cool, evenly moist, well drained, and well aerated. Keep rhododendrons and azaleas away from walnut trees (*Juglans* spp.), which release into the soil a substance that is toxic to *Rhododendron* spp. (and many other plants). Rhododendrons seldom require pruning, but because flowers are borne on old wood, meaning wood from the previous year, prune immediately *after* flowering, if necessary.

Sarcococca spp.
SARCOCOCCA, SWEET BOX
Although relatively uncommon in gardens, sarcococca is an attractive evergreen that spreads by suckers to form a broad mound.
Grower's Choice: Himalayan sarcococca (*S. hookeriana*), which reaches a height of 4 to 6 feet, bears clusters of tiny, fragrant white flowers under dark green leaves in spring. Dwarf sarcococca (*S. humilis,* formerly *S. hookeriana* var. *humilis*) is a 1½-foot-tall plant that spreads to 3 feet. Both are hardy in Zones 6–9; to Zone 5 in a protected location.
Special Uses: Plant Himalayan sarcococca in a shrub border. Dwarf sarcococca is an excellent ground cover or edging plant for shade; use it along walkways or around shady sitting areas. Plants require loose, rich, acidic soil that

is moist but well drained. Once established, they tolerate drought.

Schizophragma hydrangeoides
JAPANESE HYDRANGEA VINE
Similar to climbing hydrangea, this species also brings lovely white flowers to summer shade gardens. In midsummer, it bears flat-topped, 10-inch-wide clusters of creamy white, lightly fragrant flowers. The leaves are dark green. The plant climbs 20 to 30 feet and attaches to walls and other surfaces with clinging rootlets.
Grower's Choice: 'Moonlight' has silver-shaded, blue-green leaves; 'Roseum' bears pink bracts on the flowers. Zones 5–9.
Special Uses: Train this species up walls and tree trunks.

Taxus spp.
YEW, TAXUS
photo on page 52
These needle evergreens have been popular garden plants for generations. Not only do they grow in sun to deep shade, but they also tolerate dry shade and acidic to alkaline soil.
Grower's Choice: English yew (*T. baccata*) is a tree or very large shrub with a pyramid shape. Many cultivars are available, including extra-hardy 'Repandens' (to Zone 5), which forms 2-foot-tall mounds and spreads from 10 to 15 feet. Zones 6–7 or 8. Japanese yew (*T. cuspidata*) is a handsome 10- to 40-foot-tall shrub or tree. Many cultivars are available, including 'Emerald Spreader', which reaches to 2½ feet tall and spreads to 10 feet, and 'Nana', which grows 10 to 20 inches tall. Zones 4–7. Anglojap, or hybrid,

yew (*T.* x *media*) ranges from 2 or 3 feet to 20 feet tall, depending on the cultivar. Cultivars include 'Brownii', a rounded 9- by 12-foot shrub; 'Densiformis', a 3- to 4-foot-tall shrub that spreads to 6 feet; and 'Hicksii', a columnar, 20-foot-tall selection. Zones 4–7.

Special Uses: Plant taxus in shrub borders, hedges, screen plantings, mass plantings, and even topiaries. Dwarf forms make a nice-looking ground cover. All require well-drained soil. Cephalotaxus, or Japanese plum yew (*Cephalotaxus harringtonia*), is an excellent heat-tolerant substitute for the South.

Tsuga canadensis
CANADIAN HEMLOCK, EASTERN HEMLOCK
photo on page 52

An outstanding native evergreen for shady sites, this species features gracefully spreading branches and dark green needles with silvery stripes on the undersides. Hemlocks range from 40 to 60 feet in height. The woolly adelgid, an aphidlike pest that appears as cottony clusters along the needles, has been a serious problem on this plant in the Northeast, but scientists have identified and are releasing biological controls, including a species of lady beetle, they hope will control it.

Grower's Choice: Many cultivars, including 1-foot-tall 'Cole's Prostrate' and round 'Jeddeloh', are available. Zones 4–7.

Special Uses: Plant hemlocks in formal or informal hedges, in shrub borders or mass plantings, or as specimen plants. Well-drained acidic soil is best, but plants will tolerate slightly alkaline

conditions. In hot areas, give plants full shade, especially in the afternoon, as they do not like heat.

Vaccinium spp.
BLUEBERRY

Spring flowers, summer fruits, and spectacular fall foliage make blueberries excellent landscape plants. All bear bell-shaped white to pinkish flowers and sweet, edible, purple-black berries. Leaves turn scarlet and purple in fall.

Grower's Choice: Lowbush blueberry (*V. angustifolium*) grows from 4 inches to 2 feet tall and thrives in dry, acidic, sandy, or rocky soil. Zones 2–8. Rabbit-eye blueberry (*V. ashei*) ranges from 3 to 15 feet tall and spreads to 12 feet. Plants are similar to highbush blueberry but are much more heat-tolerant and suitable for southern gardens. Zones 8–10. Highbush blueberry (*V. corymbosum*) ranges from 6 to 12 feet tall and spreads just as far. It grows in damp to wet soil but also tolerates ordinary well-drained garden soil. Many cultivars are available, including 'Earliblue', 'Jersey', and 'Northland'. For best pollination and fruit set, plant at least two different cultivars. Zones 3–7.

Special Uses: Plant blueberries in shrub borders. They bloom and fruit best in partial shade and require well-drained, acidic soil.

Viburnum spp.
VIBURNUM
photo on page 58

Hardworking viburnums are a must for every garden, whether sunny or shady. They bring clusters of small white, creamy white, or pinkish flowers to the garden in

spring, followed by berries and bright fall foliage. They attract birds and other wildlife and are generally undemanding, easy-to-grow shrubs or small trees.

Grower's Choice: Nannyberry viburnum (*V. lentago*), which grows from 15 to 20 feet tall and spreads to 10 feet, is a native species sporting flat-topped clusters of small, creamy white flowers in late spring. Berries are blue-black and foliage turns purple-red in fall. It tolerates moist or dry soil. Zones 2–8. Blackhaw viburnum (*V. prunifolium*), which reaches a height of 12 to 15 feet, also bears flat-topped clusters of creamy white flowers in spring, followed by edible blue-black berries. Leaves turn red-purple in fall. This is another native that can be trained as a small tree. Zones 3–9. Leatherleaf viburnum (*V. rhytidophyllum*) produces clusters of slightly fragrant, creamy to yellowish white flowers in spring on 10- to 15-foot-tall plants that spread similarly. Fruits ripen to black and leaves are evergreen or semievergreen in the North. Zones 5–8. Other native viburnums that tolerate shade include mapleleaf viburnum (*V. acerifolium*), Zones 4–8; hobblebush (*V. lantanoides*), Zones 4–7; and Kentucky viburnum (*V. molle*), Zones 5–7. Arrowwood viburnum (*V. dentatum*), Zones 3–8, will grow in partial shade.

Special Uses: Plant viburnums in shrub borders, informal hedges, or screen plantings or to thicken up the understory on the edges of a wooded site. They also make handsome background plants in perennial borders.

zone map

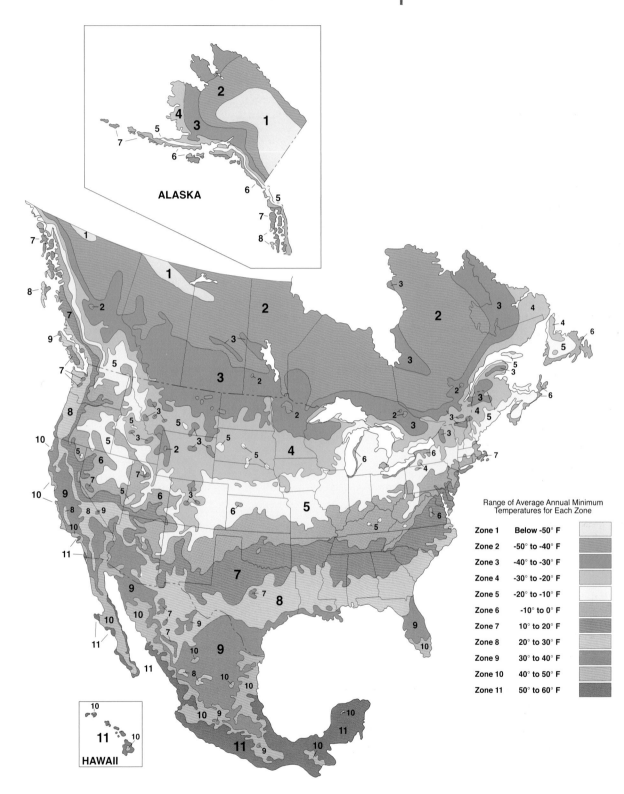

ALASKA

HAWAII

Range of Average Annual Minimum
Temperatures for Each Zone

Zone 1	Below -50° F
Zone 2	-50° to -40° F
Zone 3	-40° to -30° F
Zone 4	-30° to -20° F
Zone 5	-20° to -10° F
Zone 6	-10° to 0° F
Zone 7	10° to 20° F
Zone 8	20° to 30° F
Zone 9	30° to 40° F
Zone 10	40° to 50° F
Zone 11	50° to 60° F

index

Abelia x *grandiflora. See* Glossy abelia

Abutilon *(Abutilon* spp.), 165

Acanthopanax sieboldianus. See Five-leaf aralia

Acanthus spinosus. See Spiny bear's breech

Accent plants, 76

Access to shady retreats, 53

Acer. See Maple

Acer circinatum. See Oregon vine maple

Acer griseum. See Paperbark maple

Acer palmatum. See Japanese maple

Acer pensylvanicum. See Striped maple

Acer platanoides. See Norway maple

Acer spicatum. See Mountain maple

Achimenes *(Achimenes* hybrids), 95

Aconite *(Aconitum* spp.), 147

Aconite x cammarum. See Bicolor monkshood

Actaea alba. See Doll's eyes

Actaea rubra. See Red baneberry

Actinidia kolomikta. See Variegated kiwi

Actinidia spp. *See* Hardy kiwi

Adenophora confusa. See Ladybells

Adiantum spp. *See* Maidenhair fern

Adiantum capillus-veneris. See Southern maidenhair

Adiantum paleuticum. See Western maidenhair

Adiantum pedatum. See Northern maidenhair

Adjoining spaces design, 31–35

Aegopodium podagraria. See Bishop's weed

Aegopodium podgraria 'Variegatum'. *See* Variegated bishop's weed

Aesculus spp. *See* Horse chestnuts

Aesculus parviflora. See Bottlebrush buckeye

Ailanthus altissima. See Tree-of-heaven

Ajuga *(Ajuga* spp.), 147

Ajuga genevensis. See Blue bugleweed

Ajuga pyramidalis. See Pyramid bugleweed

Ajuga reptans. See Carpet bugleweed

Akebia quinata. See Fiveleaf akebia

Alcea rosea. See Hollyhock

Alchemilla *(Alchemilla* spp.), 147

Alleés, 8

Allegheny foamflower, 124, 159

Allegheny spurge, 71, 157

Allium spp. *See* Ornamental onions

Allium cernuum. See Wild onion

Allium moly. See Lily leek

All-weather wicker furniture, 19

Alocasia hybrids, 161

Alocasia macrorrhiza. See Giant taro

Alternanthera ficoidea. See Joseph's coat

Amelanchier arborea. See Downy serviceberry

American arborvitae, 119

American barrenwort, 160

American bittersweet, 35

American bugbane, 71, 151

American holly, 119, 168

American hornbeam, 168

American planetree, 64

American turk's-cap lily, 106, 125, 157

American wisteria, 35

Amorphophallus spp. *See* Voodoo lily

Amsonia *(Amsonia hubrectii),* 71

Amur honeysuckle, 123

Anemone *(Anemone* spp.), 147–48

Anemone canadensis. See Meadow anemone

Anemone hupehensis. See Chinese anemone

Anemone quinquefolia. See Wood anemones

Anemone sylvestris. See Snowdrop anemone

Anemone tomentosa. See Grape-leaved anemone

Anemone x hybrida. See Japanese anemone

Angel's trumpets, 142

Angel wings, 161

Anglo-Japanese yew, 119, 173–74

Annuals

  designs using, 76, 80, 83, 89, 100, 101, 131

  plants and planting, 162–65

Anthriscus (Anthriscus sylvestris), 150

Antirrhinum majus. See Snapdragons

Aquilegia spp. *See* Columbine

Aquilegia canadensis. See Wild columbine

Aquilegia chrysantha. See Golden columbine

Aquilegia vulgaris. See European columbine

Aralia racemose. See Spikenard

Arbor and lattice sitting area, 85–89

Arbors, 8, 10–11, 15, 16, 50–51, 74–76, 80–81, 92–93, 116–17, 122–23, 140–41, 142

Arborvitae, 15

Archways, 68–69, 70

Arisaema triphyllum. See Jack-in-the-pulpit

Aristolochia durior, A. macrophylla. See Dutchman's pipe

Arkwright's campion, 150

Armchairs, 128–29

Aronia arbutifolia. See Red chokeberry

Arrowwood viburnum, 174

Artemisia *(Artemisia* spp.), 143

Artemisia abrotanum. See Southernwood

Artemisia absinthium 'Lambrook Silver'. *See* Wormwood

Artemisia ludoviciana 'Silver King' or 'Silver Queen'. *See* White sage

Artemisia stelleriana. See Dusty miller

Arum italicum 'Marmoratum'. *See* Variegated Italian arum

Aruncus spp. *See* Goat's beard

Aruncus aethusifolius. See Dwarf goat's beard

Asarum *(Asarum* spp.), 148

Asarum canadense. See Canada wild ginger

Asarum europaeum. See European wild ginger

Asimina triloba. See Papaw

Aster *(Aster* spp.), 83, 148–49

Aster cordifolius. See Blue wood aster

Aster divaricatus. See White wood aster

Aster macrophyllus. See Large-leaved aster

Astilbe *(Astilbe* spp.), 40, 65, 149

Astilbe chinensis. See Chinese astilbe

Astilbe simplicifolia. See Star astilbe

Astrantia major. See Greater masterwort; Masterwort

Athyrium spp. *See* Lady fern

Athyrium filixfemina. See European lady fern

Athyrium nipponicum var. *pictum. See* Japanese painted fern

August lily, 131, 143

Autumn crocus, 106, 157

Autumn daffodil, 106, 157

Autumn fern, 113, 153

Autumn snakeroot, 151

Azalea *(Rhododendron* spp.), 28, 52, 172–73

Baby blue eyes, 163

Bacillus thuringiensis ssp. *israelensis,* 100, 123–24

Bacopa *(Bacopa* spp.), 77

Ba gua, 141

Baldcypress, 64

Balloon vine, 101

Barren strawberry, 161

Barrenwort, 152

Basil, 88

Baskets, hanging, 107

Beach wormwood, 143

Beard-tongue, 136

Bee balm, 137

Begonia *(Begonia* spp.), 40, 95, 149

Begonia grandis ssp. *evansiana. See* Hardy begonia

Begonia semperflorens. See Wax begonia

Begonia sutherlandii. See Sutherland begonia

Begonia x tuberhybrida hybrids. *See* Tuberous begonias

Bellflower, 150

Bellwort, 160

Benches, 5

Berberis thunbergii. See Japanese barberry

Berm for instant privacy, 42–47

Beta vulgaris ssp. *cicla. See* Swiss chard

Bethelehem sage, 158

Betony, 150

Betula nigra. See River birch

Bicolor epimedium, 152

Bicolor monkshood, 147

Bigleaf hydrangea, 170

Bignonia capreolata. See Crossvine

Bigroot geranium, 59, 113, 154

Birdbaths/feeders/houses, 20, 21, 57, 59, 62–63, 64, 112, 118, 122–23, 123–24

Bishop's cap, 152

Bishop's weed, 28, 147

Black cohosh, 151

Black-eyed Susan, 34

Blackhaw viburnum, 112, 174

Black jetbead, 112, 168

Black snakeroot, 71, 151

Bleeding heart, 40, 151–52

Bloody cranesbill, 154

Bluebell, 150

Blueberry, 174

Blue bugleweed, 29, 147

Blue corydalis, 151

Blue-eyed Mary, 150

Blue holly, 119

Blue lobelia, 65

Blue passionflower, 130

Blue throatwort, 163

Blue wood aster, 148–49

Boneset, 152

Borage *(Borage officinalis),* 40, 163

Borders, 13, 15

Boston ivy, 82

Bottlebrush buckeye, 167

Bottlebrush grass, 125
Bowman's root, 124
Box huckleberry, 168
Boxwood, 118
Branches, removing, 59
Broad beech fern, 29, 153
Bronze-leaved rodgersia, 158
Browallia (*Browallia* spp.), 163
Brugmansia. See Angel's trumpets
Brunnera (*Brunnera macrophylla*), 149
Buddleia davidii. See Butterfly bush
Bugbane (snakeroot), 71, 124, 151
Bugleweed, 147
Bulbs
  designs using, 16, 94, 95, 106, 107
  plants and planting, 157, 161
Burning bush, 123
Bush violet, 163
Busy Lizzie (garden impatiens, patience plant), 124, 164, 165
Butterflies, 83
Butterfly bush, 83, 143
Butterfly lily, 161
Buxus sempervirens. See Boxwood

Caladium (*Caladium bicolor*), 34, 40, 95, 124, 161
Calamint (*Calamintha* spp.), 88
Calamintha grandiflora. See Greater calamint
Calamintha nepeta. See Lesser calamint
Calendula officinalis. See Pot marigolds
Calico bush (mountain laurel), 58, 112, 171
Calla lily, 161
Calycanthus floridus. See Sweetshrub
Camass (*Camassia* spp.), 106, 157
Campanula (*Campanula* spp.), 150
Campanula carpatica. See Carpathian harebell
Campanula glomerata. See Clustered bellflower
Campanula persicifolia. See Peach-leaved bellflower
Campanula portenschlagiana. See Dalmation bellflower
Campanula rapunculoides. See Creeping bellflower
Campanula rotundifolia. See Bluebell
Campsis spp. *See* Trumpet vine
Campsis radicans. See Trumpet vine
Campsis radicans forma. *flava. See* Yellow trumpet vine
Canada lily, 106, 157
Canada violet, 161
Canada wild ginger, 124, 148
Canadian hemlock, 174
Canby paxistima, 168
Candles, 21
Canna (*Canna × generalis*), 51, 136
Canna × generalis hybrids. *See* Dwarf canna

Canopies, 10–11
Capitata Japanese yew, 119
Cardinal flower, 65
Cardiospermum halicacabum. See Balloon vine
Carex spp. *See* Sedges
Carex crinita. See Fringed sedge
Carex grayi. See Gray's sedge
Carex muskingumensis. See Palm sedge
Carex pensylvanica. See Pennsylvania sedge
Carolina allspice (sweetshrub), 58, 123, 131, 167
Carolina jessamine, 130
Carolina rhododendron, 173
Carpathian harebell, 150
Carpet, easy-care, 28
Carpet bugleweed, 47, 147
Carpinus caroliniana. See American hornbeam
Carya spp. *See* Hickories
Catawba rhododendron, 173
Catchfly, 163
Catharanthus roseus. See Rose periwinkle
Catmint, 46, 88, 118
Ceilings, shady retreats, 7, 15–16, 78–83
Celandine poppy, 159
Celastris orbiculatus. See Oriental bittersweet
Celastris scandens. See American bittersweet
Cephalotaxus harringtoniana. See Japanese plum yew
Ceratostigma plumbaginoides. See Plumbago
Cercis canadensis. See Eastern red-bud
Chai, 8
Chairs, 5, 19, 28, 122–23, 128–29
Chamaecyparis lawsoniana. See Lawson cypress
Chamaecyparis pisifera. See Sawara false cypress
Chasmanthium latifolium. See Northern sea oats; Wild oats
Checkerberry, 150
Chelidonium majus. See Greater celandine
Chelone spp. *See* Turtlehead
Cherry trees, 28
Children, shady retreats, xviii
Chilean glory vine, 136
Chimnea fireplaces, 5, 62–63
Chimonanthus praecox. See Fragrant wintersweet
Chinese anemone, 148
Chinese arbors, 140–41, 142
Chinese astilbe, 149
Chinese forget-me-not, 163
Chinese fringe flower, 168
Chinese holly, 119
Chinese juniper, 119
Chinese photinia, 168
Chinese rhubarb, 64

Chinese wisteria, 35, 142
Chionanthus virginicus. See White fringe tree
Chionodoxa spp. *See* Glory-of-the-snow
Christmas fern, 124, 153
Chrysogonum virginianum. See Green-and-gold
Cigar flower (firecracker plant), 157, 163
Cilantro, 40, 163
Cimicifuga spp. *See* Snakeroot
Cimicifuga americana. See American bugbane
Cimicifuga racemosa. See Black snakeroot
Cimicifuga simplex. See Autumn snakeroot
Cinnamon fern, 64, 153
Clearing in the woods, 120–25
Clearing on a woodland edge, 25–29
Clearing space for retreat, 125
Clematis (*Clematis* spp.), 16, 82, 83, 130
Clematis (*Clematis integrifolia*), 150
Clematis montana. See Climbing roses
Clematis terniflora. See Sweet autumn clematis
Cleome, 142
Cleome hassleriana. See Spider flower
Clethra (*Clethra* spp.), 169
Clethra alnifolia. See Summersweet
Climbing hydrangea (wood vamp), 58, 70, 169, 171
Climbing roses, 16, 136
Close spacing, 47
Clustered bellflower, 150
Cobaea scandens. See Cup-and-saucer
Colchicum spp. *See* Autumn crocus
Coleus, 34, 165
Collections for decoration, 89
Colocasia esculenta. See Elephant's ear
Color in shady retreats, 28, 34, 40, 41, 46, 53, 59, 64, 70, 76, 83, 89, 94, 100, 107, 112, 118, 124, 136, 142
Columbine (*Aquilegia* spp.), 136, 148, 159
Columbine meadow rue, 159
Comfort, 119
Connections, making, 51, 53, 143
Constructed vs. natural shade, 10–13
Container plantings, 16, 34, 40, 56–57, 59, 76, 83, 94, 95, 98–99, 100, 128–29, 136
Contrast/accent plant, 76
Convallaria spp. *See* Lily of the valley
Cooling a hot site, 29, 137
Coralbells, 154–55

Coral lily, 106, 157
Coreopsis, 46
Coreopsis rosea. See Pink coreopsis
Coreopsis verticillata 'Moonbeam', 83
Coriandrum sativum. See Cilantro
Cornelian cherry dogwood, 40, 41, 169
Cornus spp. *See* Dogwood
Cornus alternifolia. See Pagoda dogwood
Cornus amomum. See Silky dogwood
Cornus florida. See Flowering dogwood
Cornus mas. See Cornelian cherry dogwood
Corydalis (*Corydalis* spp.), 151
Corydalis flexuosa. See Blue corydalis
Corydalis lutea. See Yellow corydalis
Cosmos, 83, 142
Cotinus coggygria. See Purple smoke trees
Cow parsley, 150
Cowslip, 150
Cozy nook on a terrace, 36–41
Crab apples, 28
Cranesbill, 154
Creating shady spaces, 2–7
Creeping bellflower, 47, 150
Creeping Jacob's ladder, 124
Creeping Jenny, 150
Creeping juniper, 118
Creeping periwinkle, 47
Creeping phlox, 157
Crimson glory vine, 82, 89, 136
Crossvine, 130
Cup-and-saucer vine, 80, 101, 118
Cuphea ignea. See Cigar flower
Curcuma spp. *See* Pinecone ginger
Curry plant, 77
Custard apple, 168
Cyclamen spp. *See* Hardy cyclamen
Cyclamen coum. See Hardy cyclamen
Cyclamen hederifolium. See Hardy cyclamen
Cynoglossum amabile. See Chinese forget-me-not
Cypress vine, 101, 136
Cypripedium spp. *See* Orchids

Daffodil, 59, 107, 157
Dahlia, 142
Dalmation bellflower, 150
Dalmation cranesbill, 154
Dame's rocket, 163
Daphne (*Daphne* spp.), 168
Darmera peltata. See Umbrella plant
Dasheen (elephant's ear), 100, 161
Datura spp. *See* Angel's trumpets
Daucus carota. See Queen Anne's lace
Davidia involucrata. See Dove tree
Daylily, 40, 46, 88, 105, 136, 150

Deadnettle, 155
Deck in the woods, 66–71
Decks, 8, 56–57, 92–93
Decorations, 5, 7, 19–21, 28
Decumaria barbara. See Wood
    vamp
Designing shady retreats
    examples of, 23–143
    planning, 14–17
Dianthus spp. *See* Pinks
Dicentra spp. *See* Bleeding heart
Dicentra eximia. See Fringed bleed-
    ing heart
Dicentra formosa. See Western
    bleeding heart
Dichelostemma ida-maia. See
    Firecracker plant
Digitalis grandiflora. See Yellow fox-
    glove
Digitalis purpurea. See Foxglove
Digitalis x *mertonensis. See*
    Strawberry foxglove
Disanthus (*Disanthus cercidifolius*),
    168
Disporum spp. *See* Fairy bells
Divided spaces, 41
Dogwood, 169
Doll's eyes, 124
Doors, 98–99
Double-flowered creeping butter-
    cup, 150
Dove tree, 168
Downy serviceberry, 168
Drooping leucothoe, 168
Dryopteris spp. *See* Wood ferns
Dryopteris erythrosora. See Autumn
    fern; Japanese sword fern
Dryopteris filix-mas. See Male fern
Dry shade designs, 105, 112, 113
Dusky cranesbill, 154
Dusty miller, 143
Dutchman's pipe, 16, 34, 74, 129
Dwarf Alberta spruce, 118
Dwarf canna, 77
Dwarf conifer, 118
Dwarf fothergilla, 170
Dwarf goat's beard, 148
Dwarf petunia, 51
Dwarf Solomon's seal, 158
Dwarf sweet box, 112, 163

Eastern hemlock, 174
Eastern redbud, 41, 168
Eastern red cedar, 119
Eccremocarpus scaber. See Chilean
    glory vine
Echinacea purpurea. See Purple
    coneflower
Edging lobelia, 164
Egyptian star-cluster, 77
Elephant's ear, 100, 161
Eleutherococcus sieboldianus. See
    Five-leaf aralia
English holly, 112, 119, 168
English ivy, 28, 69, 70, 170
English primrose, 150
English violet, 161

English yew, 112, 173
Enkianthus campanulatus. See Red-
    vein enkianthus
Entryways, 17
Epimedium (*Epimedium* spp.), 29,
    46, 105, 112, 152
Epimedium grandiflorum. See
    Long-spurred epimedium
Epimedium x *rubrum. See* Red-
    flowered epimedium
Epimedium x *versicolor. See* Bicolor
    epimedium
Epimedium x *warleyense. See*
    Warley epimedium
Epimedium x *youngianum. See*
    Young's epimedium
Erysimum cheiri. See Wallflower
Euonymus alatus. See Burning
    bush
Euonymus fortunei. See
    Wintercreeper euonymus
Eupatorium (*Eupatorium* spp.), 152
Eupatorium coelestinum. See Hardy
    ageratum
Eupatorium rugosum. See White
    snakeroot
Euphorbia (*euphorbia* spp.),
    152–53
Euphorbia amygdaloides var. *robbi-
    ae. See* Wood spurge
European columbine, 148
European elder, 168
European lady fern, 153
European wild ginger, 148
Evening comforts, 65
Evergreens, 15, 26–27, 28, 41, 112
Exacum affine. See Persian violet

Fairy bells, 152
Fallopia aubertii. See Silver lace
    vine
False hellebore, 160–61
False Solomon's seal (Solomon's
    plume), 124, 159
Fan flower, 163
Featherfleece, 161
Fences, 13, 32–33, 34, 38–39,
    74–75, 76, 110–11, 113
Ferns
    designs using, 29, 40, 59, 64
    plants and planting, 153–54
Filler plants, 76
Fire cauldron, 140–41, 142
Firecracker plant (cigar flower),
    157, 163
Fireplaces, 5, 62–63, 140–41, 142
Fiveleaf akebia, 35, 74, 89
Five-leaf aralia, 52, 169
Five-spot, 163
Flag (accent) plants, 76
Flame azalea, 172
Flat space, forging, 71
Flexible furniture, 71
Flexible walls, 83
Flooring, 6, 142
Florida anise tree, 168
Flower beds, 38–39, 40, 41, 46,

50–51, 80–81, 83, 86–87, 98–99,
    134–35, 140–41
Flowering dogwood, 41, 169
Flowering ferns, 29, 153, 154
Flowering maple, 165
Flowering raspberry, 168
Flowering tobacco, 137, 142, 163
Flowering vines, 34
Foamflower, 159
Follies, 8
Forest's edge, gazebo at, 60–65
Forget-me-nots, 124
Formal garden, shady setting,
    114–19
Formosa toad lily, 160
Forsythia (*Forsythia* spp.), 15, 168
Foster's holly, 119
Fothergilla (*Fothergilla* spp.),
    169–70
Fothergilla gardenii. See Dwarf
    fothergilla
Fothergilla major. See Large
    fothergilla
Fountains (reservoir features), 21,
    110–11, 112, 116–17, 118, 119
Four-o'clocks, 89, 137, 165
Foxglove, 163
Fragrant flowers, 131
Fragrant wintersweet, 168
Freckle face (polka-dot plant), 34,
    163, 165
French doors, 140–41
Fried eggs, 163
Fringed bleeding heart, 41, 151
Fringed sedge, 125
Front porch, old-fashioned,
    127–31
Fuchsia hybrids (*Fuschia* x
    hybrida), 165
Fuchsia magellanica. See Hardy
    fuchsia
Furnishings, 5, 7, 19–21, 28, 71

Galanthus spp. See Snowdrop
Galium odoratum. See Sweet
    woodruff
Galleries, 8
Garden balsam, 164
Garden impatiens (busy Lizzie,
    patience plant), 124, 164, 165
Garden phlox, 143
Gardens
    designs using, 92–93
    formal garden, 114–19
    houses, 8–9
    maturing gardens, 47, 80, 83
    ornaments, 94
    shade and gardening, 16–17
Gates, 110–11
Gathering place, private, 138–43
Gaultheria procumbens. See
    Winterberry
Gaylussacia brachycera. See Box
    huckleberry
Gazebo at a forest's edge, 60–65
Gazebos, 9, 11, 15, 44–45
Gazing balls, 53

Gelsemium sempervirens. See
    Carolina jessamine
Geranium spp. *See* Hardy geranium
Geranium dalmaticum. See
    Dalmation cranesbill
Geranium macrorrhizum. See
    Bigroot geranium
Geranium maculatum. See Wild
    cranesbill
Geranium phaeum. See Dusky
    cranesbill
Geranium sanguineum. See Bloody
    cranesbill
Geranium sylvaticum. See Wood
    cranesbill
Giant taro, 161
Gillenia trifoliata. See Bowman's
    root
Ginger lily, 161
Glass chips, 118
Glider, 128–29
Glory-of-the-snow, 107, 157
Glossy abelia, 52, 167
Goat's beard, 65, 148
Golden columbine, 148
Golden hops, 89, 130
Goldenstar, 151
Goldflame honeysuckle, 118
Gooseneck loosestrife, 150
Grape hyacinths, 59
Grape-leaved anemone, 148
Grapes, 16, 82, 89, 136
Grass nut, 157
Gray's sedge, 125
Greater calamint, 88
Greater celandine, 150–51, 159
Greater masterwort, 150
Greater woodrush, 156
Great merry-bells, 124, 160
Great Solomon's seal, 157–58
Green-and-gold, 151
Gregg sage, 137
Grills in shady retreats, 5
Grottoes, 9
Ground covers
    designs using, 46, 47, 56–57,
        68–69, 70, 118, 124
    plants and planting, 147, 148,
        151, 152–54, 155–56, 157–58,
        159, 160, 161

Hakonechloa macra 'Aureola'. See
    Variegated hakone grass
Hakone grass (*Hakonechloa
    macra*), 156
Hamamelis spp. *See* Witch hazels
Hammocks, 5, 19
Hanging baskets, 107
Hanging chairs, 5, 19
Hardy ageratum, 71, 124, 152
Hardy amaryllis (magic lily), 106,
    157
Hardy begonia, 149, 157
Hardy cyclamen, 106, 157
Hardy fuchsia, 165
Hardy geranium, 154
Hardy kiwi, 35, 99, 101

Harebell, 150
Heavenly bamboo, 168
Hedera helix. See English ivy
Hedges, 13, 15, 116–17, 118, 119
Hedychium coronarium. See Ginger lily
Helenium autumnale. See Sneezeweed
Helianthus annuus. See Sunflowers
Helianthus debilis ssp. *cucumeri-folius* 'Italina White'. *See* Italian white sunflowers
Helichrysum italicum ssp. *serot-inum. See* Curry plant
Heliotrope (*Heliotropium arborescens*), 89, 131, 165
Hellebores (*Helleborus*), 105, 112, 154
Helleborus foetidus. See Stinking hellebore
Helleborus orientalis. See Lenten rose
Hemerocallis spp. *See* Daylily
Hemerocallis lilioasphodelus. See Lemon lilies
Hemlock, 52, 118
Henry lily, 106, 157
Hens-and-chicks, 118
Herbs, 86, 88, 92–93
Hermitage, 8
Hesperis matronalis. See Dame's rocket
Heuchera (*Heuchera* spp.), 124, 154–55
Heuchera sanguinea. See Coralbells
Heuchera x *brizoides. See* Coralbells
Hibiscus coccineus. See Scarlet rose mallow
Hibiscus (*Hibiscus* spp.), 137
Hibiscus moscheutos. See Rose mallow
Hickories, 123
Hide-and-reveal pathway, 65
Hide-and-seek pathway, 29
Highbush blueberry, 174
Himalayan sarcococca, 173
Hobblebush, 174
Hollies, 119, 168
Hollyhock, 136
Honesty, 164
Horse chestnuts, 158
Hosta (*Hosta* spp.), 29, 40, 41, 64, 100, 112, 136, 155
Hosta plantaginea. See August lily
Hot site, cooling, 29, 137
Hummingbirds, 136, 137
Humulus lupulus 'Aureus'. *See* Golden hops
Hyacinth bean, 101
Hyacinthoides hispanica. See Spanish bluebell
Hydrangea (*Hydrangea* spp.), 170–71
Hydrangea anomala var. *petiolaris. See* Climbing hydrangea
Hydrangea arborescens. See Smooth hydrangea

Hydrangea macrophylla. See Bigleaf hydrangea
Hydrangea petiolaris. See Climbing hydrangea
Hydrangea quercifolia. See Oakleaf hydrangea
Hymenocallis spp. *See* Peruvian daffodil
Hypoestes phyllostachya. See Polka-dot plant
Hystrix patula. See Bottlebrush grass

I-Ching, 141
Ilex spp. *See* Hollies
Ilex aquifolium. See English holly
Ilex cornuta. See Chinese holly
Ilex crenata. See Japanese holly
Ilex glabra. See Inkberry
Ilex opaca. See American holly
Ilex verticillata. See Winterberry
Ilex x *attenuata* 'Fosteri'. *See* Foster's holly
Ilex x *meserveae. See* Blue holly
Impatiens (*Impatiens* spp.), 124, 164
Impatiens balsamina. See Garden balsam
Impatiens walleriana. See Patience plant
Indian pink (Maryland pinkroot), 125, 159
Indian poke, 160–61
Indoors, bringing out, 77
Inkberry, 64, 168
Interrupted fern, 153
Inviting place to putter, 90–95
Ipomoea spp. *See* Morning glories
Ipomoea alba. See Moonflower
Ipomoea batatas. See Ornamental sweet potatoes
Ipomoea quamoclit. See Cypress vine
Iris sibirica. See Siberian iris
Italian white sunflowers, 142
Itea virginica. See Virginia sweet-spire
Jack-in-the-pulpit, 124
Jacob's ladder, 150
Japanese anemone, 148
Japanese barberry, 123
Japanese beech fern, 153
Japanese holly, 119, 168
Japanese honeysuckle, 123, 170
Japanese hydrangea vine, 53, 173
Japanese kerria, 112, 168
Japanese lily, 157
Japanese maple, 41, 167
Japanese painted fern, 29, 41, 153, 154
Japanese pieris, 168
Japanese plum yew, 41, 52, 168
Japanese skimmia, 168
Japanese spurge, 47, 157
Japanese sword fern, 113
Japanese tree lilac, 131
Japanese wisteria, 35

Japanese yew, 173–74
Joe-pye weed, 152
Johnny-jump-up, 40, 163
Joseph's coat, 163
Juglans spp. *See* Walnut trees
Junipers (*Juniperus* spp.), 119
Juniperus chinensis. See Chinese juniper
Juniperus conferta. See Shore juniper
Juniperus horizontalis. See Creeping juniper
Juniperus scopulorum. See Rocky Mountain juniper
Juniperus virginiana. See Eastern red cedar

Kalmia latifolia. *See* Mountain laurel
Kentucky viburnum, 174
Kentucky wisteria, 35
Kerria japonica. See Japanese kerria
Kirengeshoma (*Kirengeshoma palmata*), 155
Korean rhododendron, 173
Kudzu, 170

Lablab purpureus. *See* Hyacinth bean
Labrador violet, 161
Ladybells, 150
Lady fern, 153
Lady's mantle, 147
Lamium (*Lamium* spp.), 155
Lamium galeobdolon. See Yellow archangel
Lamium (*Lamium orvala*), 150
Landscape ties, 56–57
Lanterns, 21
Large-flowered trillium, 124
Large fothergilla, 170
Large-leaved aster, 149
Lathyrus latifolius 'White Pearl'. *See* White-flowered perennial pea
Lathyrus odoratus. See Sweet peas
Lattice, 140–41
Lattice and arbor sitting area, 85–89
Lavatera, 142
Lavender (*Lavandula angustifolia*), 86, 88, 118, 131
Lawn
  designs using, 44–45, 47, 68–69
  reducing, 29, 101
Lawson cypress, 112
Layered screen, 59
Leatherleaf viburnum, 41, 58, 174
Lemon lilies, 131
Lenten rose, 29, 154
Leopard lily, 106, 157
Lesser calamint, 88
Lesser celandine, 157
Lesser periwinkle (myrtle), 29, 47, 161
Leucanthemum vulgare. See Ox-eye daisy
Leucanthemum x *superbum. See*

Shasta daisy
Leucothoe fontanesiana. See Drooping leucothoe
Level space, making, 86, 89
Lighting, 74–75, 77, 143
Ligularia (*Ligularia stenocephala, L. dentata, L. przewalskii*), 64
Ligustrum spp. *See* Privets
Lilac, 129
Liliturf, 46
Lilium spp. *See* Lily
Lilium canadense. See Canada lily
Lilium candidum. See Madonna lily
Lilium henryi. See Henry lily
Lilium Martagon Hybrids. *See* Martagon lily
Lilium Oriental hybrids. *See* Oriental lilies
Lilium pardalinum. See Leopard lily
Lilium pumilum. See Coral lily
Lilium speciosum. See Japanese lily
Lilium superbum. See American turk's-cap lily
Lily, 106, 131, 136, 143
Lily leek, 106, 157
Lily of the valley, 151
Lilyturf, 155–56
Limnanthes douglasii. See Fried eggs
Lindera benzoin. See Spicebush
Liquidambar styraciflua. See Sweetgum
Liriope (*Liriope* spp.), 155–56
Lobelia (*Lobelia* spp.), 65
Lobelia cardinalis. See Cardinal flower
Lobelia erinus. See Edging lobelia
Lobelia siphilitica. See Blue lobelia
Lobularia maritima. See Sweet alyssum
Location importance, 35
Longleaf lungwort, 158
Long-spurred epimedium, 152
Lonicera japonica. See Japanese honeysuckle
Lonicera maackii. See Amur honey-suckle
Lonicera periclymenum. See Woodbine honeysuckles
Lonicera x *heckrottii. See* Goldflame honeysuckle
Loropetalum chinense. See Chinese fringe flower
Lowbush blueberry, 174
Low-maintenance plants, 46
Lunaria (*Lunaria annua*), 164
Lungwort, 59, 105, 112, 158
Luzula sylvatica. See Greater woodrush
Lychnis coronaria. See Rose campion
Lychnis x *arkwrightii. See* Arkwright's campion
Lycoris squamigera. See Hardy amaryllis
Lysimachia clethroides. See Gooseneck loosestrife
Lysimachia nummularia. See Creeping Jenny

Lysimachia punctata. See Yellow loosestrife

Madonna lily, 143
Magic lily (hardy amaryllis), 106, 157
Magnolia virginiana. See Sweet bay magnolia
Mahonia *(Mahonia aquifolium),* 112, 172
Maiden fern, 29, 153, 154
Maidenhair fern, 153
Male fern, 29, 113, 153
Mallow, 142
Malus spp. *See* Crab apples
Mandevilla *(Mandevilla* x *amoena* 'Alice du Pont'), 130
Maple, 167
Mapleleaf viburnum, 174
Mapping shade patterns, 12, 14, 27
Marigolds, 83
Martagon lily, 157
Maryland pinkroot (Indian pink), 125, 159
Masterwort, 65
Matteuccia struthiopteris. See Ostrich fern
Maturing gardens, 47, 80, 83
Maypops, xviii
Mazus *(Mazus repens),* 150
Meadow anemone, 148
Meadow buttercup, 150
Meadow foam, 163
Meadow rue, 65, 159
Merry-bells, 160
Mertensia pulmonarioides. See Virginia bluebells
Metal furniture, 19
Mexican fireplaces, 5
Mexican mint, 164–65
Mexican sunflowers, 83
Microbiota decussata. See Russian arborvitae
Mignonette, 89, 163
Mile-a-minute plant, 170
Mintleaf, 164–65
Mirabilis jalapa. See Four-o'clocks
Mistflower, 152
Mock orange, 15
Monarda didyma. See Bee balm
Mondo grass, 156
Money plant, 164
Monkshood, 147
Moonflower, 101, 142
Moon garden, 142, 143
Moosewood, 167
Morning glories, 16, 131
MosquitoDunks, 100, 123–24
Mountain laurel (calico bush), 58, 112, 171
Mountain maple, 167
Mourning widow, 154
Moveable privacy, 77
Mulch, 16
Mulched terrace under trees, 55–59
Multiple spaces, 31–35, 125
Muscari spp. *See* Grape hyacinths

Myosotis spp. *See* Forget-me-nots
Myrica pensylvanica. See Northern bayberry
Myrtle (lesser periwinkle), 29, 47, 161

Nandina *(Nandina domestica),* 168
Nannyberry viburnum, 58, 174
Narcissus spp. *See* Daffodil
Natural vs. constructed shade, 10–13
Nemophila maculata. See Five-spot
Nemophila menziesii. See Baby blue eyes
Nepeta spp. *See* Catmint
New York fern, 29, 153
Nicotiana spp. *See* Flowering tobacco
Nodding onion, 106, 157
Nook on a terrace, 36–41
Northern bayberry, 168
Northern maidenhair, 153
Northern sea oats, 71, 156
Norway maple, 123
Nyssa sylvatica. See Tupelo

Oakleaf hydrangea, 3, 52, 170
Oaks, 28, 123
Obedient plant, 150
Ocimum basilicum. See Basil
Octagonal flower bed, 38–39, 40, 41
Old-fashioned front porch, 127–31
Omphalodes verna. See Blue-eyed Mary
Onoclea sensibilis. See Sensitive fern
Open screens, 143
Ophiopogon *(Ophiopogon* spp.), 156
Ophiopogon japonicus. See Mondo grass
Orchids, 125
Oregano, 86, 88
Oregon holly grape (Oregon grape holly), 112, 172
Oregon vine maple, 167
Oriental bittersweet, 123, 170
Oriental lilies, 89
Origanum vulgare. See Oregano
Ornamental grasses
  designs using, 46, 86–87, 125
  plants and planting, 156
Ornamental onions, 106
Ornamental sweet potatoes, 77
Ornamental trees, 26–27, 28, 41
Osmunda spp. *See* Flowering ferns
Osmunda cinnamomea. See Cinnamon fern
Osmunda claytoniana. See Interrupted fern
Osmunda regalis. See Royal fern
Ostrich fern, 29, 153, 154
Oxalis *(Oxalis* spp.), 95, 161
Ox-eye daisy, 142
Oxlip, 150

Pachysandra *(Pachysandra),* 156–57
Pachysandra procumbens. See Allegheny spurge
Pachysandra terminalis. See Japanese spurge
Pagoda dogwood, 169
Palm sedge, 125
Pansy, 40, 163
Papaw, 168
Paperbark maple, 40, 167
Parrot leaf, 163
Parthenocissus spp. *See* Woodbine
Parthenocissus quinquefolia. See Virginia creeper
Parthenocissus tricuspidata. See Boston ivy
Passiflora spp. *See* Passionflower
Passiflora caerulea. See Blue passionflower
Passiflora incarnata. See Maypops
Passionflower, 130
Pathways, 17, 26–27, 28, 29, 62–63, 65, 74–75, 80–81
Patience plant (busy Lizzie, garden impatiens), 124, 164, 165
Pavers, 74–75, 76, 99–100, 116–17, 122–23
Pavilion, terraced garden, 102–7
Pavilions, 9
Paxistima canbyi. See Canby paxistima
Peaceful places, xviii–ix, 2, 3, 5
Peach-leaved bellflower, 150
Pelargonium spp. *See* Scented geranium
Pennisetum setaceum 'Purpureum'. *See* Purple fountain grass
Pennsylvania sedge, 125
Penstemon spp. *See* Beard-tongue
Pentas lanceolata. See Egyptian star-cluster; Star cluster
Perch in the trees, 132–37
Perennials. *See also* Ground covers
  designs using, 16, 26–27, 28, 44–45, 62–63, 64, 70, 71, 76, 77, 83, 86–87, 89, 100, 101, 105, 106, 107, 118, 128–29, 131
  plants and planting, 71, 146–61
  tender perennials, 165
Perfoliate bellwort, 160
Pergola for strolling, 96–101
Pergolas, 9, 11, 140–41
Persian shield, 165
Persian violet, 163
Persicaria (Persicaria capitata), 163
Persicaria orientale. See Prince's feather
Personalizing retreats, 89, 95
Peruvian daffodil, 161
Petunia, 83, 131, 136, 142
Phalaris arundinacea 'Picta'. *See* Ribbon grass
Phaseolus coccineus. See Scarlet runner beans
Philadelphus spp. *See* Mock orange
Phlox *(Phlox* spp.), 136, 157

Phlox divaricata. See Wild blue phlox; Woodland phlox
Phlox paniculata. See Garden phlox
Phlox stolonifera. See Creeping phlox
Photinia serratifolia. See Chinese photinia
Physostegia virginiana. See Obedient plant
Picea glauca var. *albertiana* 'Conica'. *See* Dwarf Alberta spruce
Picnic tables, 5
Pieris japonica. See Japanese pieris
Pinecone ginger, 161
Pink coreopsis, 71, 150
Pinks, 131
Pinkshell azalea, 172
Pin oak, 64
Pinus strobus. See White pine
Pinxterbloom azalea, 172
Planter boxes, 50–51
Planting pockets, 71, 107
Platanus occidentalis. See American planetree
Plectranthus *(Plectranthus* spp.), 164, 165
Plectranthus amboinicus. See Spanish thyme
Plectranthus madagascariensis. See Mintleaf
Plumbago, 47
Plumleaf azalea, 70
Polemonium caeruleum. See Jacob's ladder
Polemonium reptans. See Creeping Jacob's ladder
Polka-dot plant (freckle face), 34, 163, 165
Polygonatum spp. *See* Solomon's seal
Polygonatum biflorum. See Solomon's seal
Polygonatum commutatum. See Great Solomon's seal
Polygonatum humile. See Dwarf Solomon's seal
Polygonatum odoratum var. *thunbergii* 'Variegatum'. *See* Variegated fragrant Solomon's seal
Polygonum aubertii. See Silver lace vine
Polystichum spp. *See* Shield fern
Polystichum acrostichoides. See Christmas fern
Polystichum munitum. See Western sword fern
Ponds, 15
Pool house, relaxing, 72–77
Pools, 116–17, 118
Pop-up plantings, 107
Porches, 11, 127–31
Potato vine, 130
Pot marigolds, 40
Pots, 50–51. *See also* Container plantings
Potting sheds, 92–93, 94

Primrose, 150
Primula elatior. See Primrose
Primula vulgaris. See English primrose
Prince's feather, 163
Privacy (screens), ix, 2, 12–13, 39–40, 59, 77, 89, 143
Private gathering place, 138–43
Private space in busy yard, 109–13
Privets, 15
Prunus spp. *See* Cherry trees
Pueraria lobata. See Kudzu
Pulmonaria (*Pulmonaria* spp.), 59, 105, 158
Pulmonaria longifolia. See Longleaf lungwort
Pulmonaria saccharata. See Bethelehem sage
Pumps for fountains, 118
Purple bell vine, 101, 131
Purple coneflowers, 46
Purple fountain grass, 77
Purple heart, 136, 165
Purple smoke trees, 136
Puttering place, 90–95
Pyramid bugleweed, 147

Quamash, 106, 157
Queen Anne's lace, 142
Quercus spp. *See* Oaks
Quercus michauxii. See Swamp chestnut oak
Quercus palustris. See Pin oak

Rabbit-eye blueberry, 174
Ranunculus ficaria. See Lesser celandine
Ranunculus repens. See Tall buttercup
Ranunculus repens 'Pleniflorus'. *See* Double-flowered creeping buttercup
Reasons for shady retreats, xviii–ix, 2, 3, 5
Red baneberry, 124
Red chokeberry, 167
Red-flowered epimedium, 152
Red-vein enkianthus, 168
Relaxing pool house, 72–77
Reseda odorata. See Mignonette
Reservoir features (fountains), 21, 110–11, 112, 116–17, 118, 119
Retaining walls, 104–5
Retrofitting terrace, 53
Rheum palmatum. See Chinese rhubarb
Rhodochiton atrosanguineus. See Purple bell vine
Rhododendron (*Rhododendron* spp.), 28, 52, 172–73
Rhododendron arborescens. See Sweet azalea
Rhododendron calendulaceum. See Flame azalea
Rhododendron carolinianum. See Carolina rhododendron

Rhododendron catawbiense. See Catawba rhododendron
Rhododendron mucronulatum. See Korean rhododendron
Rhododendron periclymenoides. See Pinxterbloom azalea
Rhododendron priniphyllum. See Roseshell azalea
Rhododendron prunifolium. See Plumleaf azalea
Rhododendron schlippenbachii. See Royal azalea
Rhododendron vaseyi. See Pinkshell azalea
Rhododendron viscosum. See Swamp azalea
Rhododendron yakushimanum. See Yako rhododendron
Rhodotypos scandens. See Black jetbead
Ribbon grass, 118
Rill, 116–17
River birch, 64
Rocky Mountain juniper, 119
Rodgersia (*Rodgersia* spp.), 158
Rodgersia podophylla. See Bronze-leaved rodgersia
Rohdea (*Rohdea japonica*), 158–59
Room, making an outdoor, 83
Rooms with a view, 35
Root (tree) rules, 71, 107
Rose campion, 150, 163
Rose mallow, 137
Rose periwinkle, 163
Rose (*Rosa* spp.), 82, 83, 89
Roseshell azalea, 172
Royal azalea, 172
Royal fern, 64, 153
Rubus odoratus. See Flowering raspberry
Rugosa rose, 131
Russian arborvitae, 112

Sacred lily, 158–59
Salvia/sage (*Salvia* spp.), 40, 51, 88, 137, 163, 165
Salvia greggii. See Gregg sage
Salvia splendens. See Scarlet sage
Sambucus nigra. See European elder
Sarcococca hookeriana. See Himalayan sarcococca
Sarcococca hookeriana var. *humilis. See* Dwarf sweet box
Sarcococca (*Sarcococca* spp.), 173
Sasa bamboo (*Sasa veitchii*), 168
Sawara false cypress, 118
Scaevola aemula. See Fan flower
Scarlet rose mallow, 137
Scarlet runner beans, 16, 80, 136
Scarlet sage, 137
Scented geranium, 77
Schizophragma hydrangeoides. See Japanese hydrangea vine
Screens (privacy), ix, 2, 12–13, 39–40, 59, 77, 89, 143
Sculptures, 21, 46

Seating areas, 5, 26–27, 28, 38–39, 122–23, 140–41
Sedges, 125, 156
Sedums (*Sedum* spp.), 118
Sempervivum spp. *See* Hens-and-chicks
Senecio cineraria 'Silver Dust' or 'Silver Queen'. *See* Dusty miller
Sensitive fern, 153, 154
Shady garden retreats, xviii–21. *See also* Designing shady retreats; *Specific plants*
Shady setting, formal garden, 114–19
Shasta daisy, 143
Sheltered seats and alcoves, 9
Shield ferns, 153, 154
Shore juniper, 118
Shrubs
  designs using, 13, 16, 26–27, 28, 38–39, 41, 44–45, 53, 56–57, 68–69, 86–87, 110–11, 128–29, 131, 134–35, 140–41
  plants and planting, 166–74
Siberian bugloss, 149
Siberian iris, 65
Silene armeria. See Sweet William
Silky dogwood, 123, 169
Silver lace vine, 170
Simplicity for designs, 95, 125
Site, matching plants to, 65, 71, 113, 137
Sitting area, arbor and lattice, 85–89
Sitting areas, 32–33, 41, 92–93, 107
Skimmia japonica, 168
Sleek design, 53
Small lot, two shady spaces, 31–35
Small spaces, dressing up, 77
Smilacina racemosa. See Solomon's plume
Smooth hydrangea, 170
Snakeroot (bugbane), 71, 124, 151
Snapdragons, 136
Sneezeweed, 83
Snowberry, 168
Snowdrop, 107, 157
Snowdrop anemone, 148
Solanum jasminoides. See Potato vine
Solenostemon scutellarioides. See Coleus
Solidago caesia. See Wreath goldenrod
Solomon's plume (false Solomon's seal), 124, 159
Solomon's seal, 113, 124, 157–58
Southern maidenhair, 153
Southernwood, 88
Space for shady retreats, 3, 4–5, 89, 95
Spanish bluebell, 59
Spanish thyme, 164
Spicebush, 112, 123, 171
Spider flower, 83
Spider lily, 161
Spiderwort, 160

Spigelia (*Spigelia marilandica*), 125, 159
Spikenard, 125
Spiny bear's breech, 150
Spotted geranium, 154
Spurge, 152–53, 156–57
Stachys macrantha. See Betony
Star astilbe, 149
Star cluster, 137
Stenanthium gramineum. See Featherfleece
Steps, 86–87, 134–35
Sternbergia lutea. See Autumn daffodil
Stinking hellebore, 154
Strawberry foxglove, 150
Striped maple, 167
Strobilanthes dyerianus. See Persian shield
Strolling, pergola for, 96–101
Structural strengths, 119
Stylophorum diphyllum. See Celandine poppy
Summerhouses, 9, 11, 15
Summersweet (sweet pepperbush), 41, 58, 112, 131, 169
Sunflowers, 83
Sutherland begonia, 95, 161, 163
Swamp azalea, 64
Swamp chestnut oak, 64
Sweet alyssum, 163
Sweet autumn clematis, 70, 82, 136
Sweet azalea, 64, 172
Sweet bay magnolia, 131, 171–72
Sweet box, 173
Sweetgum, 64
Sweet peas, 142
Sweet pepperbush (summersweet), 41, 58, 112, 131, 169
Sweetshrub (Carolina allspice), 58, 123, 131, 167
Sweet violet, 161
Sweet William, 163
Sweet woodruff, 154
Swimming pool, 72–77
Swiss chard, 40
Sword fern, 153
Symmetry, 119, 137
Symphoricarpos albu. See Snowberry
Syringa reticulata. See Japanese tree lilac

Tables, 5, 122–23, 128–29
Tall buttercup, 150
Taro (elephant's ear), 100, 161
Taxodium distichum. See Baldcypress
Taxus spp. *See* Yew
Taxus baccata. See English yew
Taxus cuspidata. See Japanese yew
Taxus cuspidata 'Capitata'. *See* Capitata Japanese yew
Taxus × *media. See* Anglo-Japanese yew
Tender perennials, 165

Terraced garden, pavilion, 102–7
Terraces, 32–33, 38–39, 49–53, 86–87, 89, 122–23
Terrace under trees, 55–59
Thalictrum (*Thalictrum* spp.), 65, 159
Thalictrum aquilegifolium. See Columbine meadow rue
Thalictrum delavayi. See Yunan meadow rue
Thalictrum flavum. See Yellow meadow rue
Thelypteris spp. *See* Maiden fern
Thelypteris decursive-pinnata. See Japanese beech fern
Thelypteris hexagonoptera. See Broad beech fern
Thelypteris noveboracensis. See New York fern
Thuja occidentalis. See American arborvitae; Arborvitae
Thunbergia alata. See Black-eyed Susan
Thymes (*Thymus* spp.), 86, 88, 118
Thymus serphyllum. See Wild thyme
Tiarella (*Tiarella* spp.), 159
Tiarella cordifolia. See Allegheny foamflower
Tiarella wherryi. See Wherry's foamflower
T'ing, 9
Tithonia rotundifolia. See Mexican sunflowers
Toad lily, 160
Toadshade trillium, 124
Tool- and potting sheds, 9, 11
Torenia (*Torenia* spp.), 165
Torenia flava. See Yellow wishbone flower
Torenia fournieri. See Wishbone flower
Trachelium caeruleum. See Blue throatwort
Tradescantia (*Tradescantia* spp.), 160
Tradescantia pallida 'Purpurea'. *See* Purple heart
Trailer/weaver plants, 76
Tree-friendly design, 59
Tree houses, 9, 11, 132–37
Tree-of-heaven, 123
Trees. *See also Specific trees*
    designs using, 10, 14, 16, 26–27, 28, 38–39, 40, 44–45, 50–51, 56–57, 62–63, 64, 68–69, 70, 80–81, 116–17, 131, 134–35
    ornamental trees, 26–27, 28, 41
    plants and planting, 166–74
    root rules, 71, 107
Trellis windows, 131

Tricyrtis (*Tricyrtis* spp.), 160
Tricyrtis formosana. See Formosa toad lily
Trillium (*Trillium* spp.), 125
Trillium grandiflorum. See Large-flowered trillium
Trillium sessile. See Toadshade trillium
Triteleia laxa. See Grass nut
Trompe l'oeil paintings, 76, 77
Tropics, tree houses, 135–36
Trumpet vine, 82, 134, 135–36
Tsuga spp. *See* Hemlock
Tsuga canadensis. See Canadian hemlock
Tuberous begonias, 95, 161, 163
Tupelo, 64
Turtlehead, 65

Umbrella plant, 64
Umbrellas, 10, 11, 110–11, 113, 116–17
Uses for shady retreats, xviii–ix, 2, 3, 5
Uvularia spp. *See* Merry-bells
Uvularia grandiflora. See Great merry-bells
Uvularia perfoliata. See Perfoliate bellwort

Vaccinium spp. *See* Blueberry
Vaccinium angustifolium. See Lowbush blueberry
Vaccinium ashei. See Rabbit-eye blueberry
Vaccinium corymbosum. See Highbush blueberry
Vancouveria (*Vancouveria hexandra*), 160
Variegated bishop's weed, 47, 147
Variegated fragrant Solomon's seal, 113, 158
Variegated hakone grass, 40, 41, 64, 156
Variegated Italian arum, 106, 157
Variegated kiwi, 35
Variegated Solomon's seal, 29
Vegetables, 92–93
Ventilation, 95
Veratrum (*Veratrum viride*), 160–61
Vertical gardening, 34, 35
Viburnum (*Viburnum* spp.), 15, 174
Viburnum acerifolium. See Mapleleaf viburnum
Viburnum dentatum. See Arrowwood viburnum
Viburnum lantanoides. See Hobblebush

Viburnum lentago. See Nannyberry viburnum
Viburnum molle. See Kentucky viburnum
Viburnum prunifolium. See Blackhaw viburnum
Viburnum rhytidophyllum. See Leatherleaf viburnum
View considerations, 13, 59, 137
Vinca (*Vinca minor*), 29, 47, 161
Vines
    designs using, 16, 34, 74–76, 82, 83, 89, 100, 101, 118, 129, 130, 131, 136, 142
    plants and planting, 166–74
Viola spp. *See* Violet
Viola canadensis. See Canada violet
Viola labradorica. See Labrador violet
Viola odorata. See Sweet violet
Viola papilionacea. See Woolly blue violet
Viola sororaria. See Woolly blue violet
Viola tricolor. See Johnny-jump-up
Viola × *wittrockiana. See* Pansy
Violet, 161
Virginia bluebells, 124
Virginia creeper, 82
Virginia sweetspire, 58, 131, 171
Vitis coignetiae. See Crimson glory vine
Vitis spp. *See* Grapes
Voodoo lily, 161

Waldsteinia (*Walsteinia fragarioides*), 161
Wallflower, 163
Walls, 6, 12, 15–16, 21, 32–33, 34, 50–51, 83, 89, 104–5
Walnut trees, 173
Warley epimedium, 152
Water gardens, 70, 98–99, 100, 101, 117–18, 119
Water in shady retreats, 21
Wax begonia, 34, 124, 163, 165
Weaver/trailer plants, 76
Weed control, 111
Weigela (*Weigela florida*), 15
Western bleeding heart, 151–52
Western maidenhair, 153
Western sword fern, 153
Wet shade designs, 60–65
Wherry's foamflower, 159
White-flowered perennial pea, 142
White fringe tree, 168
White noise, 113
White pine, 118
White sage, 143
White snakeroot, 152
White wood aster, 125, 149

Whorled loosestrife, 150
Wild blue phlox, 124, 157
Wild columbine, 125, 148
Wild cranesbill, 154
Wildflowers, 68–69, 70, 124, 125
Wild ginger, 148
Wildlife haven, 57–58, 59
Wild oats, 125
Wild onion, 106, 157
Wild thyme, 88
Windflower, 147–48
Winterberry, 64, 125, 150, 168
Wintercreeper euonymus, 169
Winter sun, 131
Wishbone flower, 165
Wisteria (*Wisteria* spp.), 16, 35, 53, 136
Wisteria floribunda. See Japanese wisteria
Wisteria frutescens. See American wisteria
Wisteria macrostachya. See Kentucky wisteria
Wisteria sinensis. See Chinese wisteria
Witch hazels, 58, 170
Wood anemones, 124
Woodbine, 82
Woodbine honeysuckles, 34
Wood cranesbill, 154
Wood ferns, 153, 154
Wood furniture, 19
Woodland edge, clearing on, 25–29
Woodland phlox, 59
Woods, clearing in, 120–25
Woods, deck in, 66–71
Wood sorrel, 95, 161
Wood spurge, 113, 153
Wood vamp (climbing hydrangea), 58, 70, 169, 171
Woolly blue violet, 161
Wormwood, 143
Wreath goldenrod, 125

Yako rhododendron, 173
Yellow archangel, 155
Yellow corydalis, 100, 113, 151
Yellow foxglove, 150
Yellow loosestrife, 150
Yellow meadow rue, 159
Yellow trumpet vine, 136
Yellow wax bells, 155
Yellow wishbone flower, 165
Yew, 52, 119, 168, 173–74
Young's epimedium, 152
Yunan meadow rue, 159

Zantedeschia spp. *See* Calla lily
Zinnia, 83
Zone map, 175